W9-BLR-633

MEDAL OF HONOR

MEDAL OF HONOR

PROFILES OF AMERICA'S

MILITARY HEROES FROM THE

CIVIL WAR TO THE PRESENT

Allen Mikaelian

WITH COMMENTARY BY

Mike Wallace

HYPERION

NEW YORK

ISBN: 0-7868-6662-4

Hyperion books are available for special promotions and premiums.
For details contact Hyperion Special Markets, 77 West 66th Street,
11th floor, New York, New York 10023, or call 212-456-0100.

Book design by Richard Oriolo

FIRST EDITION

10 9 8 7 6 5 4 3 2 1

To All Those Who Have Served or
Are Now Serving in the Defense of Our Country

CONTENTS

INTRODUCTION   ix

THE STORY OF THE MEDAL OF HONOR   xvii

CHAPTER ONE: Dr. Mary Edwards Walker, Civil War   1

CHAPTER TWO: Leopold Karpeles, Civil War   19

A NATION OF IMMIGRANTS   41

CHAPTER THREE: Edouard Victor Michel Izac, World War I   45

CHAPTER FOUR: Samuel Woodfill, World War I   75

RETURN TO ISOLATIONISM   106

CHAPTER FIVE: David M. Shoup, World War II   109

CHAPTER SIX: Maynard H. Smith: World War II   135

CHAPTER SEVEN: Vernon Baker, World War II   162

UNEASY PEACE   189

CHAPTER EIGHT: Hiroshi "Hershey" Miyamura, Korean War   193

CHAPTER NINE: William Charette, Korean War   219

FROM THE FORGOTTEN WAR TO THE LIVING-ROOM WAR   238

CHAPTER TEN: Dwight Johnson, Vietnam War   241

CHAPTER ELEVEN: Thomas Kelley, Vietnam War   256

AFTERWORD   273

NOTES   281

ACKNOWLEDGMENTS   299

INTRODUCTION

by Mike Wallace

THROUGHOUT OUR HISTORY, WE AMERICANS have gone off to war in a spirit of optimism and even naïveté that had little to do with the reality we would soon have to face. In 1861, the Union generals, politicians, and eager volunteers thought they would whip the rebels in a matter of months. Their Confederate counterparts were just as convinced that their Yankee foes did not have the resolve to fight the kind of long and costly war it would take to defeat the South. Neither Blue nor Gray was prepared for the terrible bloodshed that would engulf them.

The doughboys of 1917 worried that there would be no Germans left to fight by the time they were trained and ready to join the struggle on the killing fields of Europe. They could not foresee that there would be another year and a half of ferocious trench warfare before the guns finally stopped blazing and, to borrow a famous phrase that defined the historic moment, it once again became all quiet on the western front. In 1941, we ignored warning signs that should have alerted us to the peril of Japanese aggression. It took the assault on Pearl Harbor to jolt us out of our complacent isolation, and then it took us months—even years—to mobilize the forces we needed to win the biggest and bloodiest war ever fought on this planet.

The pattern of unforeseen consequences continued through the wars that followed. When we sent troops to Korea in 1950, we were so confident of a swift and decisive victory that we dismissed the conflict as a mere "police action." Three years later, American soldiers were still being killed there. And even more tragic was our ordeal in Vietnam. We drifted into that war so gradually that it was difficult to know exactly when our so-called advisers took over the actual fighting. What we *do* know for certain is that the bitterly divisive war eventually tore our country apart, becoming such a national trauma that it brought on the downfall of two presidents.

When the bombs fell at Pearl Harbor in December of 1941, I was 23 and striving to make my mark in the world of broadcasting, which in those days meant radio—and only radio; that newfangled television wouldn't burst onto the scene until after the war. (I should perhaps explain that when people of my generation refer to "the war," the only war we have in mind is World War II.)

Like millions of young Americans, I answered the call and served for nearly three years in the navy; and although I spent most of my tour in the Pacific Theater—first in Hawaii, then Australia, and later at Subic Bay in the Philippines—I confess I never heard nor saw a shot fired in anger. As a communications officer aboard a submarine tender and communications hub, the USS *Anthedon,* my primary duties involved the exchange of terse encoded messages between our ship and the Seventh Fleet submarines on war patrol in the South China Sea, the Philippine Sea, and waters closer to Japan.

I felt no urge to complain about that assignment. My navy training (at Harvard, of all places) had been in communications and, as I was frequently reminded, our noncombat operation aboard the *Anthedon* was an essential part of the overall mission.

So I went to war as an armchair sailor. From time to time, I'd get together with men from the subs at our Officers' Club. More often than not, they would have just returned from war patrols for some well-earned shore leave, and as we relaxed over beers, I could sometimes get them to talk about the close calls and other harrowing experiences they'd gone through while waging war from the depths of the Southwestern Pacific. They did not regard themselves as heroes—far from it. Invariably, they would downplay their adventures; their tone was usually laconic and their manner self-deprecating. But enough came through from their stories to fill me with a vicarious pride in what they were doing. I was in awe of the terrible risks they took every time they headed away from our tender and out to sea.

The skipper of our ship, Captain Richard Hawes, known by the crew as "Spitting Dick" because of his tendency to spray spittle whenever he called us to attention and chewed us out for some misfeasance, was a gruff, avuncular man who played no favorites. Hawes was everything I'd imagined a navy captain should be; his only weakness, so far as I could tell, was that he didn't play a very good game of cribbage.

He also turned out to be a braver man than many of us realized when we first came under his command. Back in the fall of 1941, Lieutenant Richard Hawes had been the skipper of a submarine rescue vessel, the USS *Pigeon;* and three days after that wretched day in December when the Japanese launched their attacks on Pearl Harbor, they staged another air raid on the Philippines, where, at the time, the *Pigeon* was on duty in Manila Bay.

While under heavy fire from Japanese planes, Lieutenant Hawes managed to maneuver his rescue vessel in such a way that he was able to pull the submarine *Seadragon* away from the wharf, where she was tied up undergoing repairs, and out of harm's way. For that act of valor, and superb seamanship, he was awarded the Navy Cross.

When the *Anthedon* crew first heard this story via the grapevine, only gradually were we able to piece it all together; and when some of us finally worked up the moxie to ask Hawes directly about that December day in Manila Bay, he fended us off and brusquely changed the subject. Nor did I ever hear him acknowledge that he had received the Navy Cross, which is the highest commendation that branch of service bestows on its heroes.

But the ultimate award an American combatant can receive is the Congressional Medal of Honor. By the end of World War II, the Medal of Honor had taken on the aura of a sacred icon, the stuff of legend. Indeed, some of its most celebrated recipients became legendary heroes, Eddie

Rickenbacker and Sergeant Alvin York from World War I and Jimmy Doolittle and Audie Murphy from the Second World War. Yet even though I was aware of the medal's supreme stature, I didn't give much thought to it in those days, mainly because it was such a rare and extraordinary honor that I never had occasion to relate to anyone who'd earned it.

My first contact with a Medal of Honor recipient didn't take place until 1957, long after I'd returned to civilian life and resumed my career in broadcast journalism. By that time, I was doing a weekly interview show on ABC, and one night the object of my scrutiny was a U.S. Army veteran who'd been getting a lot of controversial attention—as well as the Medal of Honor—for his heroic exploits during World War II. His square name was Charles Kelly, but to those familiar with his story, he was mainly known by his colorful nickname—"Commando" Kelly. (In our interview that night, I called him Chuck.)

In introducing Kelly to our viewers, I marveled at his various feats of valor, especially at the Battle of Salerno, where, single-handed, he'd killed 40 German soldiers in a span of 20 minutes.

But the controversy about Kelly dealt with his failure to flourish in civilian life. During the postwar years he had tried his hand at a number of jobs and business ventures, and nothing had panned out very well. There were reports that his booze problems had been at the root of his failures, and we talked about that. And as I would later discover, Kelly was not the only Medal of Honor recipient who had the melancholy experience of going from war hero to washout.

Years passed. In fact, more than four decades would elapse before my professional path once again crossed that of a Medal of Honor recipient—or, in this case, recipients. In 1998, an accolade came my way from a totally unexpected source. The Congressional Medal of Honor Society selected me as that year's winner of the annual award it presents to journalists, an award named in honor of Tex McCrary, who has been a legendary presence in New York media circles for more than half a century. McCrary served with distinction in World War II as a lieutenant colonel in the Army Air Corps, where he was in charge of all combat photography. And over the years, he has been an avid and very active supporter of the Medal of Honor Society.

The Tex McCrary Award was so new in 1998 that I was only the second journalist to receive it. The first winner, the previous year, was Bernard Shaw, my former CBS News colleague who went on to become a pioneering force in the cable news operation at CNN. Since me, the recipients have been Paul Harvey, Tom Brokaw, and Tim Russert. According to the Medal of Honor Society's citation, the award is given to those "who, through their life's work, have distinguished themselves by service or unbiased coverage of the United States military through journalism."

I can't speak for Shaw and the others, but I can tell you that I found those words profoundly gratifying, especially the part about "unbiased coverage of the United States military." For there was a time—and not that long ago—when the U.S. military community had a vastly different perception of my reporting. During the worst years of the war in Vietnam, some of the stories I broadcast didn't sit well with the Pentagon brass and other ardent defenders of our military actions in Southeast Asia. For example, it was from an interview I did for the *CBS Evening News* that millions of Americans first learned about the atrocities committed by American GIs in a village called My Lai. On another occasion, when I did a *60 Minutes* story about some deserters who had fled to Canada, I was perceived and criticized as being overly sympathetic to their point of view.

Then, in 1982, long after that futile war had ended, I was the correspondent on a *CBS Reports* documentary in which General William Westmoreland was accused of having engaged in a conspiracy to deceive his superiors and the American public about the level of enemy troop strength in Vietnam. That may have been the most controversial broadcast in the entire history of CBS News—which is saying a great deal—and for years thereafter, I was regarded in some military circles as a pariah, the television bully boy who had sullied the reputation of an outstanding general and decent man. The general sued for libel, and after a long trial but before it went to the jury, he abandoned the field and withdrew his charge of libel. For me, to be chosen by the Medal of Honor Society to receive its Tex McCrary Award was another measure of vindication.

That award also brought me into contact with members of the Medal of Honor Society. A featured event on the group's calendar is its annual black-tie Awards Dinner, and each year since 1998 I've welcomed the invitation to attend. Becoming acquainted with some of these unfailingly modest men has been a special privilege.

Not long after the award, my longtime friend, Bill Adler, called with a proposal that I collaborate with a young writer by the name of Allen Mikaelian on a book about Medal of Honor recipients from the Civil War through Vietnam. Since I felt I now had at least a tenuous connection to the subject, I was receptive, but also hesitant because I knew my television commitments would leave me precious little time to work on such a book.

Adler was able to work out an arrangement whereby Mikaelian would take on the heavy lifting. That is, he would do all the research—a formidable task—and write the various stories that would appear in the book you are now holding in your hands. I agreed to take part in the process of selecting the recipients whose stories would be told and to help with the editing. I also offered to write this introduction and an afterword as well as brief commentaries, bridging one era to another, which are interspersed throughout the book.

As I became involved, I learned that the Medal of Honor may, by law, be awarded only to one who in action involving conflict with an enemy "distinguished himself conspicuously by gallantry and intrepidity." There must also be evidence that he put his own life on the line and that he acted "above and beyond the call of duty." And to my surprise, I learned that no one can receive a Medal of Honor for having acted under orders, no matter how heroically he carried out those orders, for the medal is reserved strictly for those who act of their own accord and out of complete selflessness. It is those rigorous conditions that set the Medal of Honor apart from all other military commendations.

General George Patton once said that he would have given his immortal soul for the medal, and at least two occupants of the White House—Harry Truman and Lyndon Johnson—told recipients they would rather have the medal than be president.

Incidentally, when the presentation ceremonies are held at the White House, it is customary for the president—the commander in chief of all our armed forces—to salute the recipient, who then returns the salute. That tradition extends throughout the chain of command: When a recipient is wearing the Medal of Honor, he is generally the one to be saluted first, regardless of how low his rank may be.

Earlier I referred to some of the more famous recipients who became household names. But it should be noted that in contrast to the occasional Sergeant York or General Doolittle, the vast majority of recipients quickly fade into anonymity. Most of those who survive their action return to the lives they led before they went off to war, and many of those lives have been humble. But because of what they went through to receive the Medal of Honor, they are acutely aware that their lives can never entirely be what they'd been before they acted with such valor to save lives, and perhaps help turn the tide of crucial battles. A descendant of one of the subjects in this book described her ancestor as being "captured" by a moment in history in which he'd played a vital part. I suspect that other recipients can relate to that. If they felt captured by a moment in history, it's because they know—though they'd be the last to say it—that their personal courage helped to make history.

THE STORY OF
THE MEDAL OF HONOR

THE SURVIVING MEMBERS of the "Andrews Raiders" were the first. Their failed mission, in April 1862, to steal a Confederate locomotive and ride to the Union lines, destroying track and depots along the way, had ended in a wild train chase and capture. Eight of the original twenty-five volunteers escaped, three went missing, eight were hanged (including their leader, James Andrews), and six were exchanged in March 1863, after almost a year in a Confederate prison camp.

On March 25, the survivors met with Secretary of War Edwin Stanton before he introduced them to President Lincoln. He praised their bravery and daring, and promised they would be celebrated as heroes. Then he stepped into the next room, returned with a small medal in his hand, and told the party that Congress had just passed a law ordering medals to be minted and awarded. The raiders would be the first to receive this honor. He was holding the prototype, and gave it to Private Jacob Parrott, the youngest of the group. This presentation, without ceremony or fanfare, was the first presentation of the Medal of Honor.

This medal wasn't just the highest honor a soldier or sailor could receive, it was practically the only one. George Washington had introduced the Badge of Military Merit as an award for "singularly meritorious action," but it was not continued past the Revolutionary War, and only three awards of this badge were recorded. The Mexican-American War saw the introduction of the "Certificate of Merit" for privates, and later for noncommissioned officers, but men were typically uninspired by the award, which consisted of a piece of paper and an extra two dollars a month. For officers, there was a system of brevets, whereby the honored officer could wear the insignia of a higher rank without being of that rank. But this system was so often used as compensation for political favors that by the 1860s, it was widely discredited.

The United States Navy of that time lacked the formality and rigor of the navy we know today. Officers were faced with crews that were often undisciplined and unmotivated. As he looked ahead to the massive buildup that would be required by the War of the Rebellion, Secretary of the Navy Gideon Welles proposed a medal for enlisted men and petty officers that would inspire them to duty. His wishes were contained in a bill presented to Congress for a Medal of Honor to "promote the efficiency of the Navy," which was signed by President Lincoln on December 21, 1861. The award was reserved for "petty officers, seamen, landsmen, and marines as shall most distinguish themselves by their gallantry in action and other seamen like qualities during the present war."

The design of the medal was similarly geared for "the present war." Two figures appeared on the inverted five-point star, Discord and Minerva, the goddess who represented both war and the ancient wisdom of the Athenian democracy. On the Medal of Honor, Minerva defends herself with a shield of stars and stripes while she holds for attack an axe in a fasces, a collection of tightly bound sticks that, for the Romans, symbolized authority through unity and singularity of purpose. By contrast, her opponent, Discord, is armed only with writhing serpents.

The army immediately saw that it was about to be left behind, and in February 1862, a bill was introduced in the Senate for an army Medal of Honor. Lincoln signed the bill on July 12, 1862, three months after the Andrews raid. The language of the bill giving a Medal of Honor for the army closely followed the navy's example: The Medal of Honor was for those who "shall most distinguish themselves by their gallantry in action, and other soldier-like qualities." In November, anticipating that many would "most distinguish themselves," the War Department ordered 2,000 medals for the army.

The Medal of Honor was soon granted to officers as well as enlisted men, and proved popular enough to extend beyond the Civil War, but it became a victim of its own success. There was no set procedure to determine who should be awarded the Medal of Honor, and no criteria to distinguish "soldier-like qualities" or "seaman-like qualities" from extraordinary valor. And in some cases, the Medal of Honor was given out copiously enough to verge on the promiscuous.

The 27th Maine, a regiment of nine-month volunteers, was getting ready to leave Washington, D.C., at the end of June 1863 as General Lee's Army invaded Pennsylvania. Their departure, which coincided with the departure of another Maine regiment, would, the army believed, leave the capital vulnerable if the rebel army turned south to attack. Colonel Wentworth, commander of the regiment, appealed to his captains to convince their men to remain during this national emergency. He pledged to Stanton his every effort, and Stanton told him the Medal of Honor would be awarded to all who stayed. In the end, over 300 of the 864 men of the 27th Maine remained, returning home only after Lee was defeated at Gettysburg and began his retreat on the Fourth of July.

It's doubtful that many men stayed because of the promised medals. It's doubtful any of them had heard of the Medal of Honor. Jacob Parrott had received his only a few months before. But Stanton was prepared to let medals rain down on this group of volunteers, not for gallantry, but for their "soldier-like qualities." It would be used here as a gesture, a bonus, not strictly as an honor. The meaning of the Medal of Honor was something that would have to be constructed over time. The ending of this story shows just how far America would have to go to establish the Medal of Honor as something sacrosanct: Due to a clerical error, all 864 men of the 27th Maine, those who stayed *and* those who left, were sent Medals of Honor by mail.

The actions of 1,517 others in the Civil War would earn the Medal of Honor, many of those being granted decades after the fighting stopped. The first action that earned a Medal of Honor, for example, predated by over a year Lincoln's signature on the bill authorizing the medal, and predated the start of the Civil War by several months. Bernard Irwin, an assistant surgeon with the army in Arizona, volunteered to lead a detachment of 14 troops on a 100-mile mule ride to break an Apache siege on an army outpost in February 1861. He received the Medal of Honor in 1894.

Men could apply for the Medal of Honor themselves, and, in the years after the war, it became increasingly common for veterans to do so. The great majority of them were deserving of some sort of recognition, but the fact remained that the Medal of Honor was the only recognition available, and was used to acknowledge both the great and the good. The medal was awarded to the entire party of Andrews Raiders, the entire 27th Maine, and the whole of the honor guard at Lincoln's funeral. But it had also been awarded to soldiers like Julian Scott. Scott, a 16-year-old army fifer, ran into a river so thick with splashes from enemy bullets that it looked like it was boiling. He made nine trips into the fray to rescue fallen comrades. It was also awarded to Private William Surles, who, upon seeing a rebel draw a bead on his commander, Colonel Anson McCook, threw himself in front of the commander so as to take the bullet himself (the enemy was then shot before he could pull the trigger). As the Medal of Honor was repeatedly sent to applicants in the decades following the Civil War, many in the military began to realize the detrimental effect of putting so many actions in the same class.

In 1876, following the slaughter of Custer's troops at Little Bighorn, officers who commanded detachments that survived recommended whole units for the Medal of Honor. But their commanding general, Alfred A. Terry, rejected the request. "Medals of Honor are not intended for ordinary good conduct, but for conspicuous acts of gallantry." A review of cases followed, and in the end, 24 men received the Medal of Honor for actions at Little Bighorn. This was still a large proportion by today's standards, but the idea of awarding medals to groups as a whole was finally questioned.

The next efforts to rarify the ranks of Medal of Honor holders was undertaken by the Medal of Honor Legion, founded in 1890. With a group of Medal of Honor holders lining up to defend the award against abuse, the meaning of the medal evolved quickly. In 1892, Adjutant General JC Kelton, by order of Major General John Schofield, himself a Medal of Honor recipient, drew a clear distinction between the Medal of Honor and the Certificate of Merit. The order was groundbreaking in its attempt to establish a hierarchy of honors:

> Medals of Honor should be awarded to officers or enlisted men for distinguished bravery in action, while Certificates of Merit should, under the law, be awarded for distinguished service, whether in action or otherwise, of a valuable character to the United States . . .

The order went on to establish that the Certificate of Merit is appropriate for men who have saved lives, property, or material, whether in battle or in peace. Braving a fire, the order says, would be an action worthy of the Certificate of Merit. But only if it benefits the United States of America.

The Medal of Honor, on the other hand, should strictly be awarded for distinguished service in battle. However, and this is another astounding point about this order, "such act of heroism may not have resulted in any benefit to the United States." Medals have, throughout history, been awarded almost exclusively to men who brought home victories. But in the United States, this order clearly establishes, valor and honor transcends whatever benefit it may bring to the nation. The battle may be lost, but valor exists even in defeat. The brave action may utterly fail, but that does not exclude it from being honored.

This allowed Gunner's Mate First Class Osmond Kelly Ingram to receive the Medal of Honor for his action in the First World War. On October 15, 1917, he was on the destroyer USS *Cassin*, which was hunting a German sub 20 miles south of Mind Head, Ireland. Scanning the sea for signs of the sub, he saw the trail of a torpedo headed straight for the aft of the ship. He knew that if it scored a hit there, it would set off the depth charges. He ran aft, racing the torpedo, hoping to release the depth charges. His citation reads: "The torpedo struck the ship before he could accomplish his purpose, and Ingram was killed by the explosion. The depth charges exploded immediately afterward. His life was sacrificed in an attempt to save the ship and his shipmates . . ." He received the Medal of Honor for his valor, not for success.

Theodore Roosevelt did more than any other president to further refine the meaning of the Medal of Honor, even though he had been refused a Medal of Honor for his July 1, 1898, charge on San Juan Hill, Cuba, during the Spanish-American War. Roosevelt blamed Secretary of War Russell A. Alger, who was stung by Roosevelt's public criticism of his department's shortcomings in Cuba. Roosevelt didn't receive the medal in his lifetime, but he continued to believe it was something that had to be elevated. Ever since the Civil War, the award typically had been mailed to recipients, but Roosevelt's executive order of 1905 demanded a "formal and impressive ceremonial . . . by the President, as Commander in Chief, or by such representative as the President may designate." Now that the recipients were to be decorated by the highest in the chain of command, the need to ensure that the deeds suited the occasion became even more evident. But the most significant changes to the meaning of the medal wouldn't come until 1916, as America once again prepared for war.

Ever since the Medal of Honor Legion was founded in 1890, it had prevailed upon Congress to pass legislation that would "tend to give the Medal of Honor the same position among the military orders of the world which similar medals occupy." In 1916, their efforts resulted in a bill presented by Representative Isaac R. Sherwood of Ohio to establish an "Army and Navy Medal of Honor Roll." The roll was to include only those recipients who had been honorably discharged, who had reached the age of 65 (today there is no age requirement), and who had obtained the medal for "action involving actual conflict with the enemy, distinguished by conspicuous gallantry or intrepidity, at the risk of life, above and beyond the call of duty." Those on the roll would receive $10 a month for life, in addition to any pension they already had.

Then, just months later, Congress passed a comprehensive national defense act, in preparation for the possibility that the European war would soon demand American participation. In one of the over 100 sections of the bill was a provision for "Investigation concerning medals of honor." It ordered a board of five retired officers of the army to be convened by the secretary of war. They were to "ascertain what medals of honor, if any, have been awarded or issued for any cause other than distinguished conduct by an officer or enlisted man in action involving actual conflict with an enemy . . ." If the board did discover cases in which the medal had been awarded for reasons other than these, those recipients were to have their names "stricken permanently from the official medal of honor list. It shall be a misdemeanor for him to wear or publicly display said medal . . ." It was a strongly worded amendment, designed to strengthen the meaning of the Medal of Honor as a new war loomed on the horizon. But as John J. Pullen put it, in his book on the 27th Maine, "Before Minerva and the medal she adorned could ascend to the exalted heights they occupy today, there inevitably had to be a human sacrifice."

The president of the review board was himself a Medal of Honor recipient. General Nelson Miles had fought at Fair Oaks, Antietam, Fredericksburg, and Chancellorsville. His troops defeated Crazy Horse in Montana, and he persuaded Geronimo to surrender in Arizona. He was married to the niece of General William Sherman and was retired when the onerous duty of stripping men of their medals was given to him. He almost immediately objected. The law, as written, required him to remove the names of civilians who had served honorably. He knew that among the names to be struck would be two civilian scouts who had made a stand with four members of the Sixth Cavalry against 125 Native Americans in Texas. He knew because he had written their recommendation himself, calling the actions of the six men examples of "cool courage, heroism, and self-sacrifice, which duty as well as inclination prompt us to recognize, but which we cannot fitly honor."

He requested that Congress revise the law by amending a pending army appropriations bill. His recommended wording loosened the law considerably:

> Section 122 of the Act of Congress approved June 3, 1916, shall not apply to persons who have lawfully received their medals of honor, nor to anyone who has rendered most extraordinary, hazardous and dangerous service to the Government.

The proposed amendment was killed on a point of order, despite an impassioned plea from Senator Henry Cabot Lodge. With their instructions clear, the Medal of Honor Board had no choice but to apply the strictest possible yardstick to the 2,625 cases before them.

When the board reported in January 1917, they found 911 cases that did not fit the new requirements. These included the 555 men of the 27th Maine who had received the Medal of Honor by clerical error, the 29 members of Lincoln's funeral guard, and 7 "miscellaneous" recipients. These, the review declared, had either not earned their medals in action or had been awarded the medals by mistake. They also reported on 309 members of the 27th Maine who had stayed to defend Washington, 5 civilian scouts and guides, and 6 recipients who received the Medal under a confusing and confused 1863 general order that appears to qualify *anyone* who stayed past the extension of their term. These recipients, the board declared, had received their medals legally and, in the cases of the civilian scouts and guides, while under fire. The board recommended that Congress review the 1916 law before rescinding these awards.

Congress, however, had moved on to other things, and the War Department's hands were tied. All 911 awards were rescinded. But the law wasn't widely publicized, and the adjutant general only sent out 183 letters informing recipients that their medals had been stripped. Many recipients had moved, so they never learned of the government's action. Some who got the letter had never received the original medal, so they learned both that they were recipients and now were recipients no longer in the same instant. Some, like Dr. Mary Edwards Walker, whose story is told in the first chapter of this book, were plainly outraged. Some, like Buffalo Bill Cody, who had his medal rescinded because he was a civilian, had died.

The slate had been cleared, but Congress had not yet found the words to clarify who should receive the Medal of Honor and for what. Finally, on July 9, 1918, Congress produced wording that would ensure the Medal of Honor could only be awarded in truly exceptional instances:

> . . . the President is authorized to present, in the name of Congress, a medal of honor only to each person who, while an officer or enlisted man of the Army, shall hereafter, in action involving actual conflict with an enemy, distinguish himself conspicuously by gallantry and intrepidity at the risk of his life above and beyond the call of duty.

Equally significant was the establishment of alternate awards. The act replaced the Certificate of Merit with the Distinguished Service Cross, and created the Silver Star. Valor that didn't meet the requirements of the Medal of Honor could still be honored. The temptation to use the highest award for lesser cases was completely removed.

Those who served in the navy still could earn the medal during noncombat duty if it was in the line of a sailor's "profession." Service on ships was still considered dangerous enough to allow for Medal of Honor awards if, for example, a sailor saved another from drowning, charged a shipboard fire, or exhibited gallantry during a shipboard explosion. However, these awards have been few. The last award of the Medal of Honor for an action performed outside of combat was in 1945. Owen Hammerberg saved the lives of two divers trapped under a wreck in Pearl Harbor.

He was killed as he used his body to protect one of the divers from a chunk of steel that fell as the wreckage caved in.

In 1963, by act of Congress, the requirements for all three branches of service were made the same. Now only the designs of the medals differ from one branch to the other. The navy adopted a second design in 1919 with the intention of awarding the original to seamen who earned the medal in noncombat duty. This second design was discontinued in 1942 after only a handful of awards were made. The army introduced a new design in 1904, which retained the inverted star but featured only the head of Athena, encircled by the words "United States of America." The air force adopted a new medal in 1965, after 20 years of using the army medal. Its design continues the use of the inverted star, but features the head of the Statue of Liberty. All three medals are suspended from blue ribbons worn around the neck, each ending in a "knot" embroidered with 13 stars. The air force and army medals are suspended from a bar that reads "valor," while the navy medal is suspended from an anchor.

Recipients receive $400 a month, in addition to any other pension. They may receive passage on military aircraft, if space allows. They may be buried at Arlington National Cemetery. Their children may attend any of the military academies without the standard appointment from a member of Congress. The lucky ones receive the thanks of a grateful nation, something by no means guaranteed.

The progression of the Medal of Honor, from an award intended to stimulate "efficiency" in the navy to something only for those who have utterly disregarded their own lives for the sake of others, was something that could never have come to pass only by passage of laws and issuance of regulations. The Medal of Honor has been infused with a sanctity by the recipients themselves. During the Second World War, for the first time, more awards of the Medal of Honor were made to the dead than to the living. The same was true in Korea and Vietnam. If the Medal of Honor today has an intangible and solemn halo around it, it is partly due to those men who did not survive to wear it. The survivors who wear the medal frequently acknowledge this. They very rarely speak of glory, preferring instead to speak simply of their immense gratitude.

As of this writing, there are 3,456 Medal of Honor recipients. Of those, only 147 are alive today.

A NOTE TO THE READER

As mentioned here, most of the men who have received the Medal of Honor since the start of the Second World War did not survive the action for which they are honored. However, this book is about a few of those who did. The purpose of these stories is to explore how these recipients lived after receiving the Medal of Honor. How did it change their lives? How did they change the lives of those around them?

But since so many did not survive, stories of these heroes are woven into the stories in this book. The men who did not live through their actions often crossed paths with the subjects of this book in surprising ways. And since those who were interviewed for this book spoke of them so often, it is appropriate to occasionally depart from the main story for these shorter stories.

The Medal of Honor has been awarded to many who rose to prominence after they got home. Douglas McArthur (and his father, Arthur), Audie Murphy, Eddie Rickenbacker, Alvin York, Bob Kerrey, James Stockdale, and Daniel Inouye are a few. But the overwhelming majority simply went on with their lives, or tried to. This book concentrates on them. Some stayed in the military; some rose to prominence as public servants; some lived in a constant state of financial trouble. But all of them lived lives that would be forgotten except for the efforts of relatives and, in some cases, a few dedicated historians. Those who appear in this book were selected for the variety of their life stories, but also because those stories were accessible. Many more were investigated but ruled out when we found that they had slipped completely into obscurity. A number of living recipients weren't comfortable stepping out of their anonymity for this book, and we strongly respect their wishes.

The late Gerard White, a historian and former director of the Medal of Honor society, helped guide us to Leopold Karpeles, Edouard Izac, Hiroshi Miyamura, and William Charette. Dr. Mary Walker, subject of the first chapter in this book, is a well-known and controversial figure. Vernon Baker was the subject of a great deal of press attention a few years ago, but has since slid into a comfortable anonymity. The remainder were chosen because their lives, while somewhat hidden and not always easy to uncover, were not completely undocumented.

The Congressional Medal of Honor Society helped us get in touch with living recipients. And former president of the Congressional Medal of Honor Society Paul Bucha called to our attention the story of Vietnam veteran Dwight Johnson, for which we are extremely grateful.

MEDAL OF HONOR

CHAPTER ONE

Dr. Mary Edwards Walker

CIVIL WAR

"Whereas it appears from official reports that Dr. Mary E. Walker, a graduate of medicine . . . has devoted herself with much patriotic zeal to the sick and wounded soldiers, both in the field and hospitals, to the detriment of her own health, and has also endured hardships as a prisoner of war [for] four months in a Southern prison while acting as a contract surgeon . . . it is ordered, That a testimonial thereof shall be hereby made and given to said Dr. Mary E. Walker, and that the usual medal of honor for meritorious services be given her."

— PRESIDENT ANDREW JOHNSON AND SECRETARY OF WAR
  EDWIN M. STANTON

ON A SUMMER DAY IN 1866, a crowd gathered on Canal Street in Manhattan. New Yorkers, even then, thought themselves among the most cosmopolitan people on the planet, and difficult to impress or to shock. But all their exposure to new ideas and ways of life hadn't prepared them for Dr. Mary Walker's shopping excursion in her provocative outfit.

She wore a high-necked top with a loose waist and long sleeves, buttoned down the front. Under her skirt, which was gathered loosely at the waist and fell to her knees, she wore pants of the same material. These pants were perhaps most troublesome to the assembled crowd; they were just like pants a man would wear. The entire outfit was designed to provide freedom of movement, and Dr. Walker took advantage of it. Her costume was known as the American Reform Dress, or equally often as "bloomers." Those who donned it were determined to free women from the heavy skirts and tight corsets that they felt were detrimental to women's physical health and independence.

When the police showed up, however, Dr. Walker announced herself not as a radical suffragette, but as a patriot. When asked for her address, she replied, "Anywhere the Stars and Stripes fly." She was ordered to the precinct, where a police sergeant asked for her name. She thrust the medal she wore on her chest in his face and instructed him to read the name on the back. He didn't take her up on the offer, but he couldn't help seeing the medal's front, depicting the battle between the goddess Minerva and the serpent-wielding Discord.

Although medals of all three branches of the service feature a woman—the army and the navy display Minerva, and the air force medal features the face of Liberty—Mary Walker remains the only woman ever to legitimately wear one. The reason is simple: Women were, and quite often still are, excluded from combat roles. Walker earned hers not in battle, but in service. She had to fight to perform that service; then she had to fight to have it recognized.

Even today, Dr. Mary Walker remains a controversial figure. However, with the questions of women's dress and suffrage behind us, the controversy over Dr. Walker centers around whether she deserved the medal she wore until the day she died. Two years before she passed away, the government asked for it back. Sixty years later, the government changed its mind again, and restored her name to the rolls of the Medal of Honor.

Mary Walker was the fifth child of seven born to Alvah and Vesta Walker, who farmed 33 acres in Oswego Town, New York. Alvah and Vesta's first son died in infancy, and the next five children were daughters. Mary was the youngest. They were raised doing "man's work" on the farm and wearing clothes that their father knew to be unfashionable but practical. They were brought up to believe that they should seek understanding, enlightenment, and even independence. Alvah himself was a self-taught man who read frequently across a wide range of topics and painted in his spare hours. Their small farmhouse was crowded with books, which Mary devoured.

In 1840s upstate New York, the stirrings of feminism developed alongside and in conjunction with abolitionism, agnosticism, and the temperance movement. Amelia Bloomer, the namesake of the outfit Walker would come to wear, had been born in Homer, New York, in 1818. An early women's rights convention was held in nearby Seneca Falls in 1848, and Oswego was visited by Elizabeth Smith Miller, a "bloomerite" and daughter of Gerrit Smith, who was an outspoken congressman, abolitionist, temperance reformer, and backer of John Brown. As with any place they went, Miller and her entourage of oddly dressed women were a topic of discussion throughout the town. If Mary Walker didn't see them herself, she almost certainly heard about them.

After the birth of his first son, Alvah began experiencing frequent illness, and incorporated medical texts into his reading routine. Mary Walker remembered these books well—they convinced her that she should become a doctor. Her elder sisters were pursuing careers in teaching and continued schooling, but for a woman to move into a profession that required study of and exposure to the human body was something else entirely. Walker defiantly enrolled in medical school in December 1853, at the age of 21.

Her decision to pursue this profession occurred during the brief rise of eclectic medicine as a school of thought. Eclectics believed that medicine was a science, had a preference for herbal remedies, prided themselves on a nondogmatic approach, and attempted to rise above the pitched battle between homeopathic doctors and the medical orthodoxy, which came to be known as allopathic medicine.

The homeopaths believed that small doses of remedies that produced the same symptoms as the disease would lead to a cure. The allopaths clung to aggressive therapies (which often included bloodletting and heavy doses of mercury). The eclectics professed to reject preformed philosophies, borrowing the "best" therapies from both schools. Put simply, the patient was more important than the procedure.

The eclectics freely mixed radical social theory with their medical practices. They were also the most generally dismissed group among the medical sects of the time, and educated members of the lower middle class populated their camp. They also admitted women to their colleges, opening themselves to a whole new level of public scorn. For Walker, an eclectic school was the right choice because of its independent philosophy, and the only choice because of her gender.

After two years of study, Mary Walker became Dr. Walker in June 1855. She graduated into a society unlikely to accept her degree as a validation of her abilities. "Why not grant the degree to sucking babes?" the Cincinnati *Lancet and Observer* lamented after a woman graduated from one of Ohio's medical colleges a few years after Walker received her degree. "There never was a woman fitted to practice medicine, surgery and obstetrics, no matter how long she may have studied. The duties of the physician are contrary and opposed to her moral, intellectual and physical nature."

Were it not for her independent streak, Dr. Walker would have become Dr. Miller shortly thereafter. Albert Miller was a charismatic and bright student at the college who gave a lecture on free thought at graduation. Walker moved to Columbus, Ohio, after graduation, and Miller proposed marriage from Rome, New York, where he had established a practice. Walker accepted and they were married immediately in Oswego.

Miller was eager to honor Walker's unconventionality by agreeing to a marriage that was almost scandalously unconventional for the time. Walker made it clear that she would not take his name. She wouldn't accept a wedding dress either, instead showing up on the big day in trousers and a dress coat. The word "obey" was struck from her vows, something that Walker remarked on later: "How barbarous the very idea of one equal promising to be the slave of another, instead of both entering life's greatest drama as intelligent equal parties. Our promises were such as denoted two intelligent beings instead of one intelligence and one chained."

Unfortunately for Walker, Albert Miller was in need of a few of the chains that come with marriage. She discovered an affair not long after they were wed, and found Miller rather unapologetic. But because of tough divorce laws, Dr. Walker was unable to finalize a divorce until 1869, and only after several acquaintances testified to his infidelity. She vented her spleen in her 1871 book *Hit*: "To be deprived of a Divorce is like being shut up in a prison because someone attempted to kill you."

But even after being mistreated by her husband and the law of the land, she held on to the ideal of marriage, claiming in *Hit* that "true conjugal companionship is the greatest blessing of which mortals can conceive in this life." The fact that she never found that ideal in her own life makes the U.S. Army's Mary E. Walker Award extremely curious and ironic. The army established the award in 1999 to honor army spouses. One recipient, while appreciating the recognition, claimed that she was "more old-fashioned" than the award's namesake. "I think the wife should stay home and take care of the kids," she told a reporter.

Staying home was never a part of Dr. Walker's plans. Although her practice couldn't be called thriving, she did manage to support herself as a doctor, and as she grew more confident, her opinions became more strident. If she could overcome the sexism woven into 19th-century America, she felt, there must be a groundswell brewing that would lead to full cultural and legal equality in her lifetime. In fact, she optimistically wrote in the feminist magazine *Sibyl* in 1859 that this would happen very soon. By 1862, she broached the idea in the same journal that women were not only equal to men in reasoning capacity, but superior. What some might call women's intuition was in fact, according to Walker, a mind reasoning at the speed of a telegraph. Men, whose minds moved at the pace of a stagecoach, could never keep pace.

Arriving in Washington, D.C., after the Battle of Bull Run, in 1861, Dr. Walker applied immediately for a commission in the army and then turned her attention to the wounded pouring into the city. The some 500 Union dead and 1,100 wounded seemed, at the time, utterly cataclysmic. Dr. Walker served as a volunteer working out of the U.S. Patent Office, which had been hastily converted into a hospital. Dr. Walker noted that doctors were scarce, while the wounded were many. She waited for her orders. Instead, her application for a commission was rejected.

But there was no objection to her staying on as a volunteer. As she helped wherever she could, she appealed directly to Surgeon General Clement A. Finley. The army rejected her again. At the hospital, however, she found that her orders were followed just as if she were a fully commissioned officer. And giving orders was not something from which Dr. Walker shied. Upon hearing that conditions in the deserters prison in Alexandria were fatally unhygienic, she appeared one day at the gate and proclaimed, "I am Dr. Walker of the Union Army. I command you to let me pass." Inside, she decided that a few of the prisoners were unjustly held. Because of her advocacy, they were freed on pardons from Secretary of War Edwin Stanton.

As she tended to the wounded in the early months of the Civil War, Walker encountered a reformer of a different sort. Dorothea Dix was superintendent of female nurses of the U.S. Army, overseeing recruitment, training, and placement of about 2,000 nurses. Walker knew of her and admired her for her investigations of asylums, prisons, and almshouses, but was less than pleased with her bedside manner. When Dix was walking through the hospital, Walker recalled in her "Notes on the War," if so much as a patient's foot was exposed, "she turned her head the other way, seeming not to see the condition, while I was so disgusted with such sham modesty that I hastened to arrange the soldier's bedclothing."

Feeling that she was not presently needed in Washington, and hoping that additional credentials would help sway the army, Walker enrolled at the Hygeia Therapeutic College in New York City in early 1862. The study of hygiene at the time constituted a leading edge of medical science. Another prominent woman associated with an army, Florence Nightingale, had reduced the mortality rate in British military hospitals during the Crimean War in the Black Sea from 40 percent to 2 percent by literally cleaning them up. A similar effort in the States might have prevented the number of deaths by disease from outnumbering the battle deaths in the Civil War by six to one.

Dr. Walker returned to Washington in fall 1862 and was then sent to the headquarters of General Burnside in nearby Warrenton, Virginia, where there was an outbreak of typhoid fever. This time, although she was still a volunteer civilian, she wore an officer's uniform: gold-striped pants, a felt hat, and a surgeon's green sash. It may not have been fully regulation, but it certainly became useful when the camp was evacuated in a retreat. The officers left Walker and her trainload of patients behind, and the engineer would not move without orders. Walker explained to him, in short, sharp words, to look at her uniform and move the train. But her moment basking in the glory of authority was short-lived. When she got to Washington and got in line for a sandwich, she was told that the food was for soldiers only. Her services may have been accepted, but she herself would never be accepted until she was fully admitted into the army.

Bristling, she wrote directly to the president. While she would accept a position in a female ward, she told him, her preference was for a battlefield assignment where, she wrote, "her energy, enthusiasm, professional abilities and patriotism will be of the greatest service in inspiring the true soldier never to yield to traitors, and in attending the wounded brave. She will not shrink from duties under shot and shells, believing that her life is of no value in the country's greatest peril if by its loss the interests of future generations shall be promoted." The reply came in less than a week, written by Lincoln himself on Walker's letter. He could not, "with strong hand," force army commanders to accept anyone, "male or female, against their consent."

But she continued to behave like a Union army regular, traveling to

Falmouth in December 1862, and then on to Chattanooga and the Tennessee front. She arrived as tens of thousands of wounded from the Battle of Chickamauga, fought on September 19, 1863, poured into the city. But her services as assistant surgeon were soon requested at Gordon's Mill, southeast of Chattanooga. Here, her presence became a point of contention.

Major General Alexander McCook thought Dr. Walker a godsend, and put her to work immediately. The medical director of the Army of the Cumberland, Dr. Perin, thought otherwise. He ordered her examined by a medical board of five doctors. In their scathing report, they said it was "doubtful whether she has pursued the study of medicine," adding that her knowledge of diseases was "not much greater than most housewives." Their recommendation was to keep her as far from the troops as possible.

Their report is often quoted by those who feel Dr. Walker should never have received the Medal of Honor in the first place, much less have it restored, as it was in 1977. But it is quoted just as often by Walker's champions, who hold it up as an example of the overt and pervasive sexism that she faced head-on. But while gender discrimination was a likely factor, so was conflict over wildly different medical philosophies. As an eclectic practitioner, Walker championed herbal medicines that looked, to traditional practitioners, like home remedies. Her advocacy of hygienic practices and her criticism of army hospitals—unhygienic places indeed—looked on the surface like criticism of the army itself. Perhaps most controversial was her campaign against amputations, most of which she felt were unnecessary. After she found that her loud protests against the hasty removal of limbs were met with equally loud claims of lives saved, she began quietly counseling patients to refuse amputations when their turn came. This subversive activity on the losing side of the greatest medical debate of the war did not ingratiate her to her staunchly traditional colleagues.

The vitriol of the medical board's report was clearly intended to extinguish her career, but surprisingly, nothing changed. This was probably due to the influence of McCook and Major General George H. Thomas, the "Rock of Chickamauga," who'd witnessed some of Walker's energy after the crushing Union defeat at Chickamauga. The severe shortage of doctors in the Union army probably played a role also. So Walker stayed with McCook, wearing an army uniform but still very much a free agent.

It was during this time, late 1863 and early 1864, that Walker began the most dangerous and mysterious phase of her service. Civilians in the surrounding areas, especially to the south, were suffering horribly from privation and disease. Dr. Walker traveled frequently behind enemy lines, on horseback and in full uniform, carrying Union medical supplies through country thick with Confederate troops. For a woman to travel alone in an unmistakable uniform was far above and beyond any call of duty.

But there may have been more to her trips: Walker never mentioned it in her personal papers, but she and others claimed years after the war that she was actually spying for the Union. Even one of the doctors who sat on the examining board that pronounced her unfit to be a doctor acknowledged the possibility in a vicious attack on Walker written for the *New York Medical Journal* in 1867. Further, a message to Major General Thomas, dated August 21, 1864, asked if "anything [is] due the woman Mary Walker, and if so, what amount for secret service or other services." Dr. Walker's *recommendation* for the Medal of Honor stated that "she frequently passed beyond our lines far within those of the enemy, and at one time gained information that led General Sherman to so modify his strategic operations as to save himself from a serious reverse and obtain success where defeat seemed to be inevitable." However, there is no mention of clandestine operations in Walker's Medal of Honor *citation*, and she didn't mention secret service in her consistently detailed journals.

Perhaps no one involved wanted to admit that the Union army used medical personnel to achieve strategic ends. A doctor sent forth as a spy, if discovered, would jeopardize all doctors who work in the battlefield.

But if she was collecting information, she had the perfect cover. On one of her sojourns, she was stopped by a group of rough-looking Confederates, and explained to their leader that she was attending a family in need of her help. She even had the cheek to ask them for an escort. The group's leader replied that if she was indeed the woman doctor he'd heard so much about, the one who had saved so many civilian lives, she could certainly pass. Much later, Walker saw a picture of the notorious bushwhacker Champ Furguson, who had vowed to kill every "bluecoat" who crossed his path, and recognized him as the man who had briefly detained her that day.

The next time she was stopped, Dr. Walker was not so lucky. On April 10, 1964, she was captured by a Confederate sentry south of Chattanooga and delivered to General Johnston of the Confederate army. Finding a shortage of doctors in his camp, she treated some of the wounded soldiers. Along the route to Richmond, news of Dr. Walker traveled by telegraph, and crowds turned up at rail stations to gawk at the oddity of a woman doctor who not only wore pants, but even dared to wear an army uniform. The greatest crowd was in Richmond itself, where Confederate Captain Joseph Semmes experienced a profound loathing, which he shared with his wife in a letter: "[We] were all amused and disgusted . . . at the sight of a *thing* that nothing but the debased and depraved Yankee nation could produce . . . she was dressed in the full uniform of a Federal surgeon . . . not good looking and of course had tongue enough for a regiment of men . . . she would be more at home in a lunatic asylum." According to Walker, this reaction was in stark contrast to those of the residents around Chattanooga, who had welcomed her despite her dress and demeanor.

In letters home from prison camp, she was cheery and optimistic about her chances of release. In her personal journal, however, she described mattresses full of insects and rats racing around on the floor. She annoyed her keepers with requests for medical supplies, better food, and cleaner conditions for all prisoners, while rebuffing their attempts to get her to wear clothes "more becoming to her sex." Like most prisoners during the Civil War, Union and Confederate, she suffered horrible privation. By the time she was released, her eyesight was deteriorating painfully because of malnutrition. After four months, she was transported via the steamer *New York* with several hundred other prisoners to Fortress Monroe on the James River in Virginia, then safely behind the Union lines, and exchanged for a Confederate major. This swap, Walker felt, was appropriate and conferred on her an air of honor and legitimacy.

Dr. Walker received the totally unexpected sum of $432.36 for her services from March to August 1864, which she felt further legitimized her position. Within weeks she was appointed acting assistant surgeon, United States Army, and given a salary of $100 a month. Behind the scenes, McCook and Thomas had been strong advocates. Except for the word *acting* stuck on her title, she was fully legitimate. But she still was a contract surgeon and thus a civilian.

The battlefield duty she preferred and requested was still denied. Instead, she was named surgeon in the Women's Prison Hospital in Louisville, Kentucky. Although chafing at the mundane duties, she won a review from her medical director that made her sound like an entirely different person from the one who'd received a drumming at the hands of Dr. Perin's medical board when she was in Chattanooga: "I bear testimony," wrote Dr. Edward Phelps, "to the superior talents and acquirements of Dr. Mary E. Walker . . . While performing her complicated duties, she evinced the same active, energetic, and persevering spirit which has characterized her in her whole military career."

After six months of this duty, she was next assigned to an orphanage in Clarksville, Tennessee, where she tended to refugees, mostly women and children, until the end of the war. Her contract ended on June 15, 1865, and Dr. Walker was released from service.

She had always intended to return to her private practice, but her damaged eyesight made this nearly impossible. She received a disability pension of $8.50 a month, but never fully recovered, and was, as she said in her claims, unable to continue working as a doctor. It wasn't until 1899 that she succeeded in having her pension raised to $20 a month, after a great deal of lobbying.

The Congressional Medal of Honor was, in 1865, awarded to those who "most distinguish themselves by their gallantry in action, and other soldier-like qualities," and was awarded liberally. Mary had certainly shown "soldier-like qualities," even if she hadn't seen any "action" per se. She had made an impression on two heroes of the war, generals Thomas and Sherman, who recommended her for an award as the war wound down. Presidents Lincoln and Andrew Johnson both knew about Walker and her seemingly endless reserve of loyalty in the face of rejection. After Lincoln's assassination in 1865, it fell to President Johnson to decide how to honor Dr. Walker.

Within months of assuming the presidency, Johnson requested Secretary of War Edwin M. Stanton to inquire about whether it was both legal and advisable to award the medal to a woman who had never been commissioned. The duty was passed to Judge-Advocate Joseph Holt, who submitted a 12-page report on Walker's service. He concluded that because of her patriotism, her exposure to peril, and her hardship during imprisonment, she constituted "an almost isolated [case] in the history of the rebellion; and to signalize and perpetuate it as such would seem to be desirable." President Johnson made the decision quickly and signed Dr. Walker's Medal of Honor citation himself.

Dr. Walker's citation is remarkable for its length—most citations from the Civil War are not more than a few lines—and the way in which it offers an explanation for why she was given the Medal of Honor:

> Whereas by reason of her not being a commissioned officer in the military service a brevet or honorary rank cannot, under existing laws, be conferred upon her; and
> Whereas in the opinion of the President an honorable recognition of her services and sufferings should be made;

It is ordered, That a testimonial thereof shall be hereby made and given to the said Dr. Mary E. Walker and that the usual medal of honor for meritorious services be given her.

Rather than calling out a specific event or deed of heroism, the citation listed her efforts at the Louisville hospital, her "patriotic zeal" in dealing with sick and wounded soldiers, and her time as a prisoner of war. This general citation was meant to honor her entire service.

Walker's newfound stature helped her win the presidency of the National Dress Reform Association shortly after the end of the war. In her inaugural speech, she jokingly proposed punishment for Confederate President Jefferson Davis: Treat him like a woman. He should be forced to wear hoop skirts and a tight corset, and do housework in a four-story home. This, Walker claimed, would be a worse punishment than any prison term. In the same speech, she predicted equal rights for women within ten years. At the time, with the slaves freed and the suffrage movement gaining momentum, this forecast might not have seemed like a fantasy.

While attending a social sciences conference in England in 1866, Walker discovered that people would actually pay to hear her speak. After the London press had made her a minor celebrity, she offered a lecture on her civil war experiences, women's dress, and equal rights. After several such lectures to packed houses, she realized that she could make a career out of these "performances" while promoting her cause. For a year, she traveled in Europe from one speaking engagement to the next, and returned to the States with an ever-growing confidence.

Walker's turn afoul of the law in New York, detailed at the start of this chapter, was just the beginning of a series of arrests, all of which she saw as an opportunity to tear into the unfortunate policemen who arrested her and the judges who heard her cases. To the New York City police commissioner, she testified that she had worn a more formal version of the outfit to the houses of generals and congressmen, and that if there were indeed a law prohibiting such dress, she would fight it to the highest court in the land. She'd become a feature in the New York papers, with most taking her side, and many mocking the police. The commissioner instructed the lawmen to not arrest her again.

In Kansas City, where she visited in 1869 to give a lecture, she was arrested for dress violations; the case was dismissed. In New Orleans soon after, she was let off with a warning, which she ignored during her several months in the city. But as public interest in the war waned and her speaking engagements became fewer and further between, she returned to Washington to focus her energies on the women's suffrage movement.

Dr. Walker shared a home in the District of Columbia with lawyer Belva Lockwood, the first woman to practice before the Supreme Court of the United States and presidential candidate in 1884 and 1888 with the National Equal Rights Party. Although Walker was much more radical and confrontational than most women in the movement, she shared stages with the mainstays—Lockwood and Susan B. Anthony, cofounder of the National American Woman Suffrage Association—and often was the crowds' favorite. At a public meeting of the Woman Suffrage Association in Cincinnati, Ohio, the calls for Dr. Walker drowned out applause for Susan B. Anthony's speech. Mistaking the men's shouts for catcalls, one woman took the stage and scolded the audience for their ungentlemanly behavior, until Dr. Walker stepped forward. The enthusiasm was due to her service with the Ohio regiments, she explained, and no offense was taken.

The suffragette's strategy at the time was to work through the courts. Women attempted to register to vote, were refused, and took their cases to court. Many felt these cases would result in a Supreme Court decision in the women's favor. But as these cases were thrown out of state and federal courts, the tenor of the movement changed. Instead of directly confronting the system, they began to work quietly toward a constitutional amendment. And as the movement grew more conservative, Walker became a liability.

During the war, Walker once entered the private room of General Sherman and demanded a commission. The discussion quickly turned to clothing—Mary was at the time wearing her bloomer outfit. "Why don't you wear proper clothing!" Sherman berated her, "That clothing is neither one thing nor the other." By the 1880s, Walker finally yielded to this argument: She gave up on women's clothes altogether. Whether in Washington or in Oswego, her typical outfit consisted of trousers, a high-collar shirt with a tie, and a frock coat. She accessorized with a silk hat and a walking stick.

This was too much even for her suffragette peers. Belva Lockwood once asked Dr. Walker to change her clothing choices, but, according to Belva's daughter's memoirs, the doctor "flew into such a rage that the subject was never again mentioned." By 1901, she was a pariah, completely shut out of a convention in her own hometown—an event that was noted even by the *New York Times*.

With opportunities for speaking engagements dried up, she signed with a professional booking agency that specialized in sideshows and dime museums. The *Toledo Blade* lamented that she had gone from "the platform of princes to the stage of freaks." In her letters, however, she seemed excited about the opportunities to continue speaking, no matter that she had been relegated to the role of a curiosity.

The Medal of Honor had long given Walker something the army never had: a tangible, honorable designation. The decoration hanging from her frock coat spoke to a degree of acceptance by an all-male military, and even those who hated the sight of her clothing choices and the sound of her sharp tongue couldn't argue that she wasn't a true patriot. But in 1917, she was stripped of her military honor.

Although the newly formed Medal of Honor review board admitted that it let stand cases in which evidence was missing, and cases in which "rewards which these men received were greater than would now be given for the same acts," they were unforgiving when they reviewed Dr. Walker's case. "This was a contract surgeon," the report reads, "whose service does not appear to have been distinguished in action or otherwise." Walker's civilian status would have been enough to disqualify her for the medal, but, it could be argued, her undoing was guaranteed by the general tone of her citation, a citation that honors a wartime career rather than a specific instance.

Walker, when asked why she'd received the honor, reflected that it was due her because of her time behind the lines, tending to civilians when "no man surgeon was willing to respond, for fear of being taken prisoner . . ." But these actions were not cited. Other citations, typically brief, honored men for traveling behind the lines and returning with information, not necessarily for action "involving actual conflict with the enemy." But President Johnson and Secretary of War Stanton, who also signed Walker's citation, had no reason to suspect that their decision would be reviewed and superseded.

In 1907, the army had issued medals with a new design. Now, in 1917, they asked Dr. Walker for both medals back. She refused. "One of them I will wear every day, and the other I will wear on occasions." Although her public display of medals that the government now said were undeserved was a misdemeanor, no one, it seems, had the heart to prosecute a woman in her eighties. Walker continued to fight for the return of her name to the Medal of Honor roll, but on one of her sorties, she slipped and injured herself on the Capitol steps. She never fully recovered.

By this time, Dr. Walker was living on the old family farm in Oswego, and had a reputation as an eccentric. In one unfortunate incident, she attempted to have her farmhand arrested for a sensational murder in New England. He sued her for libel, and won a nominal sum of $.06. As she descended into isolation, she became the butt of jokes and pranks, the townspeople completely unaware of her military service and her activism. "Now I am alone," she said in one of her last interviews, "with the infirmities of age weighing me down and practically penniless, and no one wants to be bothered with me." Dr. Mary Walker died on February 21,

1919, months before the ratification of the 19th Amendment. She never got a chance to vote.

Walker's memory was kept alive by distant relatives—one in particular. Grandniece Anne Walker made restoration of Dr. Walker's medal a full-time job, and finally got the ear of several lawmakers. In January 1977, Les Aspin, a Wisconsin Democrat in the House, introduced a measure to return Mary Walker's name to the Medal of Honor roll. "There are many people who believe Dr. Walker's involvement in civil libertarian causes is the reason it was revoked," Aspin claimed. That claim is complicated, however, by the fact that citations were sent to the 1916 review board with all identifying information obscured.

In the Senate, Edward W. Brooke, a Republican from Massachusetts, and Birch Bayh, a Democrat from Indiana, sponsored a similar resolution. The consideration eventually fell to the Army Board for the Correction of Military Records, which recommended to Secretary of the Army Clifford Alexander that the medal be restored. The 1916 review board, the 1977 board stated, "may have erred although there was no one particular act of heroism on Dr. Walker's part." On June 10, 1977, Secretary Alexander fully restored official recognition. As it had never been reclaimed from Dr. Walker, the original medal remains on display in the museum of the Oswego Historical Society.

There are many who denounce the return of Mary Walker to the Medal of Honor roll. As she was a civilian and was not in actual conflict with the enemy, her inclusion, her critics argue, dilutes the meaning of the nation's highest military honor. They express concern that the return of the medal was spearheaded by politicians and not soldiers, and that she was returned to the roll simply because she was a woman. Now, according to these critics, the floodgates are open. While the flood may not have come, many medals were similarly restored to civilians, including the scouts who distinguished themselves during the conflict with the Kiowas and Comanches. When Walker's name was restored, a precedent was certainly set.

Most of Dr. Walker's bravery was exhibited in her life outside the army—her unflinching dedication to her causes, her determination to wear clothing that was sure to draw ridicule or even arrest, her courage in arguing unpopular views. In 1871, she helped organize a procession that included prominent figures of the women's suffrage movement and former slave, abolitionist, and journalist Frederick Douglass. Their mission: to walk up to the registrars of the District of Columbia and register to vote. They were, of course, denied. Walker told those who had locked them out, "Gentlemen, these women have assembled to exercise the right of citizens of a professed-to-be republican country, and if you debar them of the right to register, you but add new proof that this is a tyrannical government, sustained by force and not by justice." Here again, her masculine clothing was noted by her audience. Here again, her clothing, itself a statement in linen, was accentuated by the nation's highest military honor pinned to her chest.

And yet, she loved her country deeply, always rising to defend its principles. The following anecdote further reveals how Dr. Walker lived from her earliest days, and how she believed all Americans should live—unfettered by convention.

During her time in Washington, she claimed, she once met the Chinese minister to the United States at a reception. He asked her, as many did, why she wore pants. She in turn asked him about why he wore his exotic national costume.

"It is the custom of my country," explained the minister.

To which Dr. Walker replied, "It is the custom in my country to do as one pleases."

CHAPTER TWO

Leopold Karpeles

CIVIL WAR

"While color bearer, rallied the retreating troops and induced them to check the enemy's advance . . ."

— MEDAL OF HONOR CITATION

IT'S STRIKING HOW OFTEN flags are mentioned in the Medal of Honor citations for the Civil War. Out of 1,520 Medal of Honor actions during the Civil War, 467 were given to men who either defended the flag of their side or captured a flag of the Confederate. Some "seized the colors" from fallen comrades and with them rallied their comrades still standing. Others struck out to the foremost part of the line and proved their "soldier-like qualities" by returning with the flag of the enemy. These actions are typically covered very briefly in the recipients' official citations. For example, John Simmons of Bethel, New York, has perhaps the most succinct Medal of Honor citation there is: "Capture of the flag."

Such citations hardly do justice to what happened to these men. The flag—the regimental colors, in this case—was at the center of the storm, and the man who held the colors was often the most vulnerable in the regiment. He carried no weapon, fired no bullets, and was always at the head of a charge. His mission was to give his comrades an indication of where the line stood, and whether they were advancing or retreating. All sets of eyes kept one eye on the flag, one on the enemy. And the enemy, of course, kept the flag and flag bearer in their sights.

Bringing the flag bearer down, everyone knew, was the most effective way of dismantling an attack. Not only did the loss of a color-bearer demoralize a regiment, it created confusion by leaving in question exactly where the point of the attack lay. Both officers and enlisted men relied on the flying colors to define the position of the regiment and its progress. As a regiment advanced, they followed the flag. The command "rally 'round the flag" was used not simply to inspire patriotism, but to prevent a rout. Many color-bearers fell. Very few held the job throughout the war. But such was the need for a visible sign, and such was the patriotic zeal that these colors inspired, that, in the words of Fairfax Downey in *The Color Bearers*, his book on these extraordinary men, "When bullets, shell fragments, and canister balls loosened grips on staffs, almost always other hands caught the colors before they fell. . . ."

It took inconceivable courage to participate in most any of the charges of the Civil War. But to do it with no weapon—to rush ahead of your comrades into a wall of fast-moving soft lead, and to do it again and again knowing that your chances for survival are slim—takes a believer. It's worth noting that color-bearers volunteered for the position (an unreliable, uncommitted bearer would do more harm than good) and they saw their task as one of highest honor.

Leopold Karpeles served longer than most flag bearers were able to serve without receiving a crippling or mortal wound, and wrote in an

1863 letter, "I am aware that while I'm providing a rallying point and courage for my comrades, I'm also a prime target for the enemy. I vowed to accept that risk when I assumed this obligation which I consider a privilege and honor." Karpeles then continued to explain why he accepted this duty: "My dedication to my country's flag rests on my ardent belief in this noblest of causes, equality for all. If my future rests under this earth rather than upon it, I fear not."

For his actions on the second day of the Battle of the Wilderness, May 6, 1864, made possible by a bravery fueled only by his desire to see "equality for all," Karpeles was awarded the Medal of Honor. Like so many of the sparse Civil War Medal of Honor citations, his—"While color bearer, rallied the retreating troops and induced them to check the enemy's advance"—understates terribly what actually happened that day.

Karpeles's journey to the Wilderness began on a ship from the Old World to the Wild West. When he was 11 years old, Karpeles landed at the port of Galveston, Texas. It was 1849. It's impossible to say what fantasies of cowboys and Indians sustained this boy as he made the long trip alone from Prague, then contained by the violently unstable Hungarian Empire. But we do know, from what he told his eldest daughter, Theresa, or "Tasy," that the life waiting for him wasn't what he expected or wanted. Leopold's brother, Emile, had immigrated to Galveston several years earlier and established a small but thriving dry goods store. News that his younger brother was on his way, probably to avoid conscription, prompted Emile to enroll him in school and prepare the store for an apprentice.

Galveston had served as a gateway to the West for several decades, but after the Mexican-American War of 1846–1848, European immigration stepped up markedly. In the year after Leopold landed, over half the town was German born, and there were small pockets of French, English, Polish, Norwegians, Greeks, Italians, Belgians, and Spaniards. But for all that, Galveston was still a new town with a long way to go. Its first bank opened its doors just the year before Leopold landed, and there wouldn't be a railroad link to Houston until ten years later. The town was flat, violent, and uninspiring. The square and plain buildings were erected quickly for shelter, not for beauty. A visiting reporter from the *New York Sun* wrote in 1847 that Galveston's streets were "wide and straight, but their cleanliness is about on a par with New York, which is no compliment."

Daily life was drab, but a crisis could always rouse the people to action. Every home was an arsenal, every day a day that could bring the feared Mexican invasion. People kept to themselves, but still looked after one another. When a group of new arrivals from Germany lost everything they had after their ship went down just outside the harbor, the town rushed to the relief of the passengers. A number of these new immigrants were given jobs with the city, cleaning the wide straight streets until they had enough to settle down or pay for passage further west.

Leopold probably didn't expect to see the medieval splendor of Prague duplicated here in Texas, but nor could he have expected the "Wild West" to be so mundane. In Prague, he had been born into a prominent family, and spent as much time as possible outside the city on farms and ranches. This is where he learned to ride, and that is probably what he expected to do more of in Texas. Instead, he found row after row of neatly stacked shelves of dry goods and a brother who thought working among them constituted an exciting life. As Tasy related in her book, *Memoirs: My Father's Life and My Life*, Leopold "cringed inwardly, but pretended to be receptive, realizing his fate lay in Emile's hands for the present."

In addition, Emile had unexpectedly embraced Catholicism. Both brothers had been baptized in Prague—a requirement for attendance in Catholic school—but their heritage was Jewish. Although Leopold's family raised him to "lay low" in matters of faith, Leopold wasn't ready to follow Emile to a new one. In this and other regards, his brother, older by seven years, had become like a stern parent. "Emile imposed his unrelenting will upon his young charge. School studies and store duties comprised

Leopold's routine, with a few exceptions," Tasy wrote. As the months dragged on, "his devotion toward his older brother ebbed away, replaced by mistrust and bitter loathing." According to Joyce Blackman, Karpeles's great-granddaughter, her ancestor was "not the most patient man." Blackman has a passion for seeing to the preservation of Leopold's memory. She holds the family records and has fleshed them out with her own research. Were it not for her bank of knowledge about Karpeles, our knowledge about him would be limited to his Medal of Honor action, which amounts to only one moment in a life filled with danger.

The dry plains beyond Galveston offered escape from his brother's "unrelenting will" and just the sort of adventure Leopold dreamed of when he came to America. After several months of cajoling, he finally got permission to accompany the supply convoys by which Emile shipped goods. The Republic of Texas might have given up its independence to become the Lone Star State, but the residents knew that when it came to their defense, they were still very much alone. The United States and the Comanches were frequently at war, and many Mexicans were very much in favor of taking Texas back. The Texas Rangers, mustered out after the Mexican-American War, were resurrected in 1849, albeit on a much more informal level than most military units. When they weren't involved in a campaign, many of them joined caravans. More than a few of them encountered a precocious and determined boy named Leopold Karpeles who spoke five languages—English, French, German, Greek, Czech— and was gaining fluency in five weapons—knife, lasso, rifle, pistol, saber.

For Leopold, this was the life. On the convoys, he met a variety of people—southerners, Mexicans, Indians—repelled attacks, protected important passengers, and fought the elements. After sundown, Leopold heard stories that made his future look full of promise and adventure. He also paid a great deal of attention to his surroundings. The desert, he wrote in a letter, was "beautiful, but humbling. One really sensed a greater power there, much more than in any church."

Karpeles would join the Rangers on expeditions much more serious

than the escorts, even fighting across the border in Mexico. The Texas
Rangers furnished their own horses, saddles, pistols, and knives. All Texas
provided was a rifle and $24 a month. The Rangers traveled light, prefer-
ring to hunt for their food rather than carry provisions, and slept in the
open rather than burden themselves with tents. It was about as informal
as military service gets, with men going AWOL for days at a time without
comment or punishment. Men and officers were on equal terms, address-
ing each other by first names or nicknames. This informality extended
into combat, as witnessed by Frederick Law Olmsted (a journalist who
became the principal architect of New York's Central Park), who traveled
with the Rangers in the 1850s: "They fought, when engaged, quite independently, the only order from the commander being—'All ready, boys?
Go ahead.'"

It was the perfect place for a young and impulsive man, but unfortunately it was also the perfect place for thugs. Karpeles was associated with
the Texas Rangers during a time of horrid brutality toward Native Americans and Mexicans, of massacres and illegal raids across the border. The
Rangers were a paramilitary force for the protection of the white settlers,
often against all others. Karpeles abhorred this violence, especially when
it was directed toward women and children, which happened far too often. He tried to align himself with Rangers who felt the same way, and
put distance between himself and those who enjoyed the violent side of
their work too much.

He also distanced himself from Emile. The more he stayed away, the
more the teenage Leopold realized he could survive independently, even
in the Texas badlands. But on his long trips, he saw much that disturbed
him deeply, in ways his youthful mind couldn't fully comprehend. He
might not have needed much practical instruction in horseback riding or
shooting, but he craved moral instruction. Knowing he wouldn't get it
from his brother, who increasingly saw his business as his only love and
who had begun harboring bigoted and anti-Semitic views, Leopold happily found it in a sad-faced man named Sam Butterfield.

They became friends in 1854, and made a curious pair. Leopold was 16, ten years younger than Butterfield, and still impulsive and full of enthusiasm. Butterfield was a drifter who approached life with a heavy heart. He had once loved a woman, who married him despite her family's disapproval. She was a Mexican, Sam an American. When she died while giving birth to their child, her family called it a fitting punishment for abandoning their wishes. Butterfield had loved her more than anything, and he shouldered a nearly crippling guilt over her demise. He said he would forever be "doing penance." This man's sincerity and his compassion for those on the lower rungs of the Texas caste system drew in young Leopold, who followed him to Brownsville, Texas.

At the southernmost point of Texas, Brownsville was a focal point of tension between Mexico and the United States. Fort Brown, established in 1845, leered defiantly across the Rio Grande at Matamoros, Mexico. Many men whose names would become prominent in the Civil War—Sheridan, Sherman, Steward, Grant, Lee—passed through Brownsville. But the presence of the Federals wasn't enough to protect the traders and caravans, who looked to militia-type organizations like the Brownsville Guard and the Brownsville Tigers for protection. Karpeles served time with both of these organizations in the late 1850s, and family lore holds that he fought in skirmishes in Mexico, though details as to where and why are missing.

In Brownsville, white Americans were surrounded by and mixed in with groups of people who had been wronged by the expanding nation. Mexicans, Seminoles, and black slaves were all there or nearby in numbers, making the town a very uneasy place. Butterfield helped Karpeles understand the causes behind the tensions. He had a connection to and a great depth of feeling for the plight of the Mexicans. He knew that in Brownsville and directly across the border were families who, following the Mexican-American War, had watched Anglos strip them of land they had held for generations. He also had experience with slavery, which he abhorred, and so he enlisted Karpeles in one of his secret causes.

The Underground Railroad didn't only run north. Slavery was illegal in Mexico, and was within reach for escaped slaves from Texas and Louisiana. Being a point of trade with Mexico, Brownsville became a final stop for "contraband" on their way to freedom. Thus Karpeles and Butterfield became the last link in a chain. Sometimes they hid their charges in wagonloads of goods they escorted over to the other side, and sometimes they ran with the escapees across the Rio Grande under cover of darkness. Either way, it was dangerous work—bounty hunters who sought escaped slaves didn't mind killing a white man to capture a black one. But, as Karpeles told his family in later years, he was compelled by the satisfaction of seeing someone born and raised in bondage walk into freedom. After leaving a grateful traveler with sympathetic Mexicans and Seminoles, he could return to Texas with the knowledge that he had helped change a life.

Karpeles's frequent border crossings weren't, however, always for altruistic reasons. At one point, he was involved in a dangerous affair with the wife of a Mexican official. "He was a young man who liked women," relates Joyce Blackman, "and he always did, for the rest of his life." This affair went on long enough to be a significant chapter in Karpeles's life, and long enough for him to fall in love very deeply. When he finally broke it off—knowing that discovery would have meant death—he did so with difficulty and regret. To Joyce Blackman, it's a chapter that fits in with the rest of his experiences: "He was always on the edge of getting into big trouble, all his life."

Karpeles couldn't have grown up to be more different from his brother. As Leopold was smuggling slaves out of the country, Emile was proclaiming his faith in the economic rightness of the southern system. While Leopold admired a country lawyer named Abraham Lincoln and his stand against slavery, Emile firmly hated the man. When secession began to seem inevitable, Emile proclaimed his loyalty to the Confederacy and promised to join its armed struggle. The fact that this quiet shopkeeper was moved to wear a uniform and carry a rifle for the Confederacy speaks to the level of passion and anger that flowed through Texas in 1861. Leopold, however, proclaimed opposite loyalties. He was clearly out of step with his brother and his adopted state, and prepared to leave behind the wide open spaces he had come to love.

Texas voted to secede on February 23, 1861, and Leopold Karpeles moved away, feeling like a political exile. He was leaving behind his only family in America, his friends, his beloved landscape, but, as he later told his daughter, "Despair and sadness were relieved by the realization that my future belonged only to me."

Everywhere in New England, anger over the audacity of secession and the outrage of the first shots of the war at Fort Sumter, on April 12, 1861, was palpable in the streets, homes, and pubs. But Springfield, Massachusetts, which Karpeles chose because of the promise of a job with one of his brother's business contacts, was even more charged. John Brown's destruction of the Harpers Ferry Arsenal and Armory in 1859 had left the Springfield Armory the most important manufacturer of small arms in the north. The town's residents were fully aware of the important role they played, and took pride in the astounding increase in production—from 1,200 rifles a year before the war to capacity for 300,000 a year by June 30, 1864. In all, Springfield sent nearly 800,000 muskets into battle.

Karpeles took a job as a shop clerk, and was swept up in the intellectual and moral furor over slavery and secession. As he had in Texas, he found a mentor—prominent community leader and abolitionist Sam Spooner—who instructed him in the unfamiliar culture and took him to lectures and meetings on the twin issues of the day. With his new friend, he ferried slaves to freedom, just as he'd done in Texas, by becoming a station in the Underground Railroad to Canada. His work was not as dangerous as what he'd done before, and the fact that he didn't see the end of the escaped slaves' trail made him feel less connected to this particular job. In the South, Karpeles had seen slavery firsthand; now he looked at it from afar with an even more critical eye. His belief that this institution was an affront to humanity and the true essence of the Constitution deepened to the point where he was ready to put his life on the line. As his friend Sam Spooner entered the Union army in 1862, Karpeles followed.

Karpeles signed up with the 46th Massachusetts Volunteer Regiment and began training on September 24, 1862, with Spooner serving as a captain in the same regiment. Although he was one of the few volunteers with actual combat experience, he was unfamiliar with the drills and the disciplined methods of attack. But he was promoted to corporal before the 46th left training, and his request to be made color-bearer was accepted. In late 1862, he served with honor and distinction in the Goldsboro Expedition, a minor campaign in North Carolina undertaken to disrupt the railroad supply lines. In the words of Sam Spooner in a letter of recommendation, which was also signed by W. S. Shurtless, commander of the 46th, "The promptness with which [Karpeles] came upon the line of battle and the firmness with which he stood his ground, though his flag was several times pierced by the bullets of the enemy, were so conspicuous as to be the subject of remark and commendation."

After his nine-month term was fulfilled, Karpeles and the rest of the 46th returned to Springfield, where they were mustered out on July 29, 1863. Karpeles reflected on his military service. While he felt "inspired" by his role as flag bearer, he wrote in a letter that morale was often undermined by tedium. "Marching monotonously down country roads in lines for hours at a time breeds boredom and hostility. There is no relief from enforced routines nor protection from danger. The soldier's life is a balancing act of striving to exercise control over one's mind and body despite unhealthful, wretched living conditions."

Knowing the truth about "the soldier's life" didn't keep him from going back into the army. In October 1863, Lincoln asked the states to enlist and train another 300,000 men for what he hoped would be one last push. Karpeles responded to the call of Colonel William Francis Bartlett, a veteran who'd had his leg amputated at the knee from an injury at Yorktown during the Peninsula campaign. He got around well enough by relying on a cork prosthetic, and managed to muster 1,038 officers and enlisted men to form the 57th Massachusetts Volunteer Infantry. Although Karpeles never sought the glory of rank, he was promoted to sergeant with Company E, assigned to assist with training, and again held the flag, as he'd requested. "My estimation of his good qualities," Colonel Bartlett later wrote in a letter of recommendation, "may be judged from the fact that I entrusted him the colors of the 57th Massachusetts Infantry."

By boat, train, and foot, the 57th made its way to Washington, D.C., arriving on April 25, 1864. They camped in view of the Capitol dome, still under construction. As they paraded past President Lincoln with their new comrades in the first division, Karpeles experienced one of the proudest moments of his life. He revered Lincoln, he revered his country's flag, and here he marched in review past one while holding the other.

As the 57th left Washington to join the Army of the Potomac—the largest army to ever march on American soil—they were at three-quarters of their original strength. All along the route from Massachusetts to Washington, men had fallen ill or decided to take their soldier's pay and disappear. The regiment saw its first death on the way to the Rappahannock—a New Englander who died of sunstroke.

The majority of the regiment was from Massachusetts, but there were also soldiers from states as unlikely as Virginia, Georgia, Louisiana, Arkansas, Kentucky, and Utah. Of the original group that trained alongside Karpeles, 358 were foreign-born. Karpeles may have been the only Jew in the group, but there's no evidence that he either proclaimed the fact or was given trouble for it. The tension in the regiment was clearly between the Irish Catholics and the New England Protestants, and this tension sometimes resulted in fistfights. But among this diverse group, most of the men—all but 245—had one thing in common. They had never before "seen the elephant," that is, they'd never been in combat.

The regiment's route took them past Bull Run, in northern Virginia, the site of two Federal disasters on two separate occasions—July 21,

1861, and August 29–30, 1862. The dead were long buried, but the land still showed the scars of battle. As they approached the Wilderness, they could hear the sickening thud of cannon fire in the distance. Colonel Bartlett wrote in his diary, "It will be a bloody day. . . . I believe I am prepared to die." On the morning of May 6, 1864, the 57th, after having covered hundreds of miles in a matter of days, marched overnight and directly into what Captain John Anderson, commander of Karpeles's company, called "a veritable baptism of fire by immersion."

The Battle of the Wilderness was a fight like no other in the war. Battles were typically a much more orderly affair, with companies moving forward together in step, as Anderson called it in his memoirs, "in picture-book style," but in this jungle-like northern Virginia location, the appropriately named Wilderness, the terrain made these precise maneuvers worthless. "A consistent line of battle on either side was impossible," one veteran remembered. The visibility was cut to a few yards by the thick underbrush and the early morning fog and dense smoke from muskets and forest fires. Swamps, bogs, creeks, and ravines broke the land. The battle was described variously by fighting soldiers as one "no man saw or could see," "a battle of invisibles with invisibles," and, in the words of a Confederate captive, no more than a fight between "howling mobs." It was precisely General Robert E. Lee's hope that by attacking on this difficult ground, he would drive General Grant back across the Rapidan, inflicting heavy casualties at the same time.

The 57th marched into the fray with Company H, where Karpeles had been temporarily assigned, in the lead. They had been ordered to march past a regiment of veterans who had stopped in a position of relative safety and would not obey orders to move ahead. As they entered the jungle, they were met by terrorized men running from it. As they moved farther into the battle, they encountered the veteran regiment lying prone. The veterans shouted at the men of the 57th to take cover. But instead of taking cover, the 57th followed orders and marched forward in rows, as they had been trained. As a result, they were, as Captain Anderson recalled, "shot to pieces."

Almost half of the 548 men of the 57th who went into the Wilderness either didn't come out or didn't come out whole, and most had their fates sealed within the first hour of the battle. Fifty-four were killed immediately. Twenty-nine more were mortally wounded. One hundred fifty-six were wounded, and 20 of those were captured. Twelve were captured unharmed, and 10 went missing. Many of those still on the field suffered in a more prolonged fashion. As Karpeles remembered:

> To make matters worse, as shells ricocheted through the woodland interior toward the troops, they sliced through the trunks and branches, setting them ablaze. In turn, the brittle undergrowth received sparks that ignited it like thousands of matches. As the foliage burned, large and small branches became disconnected from the trees and crashed to earth, often trapping the men below. Rescue was next to impossible because of the separation of the men. Wounded comrades often were knocked to the ground and burned hideously, helplessly alone in their agony.

Captain Anderson later attempted to summarize the confusion, the terror, the screams of the men, the fires, and the constant threat of death by unseen hands, but found it nearly impossible: "It seemed that nothing more of horror could be added. The mind could not comprehend the hundredth part of what had already transpired. . . . The glories of war were lost in its sickening sights." Colonel Bartlett, who wrote in his diary that he was prepared to die, came within a hair's breadth. A bullet bounced off his temple and he was taken to the rear.

The 57th took heavier casualties than any other regiment there—they would eventually have a higher casualty rate than any other regiment in the war except the 2nd Wisconsin, which was in the field four times as long—but they also advanced farther than any other. However, as no one followed, and as no one was alongside, they were soon alone. That is, until the right wing of the line crumbled under the Confederate guns, bringing about what Karpeles called "a general stampede" of other regiments upon the volunteers from Massachusetts, who readily joined in the retreat. This is exactly the sort of situation the presence of a color-bearer is supposed to prevent, which is what Karpeles tried to do.

Climbing a stump that had just recently been created by an incoming shell, Karpeles shouted to Lieutenant Colonel Chandler—Bartlett's lieutenant who'd assumed command—"Colonel, the rebs are around us." Far across the field, General Wadsworth, who was leading a division to reinforce the rapidly folding wing, spotted Karpeles's colors, as Anderson relates, "floating proudly and defiantly amid the sulphurous smoke in the face of the advancing foe. He also witnessed Sergeant Karpeles standing firmly and entreating the retreating men streaming by him to re-form and make a stand against the enemy."

Karpeles retold the story for Anderson's book on the campaign. He was, he said, the only color-bearer on the field, and he chose where to make a stand. Chandler, seeing how he exposed himself to enemy fire just to make his flag more visible, shouted to the retreating men, "For God's sake boys, don't forsake your colors!" Thirty-four men from the 57th rallied, and they added to their number troops from the routed Pennsylvania and New York regiments. "We succeeded in forming these men into a fighting line and ordered them to advance on the approaching rebels, and by a rapid discharge of firearms managed to check the enemy."

Karpeles's heroism had brought order out of chaos, but although the wing had been saved for a more orderly retreat, the men he had rallied were ultimately unsupported. The Confederates advanced past them, and then passed them again when they retreated back to their side. Typical of the day, there was often no telling on which side of the line they were. Chandler used this to a small advantage when he captured a Confederate by sneaking up on him and putting a revolver to his head. In a brief lull in the fight, one young Union soldier managed to scribble in his diary, "There is about 20 of us and Lt. Col. have rallied around the flag and going [through] heated times." Finally, the small band was able to fall back to the Union lines near sunset. On hands and knees, for what seemed like hours, they made their retreat. They, with the rest of the regiment, were exhausted and shaken, but took up shovels to improve their fortifications, their newfound fear becoming a powerful stimulant. As if in taunting answer to Anderson's claim that nothing could add to the horror of the event, the fires and the wails of wounded men burning to death continued throughout the night.

Those who hold the Medal of Honor often wince at the phrases "Medal of Honor winner," or "won the Medal of Honor." For one thing, they were not involved in a contest that delivered the award. For another, most of them lived through situations comparably hellish to what Leopold Karpeles survived. To experience something like that with bravery and honor isn't the same thing as "winning." They almost unanimously prefer the term "earned."

Most of the soldiers of the 57th had walked into battle completely green, and had walked out having survived some of the hottest and most chaotic fighting of the war. Many were openly upset when they were ordered to march on what looked like a retreat, but they started to cheer after they reached a junction and again took the road south. Grant was not retreating, they realized, but executing the first of a series of sideways redeployments that would force Lee to stay on the defensive all the way to Richmond.

Their next serious engagement was on the approach to Spotsylvania, where the Union and Confederate forces hammered at each other from May 9 to 12 and then remained in a weeklong standoff. The 57th used what they had learned in the Wilderness in an inspired charge, with fixed bayonets, that sent a group of veteran rebels running. But after disengaging from the bloodletting at Spotsylvania, as the 57th marched on, they appeared utterly resigned. They had reached the point where life and death were essentially the same. Unfortunately, at the next major battle, North Anna, they fell under the command of a general who felt the same way—not about his own life, but about theirs.

Brigadier General James Ledlie was inexperienced, ambitious, impetuous, and often drunk. Or so found the court of inquiry which investigated his part in the botched Battle of the Crater of July 30, 1864. (Grant called this battle "the saddest affair I have witnessed in this war.") That judgment would come too late for the men caught up in the butchery he produced at North Anna on May 24. Ledlie was under orders to assemble his command in a defensive position and wait for reinforcements before moving forward. When he saw what he thought was an opportunity to overwhelm a Confederate brigade, he sent a messenger to ask permission to attack. The request was unequivocally denied, but by the time the messenger returned, the attack was already under way.

The men ran across open ground, opposed by artillery and musket fire from an entrenched position, and fell by the dozens. "We had seen the regiment very nearly annihilated," Karpeles remembered later, "and had lost dear friends we dearly loved." Adding to his grief was his injury—a bullet struck his leg, sending him to the ground. He recovered his posture, and his flag, and charged again. Chandler tried to pull the flag from his grip and send him to the rear, but Karpeles refused until the loss of blood made it impossible to go on. With the help of his comrades, he limped back to the rear, and learned later that day of what transpired in his absence.

Chandler was mortally wounded soon after and had to be abandoned on the field. Chandler had, at the Wilderness, where he assumed command, and here, where he tried to take the colors from Karpeles, proven himself to be an extremely brave officer by exposing himself to danger that was more typically suffered by the enlisted men alone. Karpeles, understandably but unreasonably, blamed himself. He said that he should have taken the bullet that felled Chandler. In the moment, he could not be reassured. Only later was he able to write about North Anna with some perspective. "In the loss of our colors, our pride had been humiliated, yet we felt a consciousness that the brave men who were with the 57th that day had done all, under the circumstances, that brave men can do." After the ill-advised charge undertaken by 237 men, there remained only 199 in the 57th ready for combat duty.

Karpeles fought to rejoin them, even after lying unconscious for several days. It wasn't until October, five months later, that the doctors begrudgingly allowed him to return to the fight. Once there, however, his wounds reopened and became aggravated, and he was once more sent to recuperate, in much worse condition than he was before. His service in uniform was over.

Having roamed from Prague to Texas and Mexico, to Massachusetts and then to the battlefields of Virginia, it seemed unlikely that Karpeles's next move would be to settle down. But even if the bullet wound in his leg was a deterrent against further adventure, a more powerful argument visited him at his bedside.

Sara Mundheim, age 16, along with her mother and sister, Henrietta, were volunteers at the Mount Pleasant Army Hospital in Washington, D.C., where she met Leopold Karpeles. He was an uncomplaining patient, but restless, and his good nature masked an increasingly serious condition. The leg wound, doctors said, threatened total paralysis or death if the limb was not removed. Losing a leg was completely unacceptable to Karpeles, and, once she'd fallen in love with her patient, it was unacceptable to Sara as well.

Sara interrogated the doctors, who finally conceded that Karpeles might be able to keep his leg if he had close, attentive care in a private setting. That, she thought, was something she would gladly do—but only with her parents' blessing, as the treatments Karpeles would receive would have to take place under their roof.

As her father was the first Reform Rabbi in Washington, the first question Sara had to answer concerned Karpeles's religion. Having spent long hours at his bedside, she knew how he had been baptized into an unfamiliar faith in Prague, and how he felt about his brother's growing anti-Semitism. So the first condition put down by Sara's parents—that he convert to Judaism—was something Karpeles welcomed. The second—that there would be no wedding until Karpeles was completely recovered—was something the two simply had to accept.

Under the care of Sara and the family doctor, Karpeles made a rapid recovery, only set back once—by the gloom he suffered after Lincoln's death on April 15, 1865. Karpeles was crushed by the news, and watched the funeral procession pass directly in front of Rabbi Mundheim's house on Pennsylvania Avenue. Still unsteady on his feet as he stood on the balcony, leaning on his future wife, he would have preferred to be more formally dressed for the somber occasion. But he did wear slippers embroidered with Old Glory, fashioned by his future wife and later passed down through several generations. All his sorrow and rage over the assassination climaxed as the black horse with an empty saddle passed by. Perhaps he was thinking of the day his beloved commander in chief watched him in a parade from a balcony not far away, of how unhappily their positions were now reversed.

Karpeles kept his leg, but would walk with a limp for the rest of his life. Considering how many amputees could be seen in the streets of Washington in the early years of the Reconstruction, Karpeles considered himself lucky. His wedding to Sara, in Washington's Hebrew Congregation, added to this feeling, as did the birth of their daughter, Theresa (Tasy), in December 1870, the same year he received his Medal of Honor. Civil War veterans who hadn't been recommended for the medal by their commanding officers applied for the medal by the thousands. Karpeles received recommendations from Anderson and Bartlett and filed with the Adjutant General's office on April 18, 1870. The award was granted on April 30. Karpeles was one of six Jews granted a Medal of Honor for actions in the Civil War.

Sara was a skilled milliner, and the couple set up a fancy-hats shop catering to the tastes of Washington's elite. As Karpeles's great-grand-daughter Joyce Blackman understands it, Karpeles took care of sales—"He sort of charmed the customers"—and bookkeeping while Sara took care of manufacturing. They lived in the busy Jewish community surrounding 4½ Street Southwest with Sara's sister Henrietta, and, according to city records, garnered a modest but comfortable estate. Nothing in the family remembrances hint at Karpeles chafing at the domestic life or having any trouble leaving behind his days of wandering adventures. A second child arrived in 1871, a third was on the way in late 1872, and the family's future seemed as straight and even as Washington's methodically laid out avenues.

Back in Texas, Karpeles had seen in Sam Butterfield's face the ravages of grief brought on by the loss of his wife. Thus he might have apprehended what stood before him when Sara was taken ill during the birth of their third child. Tasy wasn't even three, but later she remembered her mother asking her family to her side, knowing she was lying on her deathbed, knowing the baby had not survived. From her husband and sister, who were wrought with grief, she extracted a promise: They would marry. This was the only way, she said, she could die with the assurance that her children would have a strong, caring mother. Henrietta and Leopold could hardly refuse.

Jewish law, Rabbi Mundheim informed the future husband and wife, prescribed a year of mourning, and, not incidentally, also prescribed the match of a widower to the deceased's sister. After a year, he performed the quiet and private ceremony in his home, and Tasy acquired the mother of Sara's choice. Leopold and Henrietta would have three sons and three daughters, but Sara's second daughter died within a year following the wedding, leaving Tasy as the only offspring of the original marriage.

Karpeles became a fixture in Washington society. As a speaker, he was valued at political conventions and veterans groups. In 1875, he obtained a job as a clerk in the Treasury Department at $900 dollars a year—more than his entire estate in 1870. But, as family members have said through the years, he always managed to spend more than he earned—seldom on himself.

As Joyce Blackman explained, he "was always on the brink of disaster financially because he would entertain the needs of anybody who came to him, and threw very lavish parties and would make big loans or take people in under his roof and shelter them until they were able to function on their own." Somehow, this beneficence never quite caught up with him; his family did not go without, but neither did they acquire wealth. There was still something of the impetuous, idealistic youth in Karpeles, something still attached to the unfortunate, especially if they had served in the defining event of the era. The Civil War was, as Blackman concludes, "a moment in history that captured him forevermore."

By the mid 1870s, Karpeles was often, as Tasy remembered, "seen strolling with a Senator, Representative, or key foreign ambassador and conversing heatedly . . . Father knew absolutely everyone from the President down as far back as I can remember." In a very informal sense, he became an advocate and lobbyist. Leopold was well known to President Chester A. Arthur, and knew Grant and McKinley well enough to be in regular attendance at their New Year's Day receptions.

For Karpeles, each connection was an opportunity to promote a cause. His name became, for a brief time, associated with labor legislation—specifically a shortened working day. His time in Texas happily haunted him each year when, according to Tasy, the Native Americans who befriended him there came to Washington on official business. She remembered they invited Karpeles to join them as they transformed elegant hotel rooms into ceremonial scenes of chanting and smoking.

In 1888, Captain John Anderson responded to a letter from his old comrade that reflected on the continuing duty of the Civil War veteran: "I was very glad to hear from you," he wrote from Fort Gibson in what's now Oklahoma, "and glad to find you still on the shores of mortality, where our numbers are fast diminishing. Our duty now lies in planting the principles and memory of the great struggle in the hearts of generations to follow us, endear the old flag to them that you carried so faithfully and gallantly from the Wilderness to North Anna and teach them to love the country which was saved at such sacrifice."

Karpeles was active in the Grand Army of the Republic, the powerful and influential veterans group that successfully lobbied for Memorial Day and claimed five U.S. presidents among its members. At the GAR, Karpeles went by "Colonel." He was also a founding member, and later a vice president, of the Medal of Honor Legion, the group instrumental in solidifying the meaning of the Medal of Honor, by doing away with the vague definition and the politically motivated "giveaways."

"[His] backbone was strong as steel, like his will," Tasy remembered. "He was a great patriot and unshakably loyal to his beliefs." While adventure had sustained and inspired his early life, patriotism became his driving force after the war and as he grew older. Only once did he consider going back into harm's way, after the outbreak of the Spanish-American War in 1898. He was in conversation with President McKinley and expressed his intense desire to serve. Even if he couldn't march, because of his limp, he said, he could still ride a horse. He was earnest, but the president replied simply: "This is for younger men."

Emile Karpeles had remained in touch with his brother throughout, but his letters reveal a loveless man. His anti-Semitism became stronger and more bitter. When Leopold's eldest son got engaged in 1893, Emile wrote a letter advising against a union with a Jew. All Jews, he wrote, were damned—none could be trusted. Emile gave his small fortune entirely to the Roman Catholic Church. His funds built a convent in Galveston, where he was treated after being struck with tuberculosis. He died there around 1897.

In 1909, the year Karpeles passed away and was buried in the cemetery of the Hebrew Congregation, his Medal of Honor was lost in a fire.

Each generation following him has tried to get a duplicate, but there appears to be no provision for making such copies for family members. Joyce Blackman says she has on file "promises from all kinds of senators and representatives that they would definitely get it, but it's never been done." All that remains of the original is the replica of the medal carved into the hero's gravestone.

A Nation of Immigrants

O ne of the enduring clichés about the Civil War was that it pitted
brother against brother in mortal combat. Well, that certainly
was the experience of Emile and Leopold Karpeles, and what I find so
striking about their story is that they were immigrants. During their
childhood years in Prague, the two brothers were far removed from the
passions of slavery and abolition that were driving such a deep wedge
into American life, and doing so long before they arrived in Galveston
to begin their new lives on the Texas frontier. Yet even without a family
or regional tradition to influence them, both brothers were soon caught
up in those passions, and on opposing sides of the burning issue.

In reading about the Karpeles brothers, I felt a vague twinge of kinship, and that's because I could identify with their heritage. Like them,
my parents were Eastern European Jews who came to America in
search of a better life. They were among the many immigrants who
made the long and difficult journey from Tsarist Russia in the 1890s,
three decades after the Civil War. Yet even though my American roots
do not extend back to that epochal event, I've always regarded the Civil

War as part of my history, too—and that's probably because of where I grew up.

I was born and raised in the Boston suburb of Brookline, and it is all but impossible to live in that region without absorbing its rich sense of tradition. Boston lies at the epicenter of American history. From Boston, it's a mere stone's throw (so to speak) to Plymouth Rock, where the Pilgrims landed, and just a few miles northwest are Lexington and Concord, where "the shot heard round the world" launched the American Revolution. No less definitive was Boston's role in the abolitionist movement. The two most eloquent and fiery leaders of that crusade—Wendell Phillips and William Lloyd Garrison—were Bostonians who ran their campaigns out of that city, and another New Englander, Harriet Beecher Stowe, wrote *Uncle Tom's Cabin,* the book that became the bible of the antislavery cause. All this imbued the region with a powerful legacy, one that greatly helped to shape the values and principles of later generations of New Englanders, even including some of us who could not trace our lineage back to the *Mayflower* or the Minutemen, or to the Yankee soldiers who fought to free the slaves and preserve the Union.

The outcome of the Civil War not only saved the Union, but significantly strengthened and solidified it. So much so that never again would the federal government have to be concerned about secession, which had been a recurring threat throughout our early history, and not only from the Southern states. (During the War of 1812, the New England states seriously considered seceding rather than support a war that disrupted their thriving trade with Britain.)

In essence, the Civil War dramatically changed the way Americans thought about themselves and their country, and no one addressed that point more succinctly than television producer Ken Burns in one of the episodes of his celebrated PBS series. Before the Civil War, Burns noted, it was customary to say, "the United States are . . ." But after that war, it would always be "the United States is . . ." And the more we became accustomed to seeing ourselves as truly "one nation indivisible," the more prepared we would be for the challenges we would have to confront when, decades later, we began to flex our muscles as a rising power on the international stage.

Comparable struggles to strengthen national unification were taking place in Europe. From Berlin, Otto von Bismarck orchestrated a series of adroit actions—including military triumphs over Austria and France—that enabled him to unite Germany under his Prussian leadership.

As the founder and first chancellor of what he proudly called the German Empire, Bismarck had ample reason to rejoice in his accomplishments. And yet he viewed the future with gloom and foreboding. He feared that the fragile alliances and treaties he had done so much to bring to fruition would not hold and that Europe was doomed to be engulfed by a terrible war. Bismarck not only envisioned the fury of World War I, but he even had a premonition of the act that would ignite it. "Some damned foolish thing in the Balkans," he predicted shortly before his death in 1898.

So along with his many other attributes, the man had a gift for prophecy. The "damned foolish thing in the Balkans"—the assassination of the Austrian archduke Franz Ferdinand in Sarajevo—occurred in late June 1914, and set off the rapid chain of events that led to what Barbara Tuchman memorably called "the guns of August." The guns that began firing that summer would continue to explode across Europe for more than four years.

—MW

CHAPTER THREE

Edouard Victor Michel Izac

WORLD WAR I

"During his stay on the U-90 *he obtained information of the movements of German submarines which was so important that he determined to escape . . ."*

— MEDAL OF HONOR CITATION

ON A BRIGHT, CLEAR DAY in the first week of June 1918, the *U-90* of the German submarine fleet was on the North Sea, speeding through uncharacteristically calm waters. The high visibility and glassy surface made it a perfect day for hunting Allied ships, but none were on the horizon. One man on deck, even more than the relaxed and confident crew, gave the impression that he was on a cruise rather than a wartime patrol. He spent the day sunning himself, casually smoking, chatting with the officers, and looking through his binoculars every now and then. He carried himself like a passenger, or maybe an observer, but he was a prisoner of war, captured from the wreckage of an American troop transport only days before. And his casual demeanor concealed the fact that he was gathering intelligence and strengthening his resolve to a course of action that would earn him the Medal of Honor.

While it was assassin's bullets—aimed at Archduke Ferdinand—that ignited the powder keg in Europe, it was the torpedoes of German U-boats that paved the way for America's entry into the conflict. Germany's submarine warfare extended even to the passenger liners *Lusitania* and *Arabic*, which were sunk in May and August 1915. Although most of the civilian deaths on these ships were British, America was outraged, and began to slide, slowly, into the war.

In spring 1917, America made a commitment of 2 million troops, but before they could get "over there," the U.S. Navy had to succeed against a new type of warfare. German subs ruled the waves, sent almost a million tons of shipping to the ocean floor every month, and by 1917 had virtually brought Britain's Royal Navy to its knees. "What we are facing," U.S. Ambassador Walter H. Page bluntly told Admiral William Snowden Sims, commander of U.S. naval forces in European waters, as America entered the war in April 1917, "is the defeat of Great Britain." This defeat appeared to be inevitable—without a single German soldier setting foot on the British Isles.

Germany had pinned all its hopes on the U-boats. From February 1915, their U-boat captains were under orders to sink any ship in British waters without warning. Although, for a time, German diplomats tried to assure America that they would abide by international law, on February 1, 1917, Germany declared a policy of unrestricted submarine warfare. If this ruthless campaign worked, Great Britain and the United States would be irrelevant. If it failed, Germany would have to face American troops and ordnance on the western front. Outside the trenches, the war hung on the balance of power in the North Atlantic. Lieutenant Edouard Victor Michel Izac, the prisoner of war on the deck of the *U-90* on that spring day, knew that every U-boat sunk meant that another American troop transport had a greater chance of getting through. He knew that German military commanders were attempting an advance on Paris in a last-ditch attempt to win the war before America could assemble enough troops to check their offensive. He knew that every day he spent on the *U-90* was a day that Admiral Sims would want to hear about.

Edouard Izac shared at least one characteristic with his father, Balthazar Izac: They both loathed dictators. The elder Izac had left his home in Alsace-Lorraine (the French region later captured during the Franco-Prussian War) shortly after Napoleon III declared himself emperor in 1852. He sailed to America, where an immigration officer changed his name to Isaacs, and he never changed it back. Neither did eight of his nine children, though they all grew up speaking French at home. Only his youngest, Edouard, reclaimed the family name as it had been, and only after the war (which is why we see his name spelled Isaacs by his captain and others). But being stripped of his name didn't strip Balthazar's desire to take America head-on. In the late 19th century, this meant heading west.

Edouard Izac's mother, Mathilda Geuth, also came from a pioneering family. Her parents had immigrated to America decades earlier from Baden-Württemberg, the German state that borders Alsace-Lorraine, and traveled west in covered wagons. Mathilda herself had been born in Philadelphia, but married Balthazar in Florenceville, Iowa, in 1867. This was the same year their home of Cresco, Iowa, became a bustling frontier town.

Cresco was one of Iowa's more successful real-estate speculations. Bought and built up in a single year, it went from a population of virtually zero to almost 1,600. Across the Atlantic, it made the pages of the *London Times*: "In six months a bald prairie is covered with stores, shops, and dwellings of a thousand inhabitants, and resounds to the hum of rushing business." Balthazar, barely educated but strong and skilled of hand, established a business building farm wagons and buggies at the rate of one per week. "They made fifty a year," recalled Izac. "No more, no less."

It wasn't the sort of operation that could make a man rich, and Balthazar never became so, but the comfortable life wasn't beyond his means in the early days of Cresco. It may have been a new town in a rural county, but the houses there would have appeared more appropriate in the Boston suburbs than on the Iowa prairies. Women's petticoats floated over planked sidewalks rather than through dusty or muddy streets. The children were well groomed and public education was said to be the best in the state. There was a real worldliness about Cresco, with its population of German, Irish, Scandinavian, and Balkan settlers. Into this milieu Edouard was born, in 1891, a year after Cresco saw its first public well and six years before its first electric streetlight.

In a town so small, with so many nationalities, there were of course many churches. But there was only one Catholic school, and that is where Edouard went. The School of the Assumption consisted of two buildings and a handful of students. One building was for boys, the other for the girls. Both had at one time been large private homes.

Edouard, being the youngest of nine children, grew up fast. As he entered young adulthood (and in his day and age, that meant his early teens), he sought his fortune with a relative in South St. Paul, another mushrooming former farm town.

Fourteen carloads of European immigrants, one historian said, poured into South St. Paul's railyard every day in the early 1900s. By 1905, the town's population was 3,458 persons; 2,108 were foreign-born, and 649 of these were German. But unlike the refined pastoral scene of Cresco, South St. Paul's draw was the stockyards. The gritty work permeated the atmosphere of the town, but the promise of steady employment kept people coming, and a civic pride blossomed amidst the cattle pens and slaughterhouses. Nowhere was this more evident than in the construction of new schools, namely the high school that Izac attended, a modern three-story structure built in 1905 with 16 classrooms and an 800-seat auditorium—more than enough room for the 40 students who attended in its first year.

Izac came to value learning above everything except God, and this is why he decided to do all he could to get into the U.S. Naval Academy. It was, he would tell his children, the only way he felt he could be guaranteed a "complete education." He knew that private colleges were completely out of reach. So he made a concentrated appeal to a congressman in Chicago and secured an appointment to the U.S. Naval Academy.

Adapting to the rigors of the Academy probably wasn't easy for him—he'd lived a landlocked life, and while the schools he had attended were academically solid, they weren't designed to produce officers or gentlemen. He didn't earn honors or great accolades, but he did win a fiancée.

Agnes Cabell was the daughter of General De Rosey Carroll Cabell, a stern West Point graduate who had entered the Chinese Emperor's Forbidden City during the Boxer Rebellion of 1900. Agnes and Izac never should have met. She was already engaged to a West Point cadet, and her father would have never allowed her to set foot on the Naval Academy's campus. But she went to a dance there as a favor to a friend, a girl who wanted a date with a friend of Izac's and needed Agnes to make the date a double. She went without her father's knowledge.

When Izac found out that Agnes was engaged, he suggested that they become "chums." She thought that funny and charming, so she called him "chum" for the rest of the night, and then for the rest of their lives. They never addressed each other by first name. Edouard was always "Chum," and she always "Sweetheart." Maybe these terms of endearment were born of her initial reaction to her future husband, which she confided to her friend later that night: "How could a man that handsome have that horrible name of Isaac?"

Agnes's father couldn't care less what this midshipman's name was. He didn't focus on the immense class difference that separated the two. Izac was navy, not army, and that was all the general needed to know. But after a thorough round of curses, he begrudgingly honored his daughter's wishes. Agnes Cabell and Edouard Izac were married the day after Izac graduated from the Naval Academy in 1915.

Izac started his naval career on the battleship *Florida*, and was at hand when the first gun crews were trained for the Naval Transport Service, the precursor to the Merchant Marine. As he was promoted from ensign to lieutenant (junior grade), he signed up for the transport service. The trips were frequent, but unlike battleship duty, they weren't open ended. Unfortunately, he did miss the birth of his first child, despite his "orders" to his wife to wait until he got back and her vain attempts to comply. And so Cabell was born in April 1916, one year before the United States entered the First World War.

The USS *President Lincoln* was built as a Hamburg-American liner, and was seized by the U.S. Navy following the April 1917 declaration of war. The German crew attempted to sabotage the ship's engines before it was pressed into service; they didn't get far enough to cripple the ship. One of two six-masted steamers in the world, the *President Lincoln* was exactly the sort of massive vessel the Naval Transport Service needed to carry American troops to France. Izac reported to the *President Lincoln* in July 1917, while she was still in dry dock, and oversaw the conversion to a man-of-war. By October, she was fitted with four 6-inch guns and had capacity for 5,000 troops and 8,000 tons of cargo. Her maiden voyage in the service of the U.S. Navy was on October 18, 1917.

Germany had declared "unrestricted submarine warfare" and was delivering on its promise, but Izac's first four voyages on the *President Lincoln* were uneventful, save for one sighting of a U-boat that was later determined to be a false alarm. In November 1917, the ship and crew conveyed Congressman Clarence B. Miller safely to France. In all, the *President Lincoln* made five trips to Europe. Izac, however, refused to let this success make him cocky. All along, he knew that his service aboard the *President Lincoln* might mean a quick trip to the Atlantic seabed. At 18,167 tons, she was a magnet for periscopes and torpedoes. Izac felt, as a result, that being drowned, shipwrecked, or wounded was an eventuality rather than a mere possibility.

May 1918 was a busy month for the *U-90*. After sneaking up on a radio installation at St. Kilda Island, about 100 miles off the coast of Scotland, and destroying it with a bombardment of 72 shells, it joined a concentration of seven U-boats hunting in the English Channel approaches. Startled observers at French listening stations tracked them closely—this strategy had never been attempted before. The U-boat pack was, thanks to warnings issued to Allied shipping, largely unsuccessful; they only got three steamers. Around May 23, the concentration broke up, with the *U-90* following a British convoy south of Ireland. On May 29, Captain Remy of the *U-90* made his first two kills of the voyage—the *Begum*, at 4,664 tons, and the *Carlton*, at 5,262 tons. He then guided his U-boat south, where his lookouts spotted a convoy of five ships, including the highly recognizable *President Lincoln*, bearing west 600 miles off the French coast. He stalked them through the dark morning hours of May 31 and, discovering that he could easily outrace them, circled around and submerged ahead of the group. Remy positioned his sub inside the convoy, just below the starboard bow of the USS *Ryndam*, and found the *President Lincoln* with his periscope. The steamer was too big to miss. He let two of his torpedoes go at a range of 800 to 1,000 yards. They struck the *President Lincoln* at 8:54 A.M.

Izac was eating breakfast in the midsection of the ship when the first torpedoes hit, one after the other, at the number-two mast just below the bridge. A third torpedo struck the stern of the ship a few seconds later. It was 9:10 A.M. when Izac, back at his aft station, reported extensive flooding to his captain, who gave the order to abandon ship. As the ship went down, stern first, the forward gun crews stayed as long as possible, firing into the water in the hopes of catching a piece of the sub, or at least scaring it away. At 9:15 A.M. the captain, executive officer, and paymaster were assured that all hands had left the ship, and they went over the side themselves. Following procedure, the other ships in the convoy left the scene without trying to pick up survivors. The *U-90*, satisfied with the great size of its kill, let the other ships go unharmed.

At 9:30, the *President Lincoln* rolled to starboard. Her nose went up in the air as the crew, now in lifeboats, watched her last moments. "As the waters closed over her," Izac wrote in his account of the sinking, "we rose and gave three cheers for the *President Lincoln,* the best ship that ever carried troops in the cause of freedom."

She'd gone down in a little over a half hour, but out of a crew of nearly 700, only 23 men and 3 officers went down with the ship. Most of these were probably killed by the initial blast. Reviewing the episode, Admiral Sims later commended the captain and crew: "The small loss of life was due to the thorough discipline of the ship's company and the excellent seamanship of the captain of the USS *Lincoln,* Commander P. W. Foote, USN." The prevailing emotion during those tense moments of the evacuation was one of calm. Once in the boats, the mood became one of camaraderie and even celebration. Later, the drifting lifeboats erupted into song every time one of their distress flares exploded in the skies above them. "Hail, Hail, the Gang's All Here," and "Where Do We Go to Now Boys?" were the favorites.

After the other ships in the convoy had moved on to a safe distance, the *U-90* surfaced and slowly maneuvered toward the flotilla of lifeboats. The *U-90*'s twin 2.10-centimeter guns, fore and aft, were manned as the sub approached. Captain Remy picked a sailor at random for a brief interrogation. The seaman he selected relaxed after he saw that Remy did not want him as a prisoner, and accepted his hospitable glass of sherry and cup of hot coffee. Remy then pressed his question: Where was the captain of the *President Lincoln?* Remy was under orders to take prisoner the senior ranking officer of any American ship he sent to the ocean floor. Captain Foote, the American replied, had gone down with the ship. The Germans were instructed to take officers as prisoners, and the Americans were determined to protect their officers, so this conversation was something of a game, with the American's answer fully expected. The sailor was returned to his lifeboat.

Remy then spotted, from a distance of some 50 yards, a flash of sunlight from an officer's insignia. Izac had been reluctant to remove his uniform—"I could not bring myself to the humiliation"—but, at the insistence of his men, had partially covered himself in a blanket. Remy pulled his sub up to Izac's lifeboat and issued a simple command in English: "Come aboard." Izac turned to his comrades with a jaunty farewell: "Good-bye, men. It is all in the game."

The German U-boat commander and the U.S. Naval officer greeted each other with salutes. The captive's sidearm was removed, and Izac then received the same refreshments offered to the first sailor picked up. Remy asked the same questions, and received the same answer. He explained to Izac his orders, and Izac explained that since the captain had gone down with the ship, he would have to take his place as prisoner. In fact, the captain was a few boats away, wearing a sailor's uniform and pulling an oar.

Satisfied with his kill and his capture, Remy half-ordered, half-invited Izac below, where he was shown to his quarters—a small berth with a hammock. The *U-90* left the scene quickly, Remy knowing full well that Allied warships had been alerted to his location. The following day, they found him.

While the American destroyer *Warrington* rescued survivors, the destroyer *Smith* gave chase. Remy took his sub to a depth of 200 feet, about as far down as he could, and Izac experienced firsthand what warfare was like for submariners. He counted 22 depth charges, 5 close enough to shake the *U-90* from stem to stern. "I was alone in the wardroom," he wrote later, "with no companions but Hope and Fear: Hope that they would 'get' the submarine and fear of that very eventuality." As the depth charges rained down, as the U-boat zigged and zagged, he did not know which side to cheer for.

Remy described those depth charges (the number of which varies from one account to the next) as particularly "unfriendly," considering that Izac was on board. But it seems from others' recollections that the *Smith* was unaware that Izac had been taken. In any case, Izac himself never betrayed a resentment toward the navy for attempting to bomb the

U-90 from the depths—each U-boat sunk meant more Americans would make it home. Izac did, however, carry away from the experience a feeling that he was in the hands of a highly trained professional: Remy never flinched during the attack. Only afterward did he confide to Izac that such events left him a nervous wreck, and that the only thing worse than being depth-charged was taking a sub through a minefield.

The experience also gave Izac food for thought. He had fully expected that he would be wounded or drowned by the Germans, but not captured. And yet, here he was, alive, unhurt, fully able to serve his country, but confined to an enemy vessel. "And the more I thought about it, the less I liked it," he reflected. Izac was already dreaming of escape.

Remy and his officers did all they could to make their "guest" comfortable. Izac dined with the officers and spent long hours after dinner playing bridge and learning German card games. He quickly found that life on a U-boat is one of intense boredom punctuated by moments of intense activity—and terror. He also found the officers, and especially the captain, strangely friendly and outgoing. This held true even during their almost nightly political debates, during which Izac got an unusual perspective on the German mindset. He concluded it was heavily influenced by propaganda. They had been told all along that America would enter the war on the side of Germany, if it entered the war at all. They believed that the only reason the United States fought alongside France and England was because of the millions the U.S. had loaned them. And finally, American participation was irrelevant: France, they asserted, would soon be conquered.

They all spoke English, a required course at the German naval academy. They were well paid and well fed. At the time Izac was on board, the entire German U-boat fleet was manned by volunteers, representing the best of the German navy. They received the highest pay and were given bonuses for each day they spent submerged. Their diet was beyond any in the service, with a generous supply of meat and eggs. They were given a leave of absence whenever they arrived in port, and received the Iron

Cross after three roundtrips. All this, thought Izac, went a long way toward explaining their gentlemanly demeanor.

Izac's experience wasn't unique. The navies of both sides were far removed from the trenches, poison gas, machine guns, and shock troops that on the Continent were dispelling any romantic notions of warfare that might have survived the carnage of the previous century. On the high seas, however, even with the introduction of the U-boat, there was still some room for chivalry. Enough room, at least, for Izac to refer to the ongoing battle between the transports and the U-boats as a "game." Similarly, when the English captain of the bark *Beluga,* John Stanley Cameron, was captured by the German raider, minelayer, and cruiser *Wolf,* he wrote that he and his wife and daughter were "treated with the utmost courtesy and consideration by the commander himself and his officers." The first thing the German captain told him as he boarded the *Wolf* as a prisoner was, "We are not the Huns you probably think we are."

But the detailed letter from Captain Remy to a member of the USS *President Lincoln* Club, a group of survivors of that ill-fated trip, is still a surprising artifact. Someone in the group had written to Remy, ten years after the sinking, to ask if he could contribute his account of events for a collection of remembrances. Remy obliged jovially in a letter, and in detail proceeded to describe the strategies he used to sink their ship. His letter reads as if he is quite pleased to hear from them. Remy's chivalry apparently had survived even the defeat of his government.

Throughout his life, Izac wanted to serve, but serve humbly. Aboard the *U-90,* cut off from his command, a way to serve presented itself almost immediately. He began taking mental notes of the sub, its route, and its operations, convinced that he would one day escape with intelligence that would lead to the destruction of many subs like the *U-90.*

Aside from the torpedo rooms, which he was never allowed to enter, Izac had full run of the *U-90.* No one was worried that he might attempt sabotage or escape, not even when he asked Remy for his pistol so he might clean it. Izac did clean it, and he also counted his bullets. There were twice as many crew members as bullets, so he decided escape lay not along this direct route. He placed the loaded pistol back in Remy's quarters, and checked frequently to ensure it was still there. Incredibly, it was never moved and never unloaded.

Charts and maps were, he decided, more useful than arms, and he borrowed them frequently. He was permitted to keep his binoculars, which allowed him to pinpoint the sub's location day by day. But even more valuable were his conversations with Captain Remy, who was pleased to have an inquisitive party on board. Only after Remy decided that his North Atlantic "hunting grounds" were too overrun with destroyers did he demur from Izac's questioning, and only in the most polite manner. "From this point on, Captain Remy requested that I question him as little as possible because of the confidential character of the information I would be likely to desire," Izac wrote in his report to the Secretary of the Navy.

What Remy was attempting to conceal, and what Izac discovered anyway, was the route and procedures used by U-boats on their return to the German port of Kiel. The English Channel had been virtually plugged up by mines and patrols, so Remy opted to take a northern route, north of even the Shetland Islands, as did many submarine captains. From there, Izac found, U-boats would run through the North Sea, hug the Danish coast, and thus pass through the Skaggerrack and Kattegat Straits, which together form an inverted V-shaped inlet to the Baltic Sea. For a conservative commander like Remy, this meant resting on the bottom for hours at a time, waiting for night to fall.

Even before the sub began its roundabout return, which added about ten days to the trip, Izac was awakened by Remy, who seemed excited to show him something. They were off the island of Rona, a solitary landfall 50 miles northwest of Scotland. They were there, Remy explained, to go hunting. Years ago, a hermit had settled on the island with a flock of sheep. After he died, the sheep thrived, and now they were a steady supply of mutton for U-boat crews. A guard on this island, Izac thought, could easily score a U-boat for the Allies.

The next vital piece of information came when Izac went up on deck for a smoke late on the night of June 9. The sub was cruising slowly, with Sweden on one side and Denmark on the other. Suddenly another U-boat surfaced about a quarter mile away, and then, not 15 minutes later, a second came up and joined the other two. They were moving slowly, apparently waiting. When a destroyer appeared in the distance, Izac realized he had discovered a rendezvous point for the subs and their escort. The information he'd gathered and the nearness of the lights of Denmark forced him to take a chance. His life preserver would aid him in swimming the four miles to shore. The subs wouldn't waste time looking for him. He chose his moment.

Captain Remy, however, saw him move toward the guardrail, and tersely ordered him below. It was an undramatic end to the first of many escape attempts by Izac. He and Remy never spoke of it again, despite the fact that Izac, under international law, could face disciplinary action for any attempt or plan to escape.

When he arrived in Keil on June 10, Izac was transferred to the battleship *Preussen*. His "joy ride" was over. He was locked in a small room, with armed sentries outside. His breakfast was "ersatz tea" made of strawberry leaves and coffee made from acorns and barley. The only other food he received was stock so thin it was essentially tasteless. Remy paid a farewell visit a few days later and remarked on the conditions before handing over a few items to make Izac's incarceration a little easier: In return for the $5 bill Izac had been carrying when he was taken prisoner, Remy brought him German marks. He also gave him toothpaste, sundries, and an item increasingly rare in wartime Germany—soap. Another officer from the *U-90* popped in a few days later. He was a captain who was with Remy on a training mission and wanted to pay his respects before he assumed his first command.

"It was then," Izac wrote, "that I realized the un-German character of the treatment I had received on the *U-90*. While there, all the officers had tried to make things pleasant for me, and although we had many arguments on the war, the discussions were friendly." A particularly unfriendly discussion highlighted this sentiment: The *Preussen* chief of staff questioned him on the progress of the troop transport efforts by the U.S. The interrogation degenerated into a series of insults, and concluded with Izac referring to all Germans as "Huns." Nothing, he found, would so upset a German officer.

Transferred to a prison camp at Karlsruhe in the south of Germany after a few days, Izac began learning the tricks of trade of a prisoner of war. The biscuits he received from the Red Cross, for example, could be given a texture almost like bread if you cut a hole in them and added water. It was either that or the German "black bread," which was doled out in rations the size of a man's fist and were fashioned out of water, potatoes, sawdust, chaff, and sand. Izac was already motivated to escape by the U-boat intelligence he had gathered; now the possibility of near starvation motivated him further.

His first attempt, which he made after two weeks, was made by bribing a guard (Izac was actually paid a "salary" of credits in camp, even though America, unlike England, had no treaty requiring this). The guard agreed to arrange an escape for Izac and a few airmen, and convey them to his girlfriend's house, where they would hide until the search had cooled down. The guard's letter to his girlfriend, however, was discovered. Izac never found out what became of the man—a Swiss teenager who had been pressed into service.

He made attempt number two just a few days later. Branches from a tree inside the camp extended over the fence, high above the ground. Izac felt that if he climbed before nightfall when prisoners were milling around, he could wait, concealed by the foliage, until the guards below moved from their station. An electric cord could then take him safely to the ground. But the sentries never budged on the night of his attempt. So he spent a cold night on his perch and climbed down the trunk the next morning, unnoticed but discouraged.

Prisoners, he observed, were moved in and out seemingly at random.

Finally, after about four weeks in the camp, he found he was to be moved to Villingen in the Black Forest. Having grown up speaking French, he naturally made many friends among the French prisoners, and when they learned of his plans for escape, they secured for him a compass, maps, money, and food. The compass and maps he sewed into his clothes, as every prisoner was searched before they left the camp.

During the daylong train ride, Izac was perpetually on the lookout for his chance. None seemed likely, as guards were sitting on either side of him, and had their guns pointed at him at all times. As they approached Villingen they hit a downgrade and started picking up speed. "I knew it had to be now or not at all," wrote Izac. With one guard half asleep and the other turning his head, Izac hurled himself through an 18- by 24-inch open window headfirst. The train was running at about 40 miles per hour.

Izac landed on the second rail track, catching his head on one steel tie and his knees on another. He recovered from semiconsciousness a few moments later, but found he couldn't bend his knees. As the train stopped and the guards commenced firing, he broke into a stiff-legged run as best he could, but when a bullet nearly missed his head, he stopped and held his hands high. They were on him in seconds, and delivered a beating for which Izac would never forgive them or their countrymen.

He described his ordeal in his memo to the secretary of the navy: "The first guard turned his gun and grasped it by the muzzle, and struck me over the head as I half lay and half sat on the side of the hill. I remember rolling downhill gaining additional impetus from their boots. They kicked me until I got up, and when I was up they knocked me down again with their guns . . . Finally in knocking me down the seventh or eighth time one of the guards struck me across the back of the head and his gun broke in two at the small of the stock." That soldier was later court-martialed—not for violating international law governing treatment of prisoners of war, but for destroying German army property, namely, his rifle. The record of the court-martial was entered into evidence when Izac sought damages before a claims commission after the war, and proved damning enough: Izac was awarded $27,000.

Izac noticed through a haze of pain that a German civilian, a farmer, was running toward the beating, pitchfork in hand. The thought that this man might try to stop the soldiers crossed his mind, but when he got there, he offered instead to help clobber Izac more thoroughly. Izac's distaste for Germans, which had been tempered by the treatment he received from Captain Remy, turned to hatred. The fact that he was part German himself, that his own mother was from the same region where he received this beating, mattered little.

As bad as the beating was, his captors had not yet tired of their brutality. The train had moved on, and Izac was now forced to march double time, or rather "as near double time as I could make it," five miles to the prison camp. He collapsed on the guardhouse steps and was informed by the commandant that if he *ever* tried to escape again, he would be shot.

The camp doctor treated his injuries—about a hundred separate wounds, he estimated. For three days, Izac's tight bandages, wrapped around him "like a mummy," prevented any motion and he drifted in and out of consciousness. Unconsciousness was preferable, he found, as his cuts and sores had become host to thousands of fleas, which he found "as poisonous as German propaganda." It was three weeks before he could walk again, and two months before he could bend his knees. On top of his forced bedrest, he was given two weeks solitary confinement for his escape attempt.

(Before America had entered the war, the State Department had sent inspectors to German camps to report on conditions. One inspector, Daniel J. McCarthy, wrote up his findings in *The Prisoner of War in Germany,* published in 1918. Some camps, he found, were run with the prisoners' welfare in mind. Others were just short of death camps. The camps' commandants, he explained, were often German army generals, and operated with near-complete autonomy. There was little central authority, which accounted for the wide variance in conditions. And no matter how well-intentioned the commandant, as the war dragged on and resources grew more scarce, conditions deteriorated across the board.)

Villingen could have been counted somewhere between the best and worst of Germany's POW camps, but there was still plenty to be depressed about, especially for an escape-minded prisoner like Izac. In the four years before Izac arrived, about 50 prisoners had escaped from Villingen. But getting past the fence was perhaps the easiest part. The small towns and farms around Villingen offered no refuge for escaped Allied soldiers, some of whom were killed and most of whom were recaptured. Only one had succeeded in making the journey to Switzerland, the nearest neutral country.

Izac knew that he would have to be in top physical shape to make the trip that had defeated 49 men before him. His regimen started with circular walks around the prison yard, and gradually moved up to include running and weightlifting as his body recovered from his previous escape attempt. All along, he was watched closely by the camp authorities: They had tried several times to extract from him a promise to refrain from flight. He even told them bluntly that it was his duty to escape. When the Germans told the prisoners to write pledges—"I will not make any attempt to escape"—Izac and others turned in the promise: "I will *now* make *an* attempt to escape."

Izac devised a coordinated but simple escape plan. First, he convinced a number of prisoners to make attempts at the same time. A mass rush, he felt, would confuse the guards and increase the chances for all. Some might be recaptured, but others could get away. The other piece of the plan was a ladder. This Izac would have to improvise himself.

There were two long pieces of wood he thought he could get his hands on in the camp—they formed the markers of the tennis court. The rungs of the ladder were "borrowed" from Red Cross crates and the slats of prisoners' beds. When other prisoners learned of his plan, they were all too happy to donate a slat or two. Constructing the ladder with nails would attract the attention of the guards, so Izac, over a period of a week, removed two screws from nearly every door in the camp until he had about one hundred. These he scattered on the ground outside his barracks. In a few days, they turned a rust color that hid them well in the gravel. Using his prison credits, he was able to bribe guards for tools. He noted in his memoir of captivity that all his plans involved bribery, and nearly all attempts to bribe guards were successful: "We use to say at the camp, 'Give me a bar of soap and I will buy the Kaiser's daughter.'" Unfortunately, he wasn't ready with a bribe when the guards searched the barracks and discovered the slats for the ladder. "It was at this time my fortunes reached their lowest ebb," Izac wrote, "but they were destined soon to brighten with the never-dying hope of success."

It wasn't just optimism that pushed him on: Throughout September, reports were coming in that the U-boats were still sinking 10,000 tons of Allied shipping every day. These reports were probably propaganda, Izac thought, but even if they were close to correct, it was a problem he could help solve. The situation in the camp was simultaneously turning more brutal. A Russian cook one day refused to work on account of illness. He didn't get his sick day—instead he received a near-fatal beating and 40 days in solitary confinement with meals only every fourth day. Izac became determined to take his chances in the German countryside and started gathering the slats for another ladder.

On October 5, 1918, the camp authorities announced that all the Russian prisoners would be moved to a separate camp in two days. Izac knew this meant two things: The camp would be turned upside-down in a search, and it would be easier for the Germans to keep a close eye on the prisoners who were left. He and another American officer, Harold Willis, hastily worked out one final plan. Four teams of Americans, each with two to three members, would attempt the perimeter at the same time. Two teams, including Izac's, would use the improvised ladders (which they would assemble after dark from the screws Izac had hidden around the camp), one would cut through the fence with wire cutters, and the fourth, Willis's party, would disguise themselves as German guards and slip through the main gates as the real guards filed out to recapture the escapees. All this would happen just as Americans who volunteered to stay behind threw chains over the camp's electrical mains. The wires were conveniently exposed and would short-circuit easily. On the outside, they would assemble into small groups. Izac arranged to meet Willis near an archeological site known as the Hun's Grave, a site that was both isolated and clearly marked.

At 10:45 P.M. on October 6, the lights went out. All the teams moved quickly to get over their section of the fence. But suddenly and inexplicably, the lights came back on. Then they went out, and then back on again. Izac quickly figured out what had happened: One of the chains was swinging back and forth across one of the wires. In a matter of seconds, he surmised, it would come to rest exactly where they wanted it to be. As they pulled the ladder—which was to form a bridge from their second-story barracks window to the perimeter fence—back inside, Izac noted the reactions of the guards outside the fence. To his relief, they appeared confused, not at all suspecting a mass escape attempt.

When the camp was finally plunged into darkness, Izac's team sent their ladder again out the window and jumped to the opposite side of the fence. The guards were close by and, already recovering from their bafflement, yelled "Halt!" twice before they leveled their rifles at close range. As Izac ran past them, he felt the muzzle flash singe his hair.

As he glanced back, he noticed that his team was the only one that had attracted the attention of the guards. All fire was directed at him and the two aviators in his team as they broke up and sought cover in the dark forest. Izac headed for his rendezvous with Willis.

There was no sign of Willis, and Izac could already hear the hounds. He ran on, and as he ran he heard another set of footfalls and the rustling of an overcoat. Izac stopped, and Willis ran past, wearing the German army coat he'd purloined for the occasion. On they ran, spreading pepper to throw off the oncoming dogs. The rest of the night they waded through shoulder-deep swamps and rivers. At six in the morning, they rested in a crag at the bottom of a cliff. They were awakened at one in the afternoon by their canine pursuers.

At the top of the cliff, the barks became whines as the dogs, confused, wandered back and forth. When their owners caught up, they collected their dogs and went away, content to let the chase pass to the soldiers, patrols, and sentries throughout the Black Forest. After seeing so many escapees caught and returned, they were confident that Izac and Willis would soon be back in their company.

The most direct route to the Swiss border was only 18 miles, but it happened to be the most heavily patrolled. So, Izac and Willis planned a 120-mile trek through the mountains and the thick of the forest to the nearest border. From the Brigach River, which flows into the Brege and then to the Danube, they crossed the mountains to the Alb river, which flowed to the Rhine and the Swiss frontier. It took them on a boomerang-shaped course and left them at a thick and fast-flowing section of the Rhine, but they were convinced it would keep them away from the determined German patrols. They believed it would take them six days.

They kept to their schedule, even though they lost a day wandering in circles, searching for a mountain pass that would take them away from the breweries, hotels, and hydroelectric plants that they discovered along the Alb. They dined on raw vegetables they found in the fields; fortunately they were in a section of Germany where almost everyone grew their own food. They slept in each other's arms for warmth, covered by the tent made by Willis's coat, heated by their own heavy breath. One night Willis woke up babbling incoherently—he'd been struck with fever while he slept. But in the morning, they still pushed on.

On daybreak of the sixth day, they heard the whistle of a locomotive and knew that they were close to the rail line that ran alongside their goal: the Rhine. After resting for the day, they made their way to the river in the darkness, wading in a narrow, quickly flowing stream. As they passed a viaduct, Willis slipped and a searchlight swung around from a distance. They were momentarily bathed in the light, but since they had covered their heads in mud, they were mistaken for stones and the light passed them over. In between flashes of the searchlight, they slowly moved forward.

They had expected a swim of 100 yards at their crossing point. It turned out to be 700 feet. The current, strengthened and made more perilous by streams on both sides, ran at seven miles per hour. But Switzerland was on the other side. Izac and Willis discussed in whispers how to traverse the Rhine. One moment, Willis was just feet ahead of Izac, who kept his eyes on the near bank, looking for patrols. In the next moment, as Izac turned to ask Willis a question, he was gone. It was "as if the earth had opened up and swallowed him." The sudden disappearance, the fact that Izac had no idea what had probably happened to his partner, filled him with dread as he removed his clothes to make the crossing. As he pulled off his pants, he discovered what had happened to Willis—the full force of the Rhine came up suddenly. Just by inching forward, he had been swept into the treacherous waters.

Weakened from his journey, Izac swam with deliberate effort. As he fought the currents to the middle of the river, he saw that he was quickly being drawn into a bend that would push him back toward the German bank. He knew that this moment would see him to success, recapture, or drowning. With every last reserve of strength, he pushed ahead until he went completely limp, 30 yards from Switzerland.

He had no fight left. "So turning over on my back I commended my soul to my God and closed my eyes. Instantly my feet touched the rocks." It was a moment he would reflect on for the rest of his life, one that, he would tell his children, made his faith solid and permanent. He remained in the river current, breathing heavily, until he found the strength to walk the remaining distance to shore. He arrived in Switzerland at 2:30 A.M. on Sunday, October 13, 1918, seven days after his escape, and knocked on the door of the first house he saw.

His Swiss host treated him with the "utmost kindness," and started a search for Willis, which ended in a small tavern two miles downstream. He also had made the Swiss bank with the very last of his strength. Of the original 13 in the escape attempt, only one other made it across the border.

When he reached London on October 23, Izac immediately received an audience with Admiral Sims, commander of U.S. naval forces in European waters. If the admiral was somewhat dismissive and distracted, Izac soon discovered why. Armistice talks were under way. The German navy was in disarray. On October 29, the sailors in Wilhelmshaven even mutinied.

Izac was ordered to report to the Bureau of Navigation in Washington, D.C. He arrived on November 11, 1918, the same day negotiators reached an armistice. The last sentence in Izac's memoir of his captivity and escape, *Prisoner of the U-90*, reflects all the irony and frustration of his timing in the simplest of terms: "I was too late!"

As Izac watched the first Armistice Day parade in Washington, D.C., others were talking about the First World War being the end to all wars. Izac was under no such delusion. He observed the first victory parade from the balcony of the old State, War and Navy Building, opposite the White House. Izac was welcomed as a hero at the Department of the Navy, not least by the assistant secretary to the navy, Franklin Delano Roosevelt. Izac's injuries kept him from returning to sea, but he was promoted to lieutenant commander within months and got a plum post at the Navy Yard in D.C., where his family joined him. He was there when he learned that he was to receive the Medal of Honor. He wondered for what reason, as did Admiral Sims, who asked why Izac was getting a medal when "all he did was to get captured."

Others disagreed, including Commander Foote, captain of the *President Lincoln*, and Secretary of the Navy Josephus Daniels, not to mention the governments of two foreign nations, which presented him with the Italian Croce di Guerra and the Cross of Montenegro. On November 11, 1920, Izac was presented with the Congressional Medal of Honor in the

Navy Yard at Washington, D.C., for his extreme bravery in escaping and persevering to the Swiss border. Presenting the medal was the same assistant secretary of the navy he'd met on Armistice Day. "Six feet five if he was an inch," Izac recalled of Roosevelt, "and clean and full of life."

Izac had been working as Director of Munitions at the Navy Yard almost from the end of the war. He lived on the site with his wife and children, along with a French family who took up residence in the basement apartment in exchange for domestic services. In the year following his receipt of the greatest honor the U.S. government could bestow, however, he was forced into retirement. His injured knees had gotten worse. His navy days were over.

His secure life in military service over, Izac faced the demands of a growing family with nothing more than a meager pension. Although it must have hurt him deeply, he accepted an offer for housing and a job from his stern father-in-law, General Cabell, who explained to him that he wasn't going to let Izac starve his daughter in D.C. Izac may have been humble about his war record, but he was definitely proud, so to require rescuing by a man who'd never wanted him as a son-in-law was quite a blow. But the options for a disabled war veteran, the son of a rural carpenter, were poignantly finite, so the family moved to a house the general provided near his own San Diego home.

Thanks to Cabell's connections, Izac earned a small salary working for the *San Diego Union* as an ad man from 1922 to 1929. He also penned articles as a freelance writer on veteran's problems, history, and English. His command of the language, his eldest daughter remembers, was obvious in both his prose and his speech. She says today that she learned more from listening to him than she ever did from her English classes at school. She and the other children also learned French at home, something that was handy after the family moved to France following the stock market crash of 1929.

His job lost, his patience over being cared for by his father-in-law at an end, Edouard and Agnes Izac returned to their roots. They rode out the beginning of the Great Depression in rural France, living cheaply—most likely off the $27,000 Izac had received from his court action against the German government for the beating and forced march on his wounded legs. In 1931, after nearly two years in France, they returned to San Diego. It would be another four years before Izac got the job offer that would change his life.

A group of San Diego veterans were tired of being pushed under the rug and watching their congressional district send well-connected and wealthy residents to Congress. After much prodding, they convinced Izac that he could and should run as representative from California's 20th district. In 1934, after securing nominations from both the Democratic and Progressive parties, he ran against millionaire banker George Burnham and lost. But in 1936, with the nation lining up behind Roosevelt, he again threw his hat in the ring.

This time the lessons of the failed campaign prepared him to use his war record and Medal of Honor as selling points. In auditoriums, on streets, in schools, he told and retold his story. Voters packed the venues to hear him; many became regulars: "They never tired of hearing it, and of course he brought down the house," recalled his eldest daughter, Cabell Berge, who worked on his campaigns and served as his "right arm" during his terms in Congress. "He talked very animatedly and grippingly on his experiences. I guess he literally relived them every time he talked. I'm sure he must have."

Izac's war stories brought in the crowds, but his promises brought in the votes. He was committed and loyal to Roosevelt's New Deal, both as a friend of the president's and as a man who knew poverty firsthand. He believed in a strong but neutral America. He promised to honor our veterans. Finally, he promised to make San Diego a strategic key to the nation's long-term military policy. He saw the small harbor transformed into the greatest naval base in the world, a project that would bring jobs and prosperity to the region, just as the WPA and the Civilian Conservation Corps were helping Americans elsewhere lift their heads above the ongoing Depression.

In 1936, he also had a small but unusual campaign fund. Forty veterans pledged $40 each. If he won, he would pay them all back. If he lost, all was forgiven. Forty dollars was no insignificant sum to many of those contributors. When they got their contributions back, San Diego heard a small but prolonged sigh of relief.

Izac was sworn into his first term with his 12-year-old son, Charles, at his side. While the backing of the veterans and his open patriotism helped him win in a district where Republicans outnumbered Democrats two to one, Izac always knew why he was elected and reelected: "I never had any illusion it was my popularity. It was Roosevelt," he once told a reporter.

Like so many who had seen the horrors of the First World War, Izac desperately wanted to keep America out of the Second World War. He made this the topic of his maiden speech on the House floor, explaining passionately and at length that the course America was on would inevitably lead to American involvement. Large portions of his speech were quoted the next day in a glowing article in the *New York Times*. He'd hit a political home run his first time at bat. But then, having stated his position, he quickly ducked out of the limelight and continued a quiet service.

Izac was one of a last generation of congressmen who governed from afar. Without passenger jets to whisk them back to their constituents for perpetual campaigning and fund-raising, most members of Congress found it difficult to return frequently to their home base. Izac's first trip home was by car, with his children in the backseat. "My dad did all the driving," his daughter Cabell remembers, "and we kept a bucket with a diaper in cold water to smack on his face to keep him awake."

Izac introduced and sponsored legislation to protect the Palomar Observatory, which still operates today; to establish a Marine hospital in San Diego; to bring aid for the construction of public schools; and to establish an infantry battalion of African Americans as part of the California National Guard. More than with any other issue, however, his record reflects an abiding concern for veterans and the widows they left behind. He strove to include disabled World War I vets in the New Deal and other appropriations. In particular, he introduced bill after bill "for the relief" of particular servicemen and their families. Many, but not all, were his own constituents.

During late-night sessions, witnessed by Izac's daughter and notetaker Cabell, the representative heard firsthand the hardship suffered by impoverished San Diegans. "And many a time," Cabell whispers, "I saw my father reach in his wallet and pull something out and hand it over. Those things never came up again. They didn't have to. And I'm sure it was manna from heaven in their eyes."

Izac was in a position—as a member of the House Naval Affairs Committee and one with ties to Roosevelt—to move into a higher post. His daughter saw this during her first attendance at a White House function, when Roosevelt pulled Izac into a bear hug and called him "My old navy associate." "I'm sure," she says with a laugh, "that my father heard that in his mind many times after that." But when his name came up in 1940 as a possible candidate for assistant secretary of the navy—Roosevelt's job at the time he presented Izac with the medal—Izac bluntly and publicly announced that he would rather be a congressman. According to his daughter, he felt he had been selected for public service by the veterans who helped him get there, and he wasn't about to use their support as a mere stepping stone to a higher level.

At the time he made this decision, he was becoming an increasingly unpopular congressman. The paper where he once worked, the *San Diego Union*, was stepping up its attacks on his voting record—particularly on his opposition to permanent status for the House Un-American Activities Committee and his vocal protests against the deportation of Pacific coast maritime union leader Harry Bridges. Voters were starting to wonder if they had placed in office a man of a more liberal stripe than they originally thought. He won his first reelection campaign in 1938 by over 20,000 votes (58,806 votes to his opponent's 38,333), saw his margin of victory shrink to 4,373 votes in 1940, and barely squeezed in by 777 votes in 1942, following a nail-biting count of absentee ballots. To San Diego voters, the call for national unity to support the war effort didn't trump Izac's opposition to the more reactionary efforts of Congress.

In 1941, months before Pearl Harbor, he told his House colleagues from his podium, "I lost all patience with my people when they came to me during the last campaign and said, 'Please don't get us into war.' I said, 'Don't look at me. I am not getting you into war, but there is one man who has the power to do that, and that is Mr. Hitler.'"

He never advocated going after Hitler, but he deeply loathed him as a dictator; as a follower of "the philosophy of force, the pagan philosophy"; and finally as a German. Izac *loathed* Germans. "That's the one word I can produce and it's perfect. Don't need any other description. He loathed them," says his eldest daughter. Once we got into the war, Izac watched as two of his sons went into overseas service.

In 1945, during his last term in Congress, Izac was given a task that would only further his loathing of the German people. In April, General Eisenhower cabled Army Chief of Staff George Marshall with the news that his army had found concentration camps as they advanced on Berlin, and advised that the legislative branch send representatives. "I can state unequivocally that all written statements up to now do not paint the full horrors," Eisenhower wrote. Izac was part of the hastily assembled team. It was a bitter job for a man who had spent time in a prison camp in Germany. Days after receipt of the cable, he and five other representatives were joined by six senators and flown to a conquered section of a country still at war with the United States.

They toured Buchenwald, Nordhausen, and Dachau. At Dachau, they saw the infamous showers; at Buchenwald, witnesses explained how prisoners were strangled and hung from hooks. Everywhere, they saw bodies—thousands of bodies—"stacked up like cordwood." The executioners had run out of coal, and also time, leaving this gruesome evidence behind. They saw many victims of starvation and medical experiments—who survived just long enough to see the liberation of their prison—die before their eyes despite the efforts of army doctors.

The experience struck Izac deeply. He bristled for the rest of his life at the notion that German civilians were unaware of what was going on in the camps. "The Germans would trail in and view the camps and say they had no idea. No idea," he said with supreme incredulity years later. The camps, the report of the joint committee claimed, were built in populated areas, near major highways, and their designers made no attempt to conceal them. When Izac returned, he spoke before the Society for the Prevention of World War III, stating that the "terroristic and fanatical" members of the Nazi party should be "eliminated."

"And the rank and file of the German people," he continued, "must also be made to suffer, at least from some of the shortages and through some of the same kind of restrictions as were the lot of their so-called inferior neighbors. Stern justice demands that much; the preservation of world peace requires it." He knew however, that his idea of a harsh peace would never be accepted by the "forgiving hearts of the Americans." War does pay, he decided, "for the aggressors."

Izac had started his naval career training gun crews on a steam-powered battleship. As a witness to Operation Crossroads, the navy's 1946 test of nuclear weapons at Bikini Atoll, he saw the new face of warfare. A fleet of 90 vessels was "attacked" in two separate tests as Izac watched from the deck of the USS *Panamint*, 22 miles from the explosion. One can only wonder what went through his mind as he watched decommissioned warships, much larger than the *President Lincoln*, consumed by the blast and waves produced by this horrifying new weapon. He said very little about his reaction to the tests, which offered a spectacular and terrifying example of how nuclear weapons could make the navy of any country obsolete.

Izac lost his seat in the 1946 election, defeated by a tall, attractive banker who joined a shift of power that gave the Republicans a majority in the House. With the war over, Roosevelt gone, and Izac's dream of a large naval base at San Diego accomplished, his opponent gained victory by focusing on local issues that Izac felt should be addressed by local bodies, rather than the federal government. In some ways, he had indeed lost touch. And in some ways, his defeat was a release.

Agnes had inherited land in Gordonsville, Virginia, where the family moved into a simple life. Izac became a farmer. He raised cattle, grew all types of fruit and vegetables, and perfected a chili sauce that became legendary. Agnes, who didn't even know how to boil water when she married, had become by that time a great cook, and adapted her skills to the ranch house's rustic wood stove. They grew most of their own food, and survived well on pensions from the navy and Congress. Izac dammed a stream to form a small lake, which is known still as Lake Izac. All of his children learned to swim in that lake.

Life slowed down considerably, but the family's retreat to a simpler pace was shattered in 1952 by the death of Izac's 19-year-old son, Forrest. Just after Christmas, he died in what the family often called a shooting accident and what the coroner called a suicide. Izac's youngest son, Andre, toyed for a long time with the idea of joining the army, which might have sent his father into a rage comparable to what Izac's father-in-law had displayed. But, to the relief of the entire family, he joined the navy instead and became a chaplain. He then followed further in his father's footsteps than anyone expected, when he took an assignment on the aircraft carrier USS *Abraham Lincoln*.

Izac lost his "Sweetheart" in 1970, but continued to live on the ranch until one day he fell off his porch and gashed his head on the concrete. This small accident convinced him that he should live with a family member. He moved in with his second daughter, Anna, for the rest of his long life, getting around in a sedan sporting the license plate "CMH-1," that identified him as the state's oldest living Congressional Medal of Honor recipient. He didn't fail his regular driving test until he was in his mid-90s.

Washington Redskins games became a regular family gathering at Cabell's house in Arlington, Virginia, where Izac would allow himself one bourbon and one cigar. On his birthday in 1989, he was honored by Willard Scott, weather reporter on NBC's *Today* who gives birthday greetings to Americans who have reached their centennial birthday. Scott was a little premature. Izac was by then the oldest living recipient of the Medal of Honor, but he was only 99. When he died in his sleep at Anna's house the following year, he had, however, seen his 100th birthday.

Having seen history in the making throughout his life, Izac reveled in a history that had always lived strongly within him. Early in Izac's "retirement," after he went from congressman to farmer, Edouard and Agnes traveled almost every year to Jerusalem. He had seen the horrors of war on the seas, in POW camps, in concentration camps, as a wartime congressman, and finally as a witness to an A-bomb test. In the Middle East, he sought a history that would bring him peace.

Izac used his visits as the basis for a book published in 1965. *The Holy Land: Then and Now* is a bridge between the Biblical scholar and the pilgrim, an invitation to walk through Palestine as Jesus walked through it. Izac, who had himself brushed against so many people and events that made history, wrote: "No one who has not visited the scenes of the most momentous events in the history of the human race will ever be able to visualize just how it all happened. You simply have to go there." As one who had, in his own life, so often "been there" as history was formed, he knew these words to be true.

CHAPTER FOUR

Samuel Woodfill

WORLD WAR I

"Inspired by the exceptional courage displayed by this officer, his men pressed on to their objective under severe shell and machine-gun fire."

— MEDAL OF HONOR CITATION

"MAYBE THERE ARE PEOPLE WHO ARE BORN with silver spoons in their mouths, but I had no such luck. However, I did come near being born with a gun in my hands. And I've had one there almost ever since." Samuel Woodfill was exaggerating only slightly with these words from his memoirs. Marksmanship was his art, passion, and occupation.

As he brought his skill to perfection, the First World War broke out. This war to end all wars was, many believed, also the beginning of riflery's obsolescence. "Whatever may have been my qualifications as a soldier," Woodfill remarked, "more than anything else I was just a woodsman and a hunter, and the time came when I was called upon to put my frontiers-man's craft into service in a war of airplanes, poison gas, machine guns, and massed artillery." The world war was supposed to be a war by the numbers, a war, as one historian put it, "by timetable." The generals and politicians believed that new technologies would edge out the importance of the individual soldier. With him would disappear independent vari-ables and unpredictable behavior, but also individual initiative and acts of heroism. If these predictions had been borne out, the Medal of Honor, designed by law to honor singular bravery outside the boundaries of or-ders and beyond duty, would have become little more than a quaint relic of the 19th century.

Perhaps that is why Woodfill's Medal of Honor action so captured the imagination of the public and the attention of General Pershing, com-mander of the American Expeditionary Force (AEF) in France. Acting alone, Woodfill earned the Medal of Honor while proving beyond a doubt that skill, intelligence, and bravery could defeat even the deadly power of the machine gun. For a very brief time, Woodfill's backwoods marksmanship brought him national fame and glory; one paper even re-marked that Woodfill's name would "live forever." But while the exploits of Sergeant York—the pacifist-turned-war hero who was later portrayed onscreen by Gary Cooper—and the tale of the surrounded but never sur-rendered Lost Battalion still linger in our national memory, Woodfill is a name largely forgotten. He may have wanted it that way. In addition to learning how to shoot in the forests of Kentucky, where he was raised, he learned humility.

Woodfill's father, John, volunteered to serve in the army for the Mex-ican-American War in 1846, and was wounded in his right arm by a bay-onet. Then, during the Civil War, he served as captain of the Fifth Indiana Volunteers. When the nation laid down its arms, he settled in Kentucky, just south of the Ohio River. He married in 1873, at the age of 50, and had two sons and a daughter by the time Sam was born, in 1883.

One of Sam's earliest memories was of his father being caught in a flash flood while building a bridge. He was knocked unconscious by a rolling boulder and pulled out by Sam's older brothers, John Junior and William. Sam's mom drained the water out of his lungs by draping him over a barrel. John Senior came to quickly and went right back to work, but the incident taught Sam a powerful lesson about the frailty of life. He decided it would be a good idea to learn how to swim.

While his dad was descended from a Welshman, Sam's mother was the daughter of German immigrants who'd traveled over in the mid-1840s. Conscription was strict and army service rough in Germany. The American frontier seemed a much safer option. Woodfill would reflect on his maternal grandfather years later: "Strange world this. Grandpap leaves the old country to keep from fightin' with the Germans and a generation later his grandson goes back across the water to fight against them."

By the time Sam was seven, he had developed an intense curiosity about the squirrel gun that was always in plain sight in their little cabin. Longer than Sam was tall, the octagon-barreled muzzle-loading rifle held him in thrall until one day when his dad let him fire it. Although he wasn't normally allowed to touch the gun, he'd watched it being loaded and fired, so he thought he knew what to do. He pointed the barrel out a window, aimed for a fence post, and pulled the trigger. When he saw he had hit his mark, he became "the happiest boy in the countryside that day."

Meanwhile, his parents were becoming concerned about one little detail in Sam's development. He's not sure why, but early in life Sam had more of an affinity for his elder sister's hand-me-downs than his brothers'. Up until age eight, no one could get him to stop wearing dresses or get near his long curly locks of hair with a pair of scissors. His brothers and the few boys who lived within walking distance would predictably and mercilessly tease him, but it had no impact whatsoever. He was just going to wear dresses. His parents thought this was a little strange, but decided to leave him alone to grow out of it. When it began to seem like he wasn't ever going to change his ways, they conspired with a neighbor, a local girl for whom Sam had a powerful crush. She was a friendly 18-year-old with dark hair and a more appropriately aged suitor. On one of Sam's visits, which he usually made after watching this competitor for her affections ride away, she told him that if he wanted to be her man, he might consider dressing the part. That brought an end to the dresses and long hair.

By age ten, Sam took to sneaking the gun down on a regular basis and terrorizing the squirrels of the neighborhood. He was so short he had to stand on a stump to pour powder into the muzzle, but his aim was deadly. He'd come home with arms full of dead squirrels before his mom got in from her chores, and he'd say that he'd been out with a friend who'd been hunting and had given him a share. His mom would shrug, not quite believing, but happy for the fresh meat, which she'd fry up like chicken, "unless we got an old boy, and then we would have to parboil him first." But it was only a matter of time before he got caught.

When he did, his mom told him that Pap would handle this punishment, and it would be severe. But when his dad saw how many rodents his boy had shot, he couldn't hide his pride. He figured that Sam must be old enough to handle a rifle, and so there wasn't any retribution except for a stern lecture and a lesson in firearm safety. After that, Sam could take the squirrel gun out anytime he liked.

To reach the schoolhouse where Sam received his only formal education, he had to hike three miles and through a stream. During the winter, it wasn't so bad when the stream completely froze over and he could walk across, but if it didn't, he faced a wade through very icy water. Risking pneumonia didn't seem worth a little "book learnin'," as Sam called it, so he and his siblings got a spotty education.

Sam was 13 when his father died. He had been out late, across the Ohio River to see some friends, and grew tired on the way back. He stopped to rest in the cold winter air, and accidentally fell asleep. He could have died right there, but he awoke and made it home one last time. The next day, he awoke with a cold that laid his 72-year-old body to rest.

As Sam tried to fill his father's shoes, the "heavy man's work" started taking its toll on him. He became a hunched-over farm boy, underfed and overworked, but somehow he managed to save up enough for a Winchester rifle. Sam and his fancy gun became well known at shooting competitions, where Sam typically had to take a 10- to 15-yard handicap.

In 1898, at the outbreak of the Spanish-American War, 15-year-old Sam tried to enlist. He was turned away, and could only dream of getting into uniform until he was 18, when he answered the call for troops for the Philippine Insurrection. The conflict started in 1899, when the guerrillas who'd fought against Spain before and during the Spanish-American War discovered that the United States wasn't going to grant them independence after all. Sam didn't really understand the situation when he signed up in 1901, just that this was perhaps the only chance he'd have to make his number-one skill pay off. "Pretty nigh from the first I qualified as an expert rifleman," Sam recalled, "and that meant an extra dollar a month when the eagle screamed."

The biggest bonus, however, was getting out beyond his corner of Kentucky, something he'd never done before. Woodfill compared his first train ride to San Francisco to being "astride a rocket headed for the moon." He felt his wings spread, only to have them clipped almost as soon as he got into training. "If there was a bigger dumbbell in the outfit than I was I didn't see him." Neither did his drill sergeant, who seemed determined to teach Woodfill every vulgarity and synonym for "idiot" in the English language. The hapless private had trouble telling left from right, and his drill sergeant would fire orders so rapidly that his "brain got left behind." The woodsman looked to everyone like he'd end up being one of those unfortunates who buy the farm on their first day in combat.

Woodfill was miserable until the army—with some trepidation—put a rifle in his hands. When he took his first shot at his first target practice, he hit the bull's-eye dead-on, and thought to himself there was no way the drill sergeant would yell at him now. In fact, he was rushing over to

Woodfill's spot on the firing line right at that moment, probably to congratulate him. Woodfill turned to him, beaming, and got the ripping of his life, in highly colorful language. He'd gotten a bull's-eye, but on the wrong target.

Service in the Philippines wasn't glamorous. Woodfill never felt he was helping make the world safe for democracy. He never itched to get into combat, and he never did. The insurrection was more active on other parts of the main island, and Sam's unit mostly performed garrison duty in a small town. Woodfill found the landscape unappealing, the food horrible, the climate insufferable, and the locals mostly unfriendly. He contracted malaria, dysentery, and dengue fever, serious illnesses that would plague him for years. His comrades were behaving as soldiers often do when bored out of their minds: drinking, gambling, and visiting prostitutes. Woodfill also was witness to several acts of brutality against locals and Chinese immigrants. Throughout all this, he claimed, he stayed outside, if not above, the bad behavior. One night he sampled everything in the town saloon, including a few glasses of something that was called *Vino*, but definitely wasn't wine. Woodfill called it "the devil's own beverage made out of something that looks like a mixture of alcohol, rat poison, and tobacco juice," and said it took only three drinks to make a Yankee go "right off his nut." His brief bender left him hungover for a week, and he drank only very lightly, if at all, from that day on. He eventually decided that he was "a bit too shy, a bit too silent" to be "much of a mixer." He would take after his father and grandfather, frontiersmen who "didn't believe much in wastin' words."

Woodfill wasn't sad to leave the Philippines in 1904, but he wasn't too thrilled about being back in Kentucky. Then he read in the paper that the Third Ohio Infantry—based just across the river—was about to be shipped out to Alaska. While most people would see this assignment as a harsh exile, Woodfill saw the opportunity of a lifetime. He made the short trip to Ohio, signed up, and arrived in Alaska in 1904, in the sunset days of the gold rush that had kicked off in 1898.

Fort Egbert was the northernmost U.S. Army outpost in the world. Woodfill knew he'd made the right decision on the boat ride up, as he watched the mountains pass by and massive chunks of glacier fall into the ocean. After he surveyed the outpost, there was nothing that could dissuade him from his love for Alaska. Not even that first winter, when the mercury dropped to 53 degrees below zero.

The army had established Fort Egbert to police the prospectors and the native Alaskans, but the gold was mostly gone, and the Siwash seemed to look upon the white men as an occasional inconvenience rather than an enemy. The one firefight that occurred while he was there involved a prospector—later deemed insane—and a lot of alcohol. There wasn't much of a mission, except to keep the telegraph wires up and keep the camp as self-sufficient as possible. During the short growing season, this meant that the soldiers had to do a lot of digging to grow crops out of the frosty earth, but to Sam Woodfill, the spring meant he had a few months to hunt down enough meat to last through the winter.

He was graduating straight from squirrel to moose, caribou, and bear, but he did his job well. Once the hunting season started, he'd head out of the base for days, sometimes with other soldiers, but often alone. His quarry was as dangerous as the elements; both brought him close to an untimely demise on many occasions.

After tracking one particular moose for the better part of a day, Woodfill and a friend knew the creature was a big one by the way it left trampled ground and a wide path through the undergrowth. Still, they weren't prepared for what came charging at them in a clearing. Woodfill emptied his clip, six shots, into the beast, but it kept coming until he stepped aside to give his partner a clear shot. The last one took it. The moose stood 10 feet high, with horns that spread 62 inches. In the inch-thick hide around its neck were lodged four of Woodfill's bullets.

He left camp the following daybreak to pick up the trail of two more moose. Thinking he'd be following them through high alpine, and it being spring, Woodfill didn't take his snowshoes. He was still a little green and didn't know that this could be a fatal mistake. While working his way down the side of a mountain, he slipped and fell, cursing, into a sitting position in a deep snowbank. That's when he spotted his prey in a clearing below. He slid down the mountain "like a toboggan" and snuck up close. With two shots, he dispatched the moose, and then, turning to his right at another sound, bagged another. Feeling pretty pleased with himself, he packed them in snow for fresh-keeping until the sleds could make it in. That's when he realized that it was getting toward nightfall and the snow-covered mountain he'd so easily slid down would resist his every effort to get back up.

He improvised snowshoes out of spruce trees. They kept him from sinking into the snow completely, but not by much. For most of the night, he struggled against the cold, feeling, the entire time, his strength slipping away. Finally, well past midnight, he staggered into camp, where his comrades assured him that they knew all along he'd make it. Woodfill himself hadn't been so sure. He scraped up against death several times, but he always said that he never came closer than he had on that night. The bowls of caribou stew he ate by the fire—enough, he said, for four burly men—were the best he'd ever tasted.

Everyone in Alaska, Woodfill found out, had a bear story. The time came when he felt he should get one too, seeing as how there was a bear coming around and causing trouble, and seeing as how bear meat made for some fine dining. He left with nothing but a moose sandwich stuck in his pocket, thinking this errand probably wouldn't take long. Fifty miles and three days later, Woodfill was weak and delirious when he finally gave up. He made up for it later when he stumbled into three bears in a clearing. The last one took him by surprise, charging him from behind and taking three bullets that Woodfill fired from his hip. Woodfill became a local legend that day; not many could remember a hunter taking three bears in one afternoon.

Maybe not as talked about, but even more incredible, was his assault on a massive herd of caribou he spotted in a valley far below him. He adjusted his scope, and after a couple shots fell short and he pushed his scope out again, he started dropping them one after the other, each with one shot. He'd learned how to find the heart on these animals—six inches back from the base of the neck, six inches down from the top of the animal's back. When Woodfill was done, his companion saw the distance at which Sam had set his scope and his mouth dropped open. The woodsman had been shooting from 1,800 yards out. Woodfill wasn't bragging when he said, "Finding the mark with my bullet was just as much second nature to me as finding my mouth with my fork."

As he stalked the mountain ranges and braved one arctic winter after the next, he started standing taller. He'd arrived in Alaska with the dengue and malaria he'd caught in the Philippines still lingering, but after a few years finally managed to shake them off. He lost his farm-boy slouch and said that his eight years in Alaska had "put another thirty pounds of beef on my frame and had pushed me up another three inches in height." Private Woodfill was, after eight years in Alaska, a muscular 5 feet, 11 inches, with a 42-inch chest and 180 pounds of "beef."

The army closed Fort Egbert down in 1911 because "nothing was being accomplished and Uncle Sam got tired of havin' us sittin' up there gazin' at the Northern Lights." He stayed at Fort Gibbon in central Alaska for about a year, but without the big game hunting, Alaska lost its luster. He left with his regiment in 1912. Stationed next at San Francisco's Presidio, he found that target practice held no challenge whatsoever when the targets weren't moving. So he was pleased when, after a few months, he got a transfer to Fort Thomas, near home, while waiting for the next adventure.

In Kentucky, Woodfill's new captain took one look at this prime physical specimen, then one look at what his superiors said about him—model soldier, loyal, faithful—and promoted him to sergeant on the spot. Ever since they closed Fort Egbert, Woodfill had been wondering what could beat his eight years there. Now he knew. A set of general's gold stars on his collar couldn't, he said, have left him more "bucked" than his instant promotion. And on top of that, he got eight weeks leave.

Woodfill spent most of his eight weeks close to home. His brother William had joined the army, but his other brother John had been missing for years. He'd left home well before Sam had, and checked in periodically from his travels around the country. Then his mom got a letter in the first years of 1900, saying he'd joined the army and was off to the South Pacific. That was the last anyone heard of him. They had no idea what regiment he'd joined, and no one Sam asked—which was just about everyone he met—had ever heard of John Woodfill. Sam remained hopeful for the rest of his life that John would turn up, but he never did.

Women made quite an impression on Woodfill during this furlough. Once he got over his initial shock and shyness, he fell in love. Tall and elegant Lorena Wiltshire, who came to be known to Woodfill as "Darling Blossom," or just "Blossom," was a local girl, about as local as they come. Her family claimed to be in a direct line from Kentucky pioneer Daniel Boone, but more important to Woodfill was the fact that she didn't get bored listening to his Alaska stories. Before he went back into the army, not knowing where he'd end up next, he proposed marriage.

In 1914, Woodfill's regiment was sent to the Mexican border as tensions between the United States and the revolutionary government of Victoriano Huerta threatened the peace. After seeing the grandeur of the Alaska wilderness, Woodfill felt the desert was disappointing and the wildlife not worth stalking. Woodfill and his men did go out almost every day to clear up rattlesnakes so they wouldn't find their way into camp—and usually killed about 40 to 50 a day. As the years dragged on, Woodfill's primary concern, now that he was engaged, was finding a way to make enough money so he could marry Lorena.

Photography was still a novelty and soldiers would pay to have a keepsake of their time in a part of the world many of them considered exotic. So Woodfill and another sergeant set up shop as "Photographers De

Luxe," and even offered hand coloring. It couldn't miss. "We were sittin' up late 'o nights figurin' out how soon we'd be able to retire on the loot. Then one day our bubble was punctured and word came that Uncle Sam had decided to take a hand in the World War." On April 6, 1917, after the United States intercepted a message from Germany to Mexico promising aid and a return of lost territories if Mexico declared war against America, Congress declared war on Germany.

Woodfill had received nothing but the best assessments from his superiors: "Honest and faithful service." "Excellent. A model soldier." And finally, "A steady and reliable noncommissioned officer." So his superiors, in desperate need of additional commanders to handle the exponentially expanding army, granted him a temporary promotion to second lieutenant. He was now one of three second lieutenants in his company, commanding one of three platoons, and he reported to the company's captain. Woodfill wasn't as pleased with this bump as he was with becoming sergeant. Did lieutenants carry rifles? Would he sit off to the side and simply give orders? One of his peers remarked that he didn't need to worry about that. In this war, the rifle didn't stand a chance against the machine gun, much less against an artillery shell or mustard gas. So it didn't matter if he went as a private or second lieutenant.

But the promotion did come with a respectable pay increase, and Woodfill figured he could now afford "the luxury of matrimony." So, he explained, he did what all good soldiers do before they head off to war— he got married. The day after Christmas, 1917, he and Lorena were wed. The day after that, he was off to join the new recruits at camp near Gettysburg, Pennsylvania.

In general, he couldn't have been more pleased with the men who'd signed up. The regulars—Hans "Swede" Nelson and Sam Gowler—who'd been promoted just like he was, became his good friends quickly, equally dedicated to whipping their men into shape for what was to come. Only one guy in Woodfill's platoon turned out to be a problem. Johnnie Pulcino, a lively man with a thick Italian accent, was the worst shot in the company, simply because he would flinch every time the gun went off, sending bullets flying wildly. He was a coward, the other men in the company decided, who had no business carrying a rifle. But when one of these critics said this to his face, Pulcino let loose with a series of challenges and insults that convinced Woodfill he wasn't a coward after all. He became Woodfill's orderly, proving repeatedly his faithfulness and courage. Whenever the call went out for volunteers, he'd jump, saying he may not be able to shoot, but he would fight with grenades. Explosions and loud noises were okay as long as they weren't right next to his ear.

Woodfill's captain went overseas ahead of the company, leaving Woodfill with the duty of finishing the company's training and getting them to France. He saw his men aboard the *Philadelphia* in April 1918 and made the voyage unscathed, thanks to the destroyer escorts that sank a U-boat as it penetrated the convoy. Although Woodfill was surrounded by one of the most enthusiastic and cocksure group of soldiers America had ever sent into war, he was more reflective. He was about to head into terror, to kill strangers and possibly die at their hands, but only because it was his duty. On that one point, he was very different from the saber-rattling youths around him. "Personally, I never had much luck workin' up any spirit of hatred against the lads we were fightin'," he later said. "Maybe I'd had too many German friends in my time. I couldn't forget how old John Ott used to make flapjacks for me up in Alaska, nor Max Bachmann with his beer and music, and my old grandfather tellin' me, 'Ve vill haf no more vars.'"

They landed safely and made their way slowly to the front. Their train sped through Paris under cover of darkness, so Woodfill wouldn't see the City of Lights until after the war. They stopped at a training camp at Champin, but didn't stay long. A steady stream of American soldiers were steaming into port, so Woodfill and his men would train a day, march a day, train a day, and then march a day. On one of these marches, they came under fire for the first time.

The first shell—the first shell Woodfill and the company in his charge had ever heard—screeched over them and exploded on impact, lifting the field behind them into the air. They had stopped at a farmhouse for a meal of stew. Behind them was a team of horses bringing up artillery. Above them was a German observation blimp, telegraphing coordinates to the artillery behind German lines. Woodfill quickly learned the results of this combination. The first shell went wide, and was well enough away to be utterly harmless, but the men dove for cover, sending soup bowls flying. Someone screamed "I'm hit, I'm hit," but it was just panic. Seated in the middle of this pandemonium, Sam Woodfill barely moved. He lifted a spoonful of stew into his mouth and chewed nonchalantly. He stared straight ahead. Inside, his stomach was doing flips, but it was his job to appear calm, even if he wasn't.

The shells started coming faster, getting closer to the artillery. Finally, one landed in the road, making it impassable. Sam and a few volunteers got up and walked over to the team of horses to help lead them around the crater. If he got this shipment on its way, maybe the Germans would leave him and his men alone. As he and the French wagon driver led the horses around, a shell landed directly between them. They froze and looked at each other. It was a dud. All the Frenchman could mutter was "Mon Dieu."

Woodfill and the others would get used to these falling shells. They were just part of the surreal landscape that Europe had become. Months later, in September 1918, as they were marching with a battalion to take part in the Argonne offensive, Pershing's final push, they were targeted by a bomber that accurately placed a dud right alongside their path. The "nice big juicy bomb," as Woodfill called it, five feet long and a foot thick, made a huge crater, and would have wiped out the entire battalion if it had gone off. The marchers, who didn't break step for a moment, merely glanced at the neutered ordnance sticking out of the ground as if it were no more than a curious native shrub.

Arriving in the Anould Sector near the Vosges Mountains of Eastern France in early 1918, Woodfill returned command to his captain. This sector, which looked across the French-German border toward Stras-bourg, then a German city, had been the scene of very intense battles at the beginning of the war before becoming one of the front's most static sectors. Soldiers here held steady in the quiet tension of a stalemate. Vines and bushes had started to reclaim the land by climbing up batteries and observation posts, giving the sector a sense of peacefulness, but at the same time giving the war an eerie sense of permanence. The Anould Sector was useful to the Americans as a training ground for troops. Here they could get used to trench life and the occasional firefight before they were needed in a more serious situation.

Not that there weren't deadly serious moments interrupting the silence of the Anould Sector. Following a night attack that left 6 Americans dead and 24 others hospitalized from the effects of mustard gas, Woodfill gathered volunteers for a venture into the no-man's-land to repair the defenses damaged by the attackers. In relating this story years later, he remarked that it was a beautiful midsummer day, as if they were heading out for a picnic rather than to reinforce the barbed wire that ran the length of the trench. Woodfill and his volunteers made it back unscathed, their small mission accomplished, but two gunners spent "a bushel or two of bullets" trying to knock him out as he slithered from point to point on his belly. They didn't seem to like him, he remarked back in the trench. "What did you expect 'em to do," growled a friend, "serve you beer and pretzels?"

With the start of the Argonne offensive in September 1918, Wood-fill's regiment, part of the Fifth Division, moved out to join nine army divisions: 60,000 French troops and one million Americans for, as Woodfill put it in his memoir, "forty-six days of rain and mud and death and general hell such as no American army had ever faced." Arriving in the last week of September, Woodfill, again filling in for his captain, had been ordered to take his company to replace a company that had been tragically destroyed in an instant. Two young women, Salvation Army volunteers, had set up a kitchen in an abandoned farmhouse. Acting against direct orders, they started serving food, naively thinking that they were alleviating the soldiers' suffering. But an observation plane spotted the concentration of troops, and the first shell that came in was a direct hit. The two women were buried with military honors.

After a few uneventful weeks, Woodfill was ordered to report to the commander of the 319th. He left his company for the moment and selected a dozen men to move with him laterally along the lines in the midst of an ongoing battle. The woods they traversed were a scene of recent horrors, according to Woodfill's memoirs, "covered with rotting horses, dead men, human hands and feet, shoes half filled with flesh and bones, blood, mud, filth, and stench." As they reached an open field, it appeared that the front line had moved forward and they were behind it, so Woodfill and his men moved across. In fact, they walked right into an intense firefight that had only momentarily subsided. The men scattered for cover, and Woodfill found himself alone, facedown in a shallow trench. He was safe, but his backpack was exposed, and a German gunner raked it with bullets. He couldn't move forward or back, or even roll over. "Then to liven things up still more that machine gunner must have invited his artillery to attend the party." A shell fell about ten paces behind him. A second shell hit closer. They were finding his range. The explosion covered him in mud as the gunner continued to shred his pack. He surmised that the next shell was certain to fall directly upon him.

Woodfill reached into his shirt pocket and pulled out a picture of Lorena wearing her wedding dress. It was always there, along with a picture of his mother. He looked at it for a moment, then turned it over and, using the stub of a pencil, wrote:

In case of Axident [sic] or Death It is my last and fondest desire that the finder of my remains shall please do me a last, and ever lasting favor to please forward this picture to my Darling Wife. And tell her that I have fallen on the field of Honor, and departed to a better land which knows no sorrow and feels no pain. I will prepair [sic] a place and be waiting at the Golden Gait [sic] of Heaven for the arrival of my Darling Blossom.

The address
Mrs. Samuel Woodfill
167 Alexandria Pike
Fort Thomas, Kentucky

Moments later the firing stopped. The 319th had finally pushed the attackers back over a nearby hill. Explosions and gunfire had shattered everything around him, but he smiled when he saw his men crawling out of shell holes. Not one had been hurt. He placed the picture of his wife back in his pocket, remembering something one of his Alaska buddies had said: "Sam, the only way they'll ever kill you is by hanging."

The commander who was relieved by Woodfill was eager to get his men out of there. He was sure that the expected nighttime barrage would wipe them out. As Woodfill watched them stumble back to the rear, he could see why. They had been up for days and were covered in mud and the blood of their comrades. They looked hardly capable of walking. Woodfill watched them knowing he and his men would be going where they had been.

The barrage came that night. There was little the group could do but disperse themselves among the shell holes, hoping against a direct hit. It rained all night, leaving almost a foot of water in the holes and trenches, but Woodfill welcomed the mud and muck. When shells struck the soft ground, they sank before exploding, sending a jet of mud straight up, rather than sending a burst of shrapnel straight out. But the conditions on the ground didn't stop a shell from exploding directly above Woodfill's head, not close enough to kill him but close enough to knock him out for several hours. He missed most of the terrible night.

With the morning of October 12 came orders to take his company forward through a wooded area to find the German line and attempt to break through. They were east of the the town of Cunel, and surrounded by woods ravaged by war. Woodfill formed his men into a long line, and they cautiously moved through the daybreak's fog with bayonets fixed. The fog was on their side until they came to a clearing, when it suddenly lifted. Three machine gun nests opened up simultaneously, and men started falling left and right. A sergeant directly left of Woodfill convulsed unnaturally, and Woodfill asked if he was hit. The man simply took three steps forward and fell. The survivors found cover, but then, as they had learned to expect, the shells started falling, seeking them out as the bullets kept them stationary.

Reflecting later on how American soldiers tipped the balance in France, Woodfill remarked, "We accomplished most of the things we did as a result of youth, pep, courage, and the 'orders be damned' individual initiative of our chaps . . ." This same spirit, along with a knowledge that, while he may be an officer, he wasn't better than anyone else, moved this "model soldier" to act: "The only thing to do was find out where that first machine gun was and get it. And I didn't believe in askin' any of my men to do something I wouldn't do myself." With that thought, he was off. This time, he left his pack.

He made it to the cover of a shell hole just in time and found the problem. From the right, fire was coming from an abandoned stable. From the left, it was coming from a church tower over 200 yards away. From dead ahead, it was pouring out of the natural cover of the forest. Woodfill couldn't see the gunner in the church tower, but he did see a window slit, and placed a bullet there. He never knew if he hit anything, but the firing stopped. Examining the stable, he noticed a clapboard had been removed. Again, he fired blindly into the place most likely to conceal a gunner. Again the firing stopped.

With the threats on his flank gone, he rushed to a fresh shell hole, then another. As he "pancaked" on the ground, he noticed he was winded, gasping for air. His hole contained a patch of mustard gas, and he moved on quickly before he took a fatal lungful. He slithered off to the side, reaching a clump of thistle that concealed him. The gun didn't attempt to seek him out.

"There's not much difference between hunting animals and hunting humans," Woodfill told a reporter later. He crept up on the machine gun nest, finding perfect cover in a ditch by a roadside. He could see the muzzle sticking out of a clump of bushes just 40 feet away. But that was all. He placed his pistol and an extra clip next to him and took aim. His vision was blurred and his eyes watery from the gas, but he focused on where the gunner should be, and waited. A ray of sunlight flashed off what looked like a helmet and he thought he could make out a face. He fired a single shot. The gunner fell, and Woodfill saw a second man push the first aside and take his place behind the gun. The woodsman waited until the gunner had taken his seat. The German fell with one of Woodfill's bullets in his head.

"The third and fourth ones must have known what to expect," Woodfill remembered thinking. "That was nerve—to take their places knowin' they would be picked off." The fifth and sixth men, after watching four of their fellows drop with flawless single shots to the head, decided the position was untenable. Woodfill killed them as they fled. He saw no movement in the nest, so he charged it with his pistol drawn. He stumbled over a German, who made a grab for Woodfill's rifle. Sam killed him with his pistol. Then he turned to signal the men in his command, still in their shell holes and stunned by what they had just witnessed, to move up.

Without waiting for them to arrive, he moved ahead in search of new targets. He snuck up on a second nest and killed another five men in the same fashion. As he penetrated farther into the enemy's line, he bumped into a group of German soldiers attempting to supply the gun he'd just taken out. They'd left their rifles behind to carry armfuls of ammunition, and they surrendered immediately. Sam sent them to the rear unescorted.

His company was spread throughout the woods. "It was every man for himself now," he recalled. "That's where American initiative stood to advantage." It seemed the German soldiers hardly expected to be attacked by a lone sniper, which allowed Woodfill to take out yet another nest, another five men, with another five well-placed shots. As he charged this third nest, another hidden machine gun fired, sending him into a nearby trench.

He dove almost directly onto a German with his pistol out, but got the draw on him and laid him down with a single shot. Another German appeared behind, crawling around a trench corner, and must have breathed a moment of relief when Woodfill's pistol, aimed directly at his heart, jammed. But as the German aimed his rifle, Woodfill reached for the nearest substitute—a pickax—and drove it into his brain. As it sank in, Woodfill felt a bullet whistle past his ear, fired by the man he thought he'd killed just moments before. He finished the job with the pick.

Poking his head above the trench, Woodfill found that the Germans were in retreat, but they were on both sides. He'd broken the line, but now he and his men were alone. A small cadre of his men found his position and informed him that they were unsupported on the flanks. Woodfill sent a runner back to request orders, and he returned promptly with the order to fall back—Woodfill and his men had penetrated more than 200 yards farther than any other group. They fell back as ordered, and once they were among friends, they found that their company had been up against four German regiments.

He quickly organized his company, placing them among the shell holes to be ready for any counterattack. It came in the form of a furious artillery bombardment that scored one direct hit after another. As Woodfill was conferring with a few of his men, he noticed a pair of his soldiers hunkering down in a foxhole. In the next moment, they were gone, transformed into a rain of "mud and rags, blood and brains and muscle" by an exploding shell. The shelling went on for hours, but it wasn't followed by a ground assault. As dusk approached, it suddenly stopped.

Woodfill retrieved his pack. He discovered that the jar of strawberry jam that he'd miraculously lucked into and even more miraculously saved for several weeks had been stolen by some "yellow-bellied son of a sea cook." He was still grumbling about it when the company cook—a man who took his job very seriously, coming up with all manner of delicacies while other companies were spooning through cans of beans—presented him with a fresh apple pie. It was, he said, a "reward for wipin' up the German army." Sitting in his foxhole, surrounded by devastation, covered with grime, full of adrenaline and the knowledge that he'd killed some 20 men, lamenting the loss of his friends and his jar of jam, this pie meant the world to him. "I don't think any medal I ever got pleased me half as much as that apple pie," he later reflected.

News started to come in about his comrades. Pulcino, the man who flinched whenever he pulled the trigger, was dead. He had been relegated to stretcher bearer, and proved he wasn't a coward by running through fields that were literally exploding. Back in the field hospital, he took a breather, and that's where a shell found him. Sam Gowler led a successful attack on an artillery position, but was mortally wounded. Hans Nelson had moved forward alone, like Woodfill had, working with grenades to neutralize a machine gun nest. Just as he moved in victoriously, a sniper shot him.

Woodfill's friends were gone. Most of his company was missing. His captain had been killed that day. He slept that night in the soggy foxhole. He woke up feeling ill from the effects of the mustard gas he'd breathed in the shell hole the previous day, coupled with yet another damp night out in the open, and so he was removed to the hospital. The following day Woodfill's regiment was sent, without him, into the Bois de Pultiere, just north of Cunel, where over a thousand men lost their lives to achieve a 550-yard advance.

General Pershing's Argonne offensive drew the war to a rapid close. The Germans and Allies reached an armistice on November 11, 1918. By the time Woodfill got out of the hospital, after ten weeks fighting off the effects of the gas, the war was well over. He served out his time in Europe as a clothing inspector for returning troops—making sure they weren't taking any lice as passengers across the ocean. In late January, 1919, when he learned that he would receive the Medal of Honor for his actions against the machine gun nests, and that it would be presented by Pershing himself, he didn't tell his captain, but simply asked him for a few days' leave. The captain learned about the medal only after the written orders came in.

The ceremony and surrounding events took place in France in February 1919, and while Woodfill wasn't much for the pomp, he was very pleased to meet General Pershing and make the acquaintance of several other Medal of Honor recipients, including Willie Sandlin, a fellow Kentuckian who'd taken out three machine gun nests on the first day of the Argonne offensive. Edward Allworth, who appears in a photograph with Woodfill, was honored for swimming the Meuse River under fire and establishing a beachhead on the far bank. It seemed like every general in the army was there, and they all wanted to shake the hands of the men they'd come to honor.

There was one other duty to fulfill: A filmmaker wanted to send something home on behalf of Victory Loan, so he had some of the heroes reenact their deeds for the camera. Woodfill's wife, back in Fort Thomas, saw this reel and learned what her husband had been through. She was visibly shaken by the experience and left the theater in a daze. When she got home, however, there was a comforting letter from Woodfill saying that he would be home within six months.

A quiet reception welcomed him home. Mustered out at Fort Thomas in early November 1919, he joyfully reunited with Lorena, who'd been working as a bookkeeper in a furniture store. Determined to support "the best wife in the whole world" as he thought she deserved, Woodfill started assessing his skills and job opportunities. It was only a matter of months before he realized that after 18 years in the army, he wasn't cut out for civilian life. Unlike the youngsters who'd signed up for the war, he was in his mid-30s and had never held a job outside the army. Marksmanship, his most finely honed skill, was useless outside the gates of the Fort Thomas army base. So he reenlisted on November 24, after only three weeks out of uniform.

The army was glad to have him back, but was in the process of contracting to its pre-war size. So he was reenlisted as a sergeant, the rank he'd held before his temporary promotion. A local reporter remarked on the peculiarity of a war hero of his stature and abilities receiving what looked like a demotion. But a few unnamed officers assured him that Woodfill would be awarded a commission in a very short time. Woodfill himself didn't ask for one. Part of his idea of being a model soldier was serving where he was needed without trying to shake up the system for his own benefit. Still, his wife and friends tried several times to have his rank increased by an act of Congress.

For two years, Sam and Lorena Woodfill lived a quiet life on a modest salary. Woodfill was with his wife, close to his mother, who was in the last year of her life, and was back to his familiar role in the army. It's certain that he would have succeeded in fading away, which is probably exactly what he wanted to do, if General Pershing, by then army chief of staff, had not made a remark to the press one day about Woodfill. In 1921, a team of heroes—Woodfill and Sergeant York among them—was called to Washington to serve as pallbearers to the Unknown Soldier. When General Pershing saw the list, he singled Woodfill out from the other, better-known names: "Why, I have already picked that man as the greatest single hero in the American forces." As they hastily jotted down this unexpected comment, reporters were asking themselves the question they knew would soon be on everyone's lips: "Sam who?"

By the time they tracked down the address of this unknown hero who'd been selected to carry the Unknown Soldier, he was already in Washington. But they descended on the residence at 167 Alexandria Pike anyway, trying to, in the words of one correspondent, "find out what sort of fellow is Sergeant Samuel Woodfill." Lorena met them gladly, and her pride had put her in an expansive mood. She said that although he had received nine honors from various governments, including France, Montenegro, and Italy, since receiving the Medal of Honor, she wanted the world to know that she had decorated him with the "M. H." award for being a "model husband." He washes dishes, she beamed, and was front and center the last time she was sick, taking care of all manner of household chores. He was grateful for the nation's attention, but would rather be home fixing things. The only problem she had with him, she concluded, was that he was just too modest. The reporters went away satisfied. The *New York Times* went with the headline: OUTSTANDING WAR HERO HELPS WITH THE DISHES.

In Washington, Woodfill was shaking hands with President Harding and nearly every member of the House of Representatives, which adjourned in his honor. He sat in the president's box at the Belasco Theater, and after one of the singers introduced him and related his story, he was mobbed in the lobby. The public was really testing the boundaries of this very shy man's endurance, asking him to recall again and again the day when he killed around 20 men, two face-to-face and hand-to-hand. "When he reached Washington," one reporter wrote, "it was evident that he would rather face German machine guns than newspapermen. When asked about the exploits for which he has been decorated by his own and foreign governments, he shifted from one foot to the other, mumbled something about wishing he could have done more than he did, and then abruptly ceased speaking."

Serving as pallbearer with Woodfill was another hero who'd received a great deal of attention as the leader of the storied "Lost Battalion." Major Charles Whittlesey had protested his orders before leading his exhausted men to fight themselves into an advanced position. Then he protested again when the flanks failed to keep up with his progress. What he foresaw happened: The units on the flanks never joined him, and on the morning of October 3, 1918, the 600 men of the 77th were cut off and surrounded with only a day's rations. On October 8, the 194 men who were left marched out of the trenches where they had been waiting for the Allies to catch up. The others had been killed, captured, or maimed. Whittlesey had held on to his fragile group through starvation, thirst, relentless attacks, and even an accidental hours-long shelling by their own troops.

Whittlesey was publicly accused of causing the separation of his battalion by overstepping his orders for the sake of personal ambition. It was a ludicrous claim, since he had twice protested those orders, but he remained tight-lipped. As he carried the Unknown Soldier, however, he was also carrying an overwhelming mental burden. Too many men had died under his command for Whittlesey to consider himself a hero. Two weeks after the ceremony, he sailed for Cuba on a luxury liner. Midway, he jumped over the side. His body was never recovered.

Woodfill spent the week following the ceremony in New York. He was feted by the Society of the Fifth Division and visited the stock exchange, which honored him by suspending trading for three minutes. He met French field marshal Ferdinand Foch, supreme commander of the Allied forces, who commented that he was honored to meet the first soldier of America. It's reported that Woodfill replied that he was honored to meet the first soldier of the world. He attended a reception at the 5,200-capacity Hippodrome, the largest, most opulent theater in New York, and had a portrait painted by Joseph Cummings Chase, America's most prolific portrait painter, who executed portraits of Theodore Roosevelt and Warren G. Harding. Then, as suddenly as it had swept him up, the whirlwind dropped him back in Kentucky. He removed his medals and put them back where they'd been before—in a cotton sack—and returned to being a U.S. Army sergeant.

The fact that he was a sergeant after having earned the medal while an acting captain bothered a number of people. The Society of the Fifth Division telegrammed key Senate members asking for quick action before Woodfill marched in the Armistice Day procession, saying that inaction would allow America to parade "her injustice and ingratitude" before the eyes of the world. The *New York Times* editorial page writers saw a tinge of classism at work, saying that it was surprising such a situation would arise in "such a democracy as ours." Throughout the years, even as late as 1939, the issue of Woodfill's rank would periodically arise in the Senate, only to be struck down.

Lawmakers were acutely aware of the perception that this man was serving well below his abilities, but they were swayed by other considerations: For one thing, the legislative branch should not, ideally, micromanage the military's personnel matters. For another, one should never put a price or a professional reward on heroism. Woodfill probably didn't have many opinions on the first point, but he was in full agreement with the second, which is why he never involved himself in any of the bills or efforts. "You fought for your country, but you don't seem to want to fight for yourself," his wife would repeatedly remind him in frustration. But he would not be swayed. If the army wanted him to be a sergeant, that is what he would be.

The only problem Woodfill had was the pay. It would have been fine for him alone—he didn't need much—but he wanted his wife to enjoy "the American standard of living," as he told a reporter, and that cost money. They had a decent house, but by 1922, they were having serious problems keeping up the mortgage. Woodfill went to his commanding officer and requested three months' leave. They were in need of help down on the dam at Silver Grove. As a carpenter, he could make $6.00 a day, and that was twice what he made from the army. He was granted the three months.

Cincinnati papers got ahold of this story and ran it without sensationalizing. The *New York Times* followed suit. His hero's welcome in Washington over, he'd stopped talking to the press, but his wife was more than happy to speak for him. "My husband went to work on the dam today because he finds it necessary to raise the money to meet the payment on our home that will fall due on January 1. He could never do it on his sergeant's pay, and the work at the dam opened a way for him." In

Cincinnati, E. F. Albee, who operated the Keith Circuit of theaters, started a campaign to raise money for Woodfill and his wife in lobbies as far away as New York. When he was done, as Woodfill was ready to leave the dam, Albee had raised $10,000, more than enough to pay off the mortgage in its entirety.

The following year was Woodfill's last year in the army. With his overseas time counting double, he'd served the 30 years to make him eligible for a pension. As he announced his retirement, at 40 years old, three master sergeants volunteered to step down so Woodfill could be promoted to master sergeant before he left. One volunteer was selected by his C.O., who subsequently promoted Woodfill just before retirement. The promotion left him with a pension of $133.86 a month, with about thirty dollars going to insurance.

His dreams now were of a simple life on a farm he and his wife had picked out, raising fruit trees. His only connection with the army was the occasional meetings of veterans organizations, where he was typically a guest of honor. His connection to Willie Sandlin, fellow Kentuckian and Medal of Honor recipient, prompted him to appeal on Sandlin's behalf to the state legislature for a grant of $10,000 to buy a farm. It probably didn't escape his wife's notice that here he was, fighting for someone in the same way he'd refused to fight for himself.

The steady stream of small events that took Woodfill away from the farm began to try his patience. It was very nice that they named an elementary school after him and called him out annually for Armistice Day, but it was hard on a modest man to put in an appearance at every pageant and American Legion convention. There are also a few indications that he didn't want to repeatedly recall what happened on that day.

"I'm tired of being a circus pony," Woodfill told his wife. "Every time there is something doing they trot me out to perform." But the duty-bound veteran seldom could muster the courage to say no. That's why he was out of town, in Massachusetts at a convention, when a drive started among an insurgent wing of the local Democratic party to recruit him as a candidate for Congress in 1924. Even if he had been home to answer reporters' questions, it's pretty doubtful that he would have started a campaign. But by now, his Lorena was an old hand in the role of spokeswoman.

She told them how Woodfill felt about being paraded around like a prop, but thought he would make a fine congressman: "My husband may not have the education of a lawyer, scholar or the like, but if reputation, honesty, service and truth were the only requisite, he is amply qualified to fill the high position to which his friends would elect him." Of course, the real problem with the proposal was that "he's so bashful" he'd never run a successful campaign. But Lorena wouldn't let the reporters go without putting in her two cents about the problem with America's elected officials: "What we need in Washington are more men who will lay aside personal feelings and self-aggrandizement and remember they are there to represent and serve their constituents who expect a fulfillment of election promises."

When Woodfill returned from New England, he removed any uncertainty by saying that he would definitely not run. From that point on, he became less a public fixture every year, and his life settled into a routine of fixing things and trying to make his farm bear fruit. A film crew caught up with him in 1928 for a short piece on what veterans were doing ten years later. Sam was wearing an apron, still helping with the dishes, and reading "instructive" books in the evening (he never had much use for fiction, he said). What they didn't discuss was the resurgence of financial problems that threatened to engulf the Woodfills.

The fruit trees had failed. To purchase more, Sam took out a mortgage. Once again, his pension wasn't enough to keep up, and the second batch of fruit trees weren't doing much better than the first. Once again, Congress considered and rejected a promotion. This time, someone had the novel idea of reenlisting him, promoting him, and immediately retiring him. Sam hit the job market again, taking a post with the Kentucky Disabled Ex-service Men's Board as an assistant to the secretary. For some unknown reason, it didn't work out. He got an audience with Gilbert Bettman, attorney general of Ohio, and said he was looking for a job as a security guard in a bank. "I felt ashamed for America," Bettman later said.

Bettman pulled a few strings to introduce Woodfill to author-adventurer Lowell Thomas, with the idea that a biography by a best-selling writer could solve his problems while simultaneously teaching the postwar generation about the sacrifices made on their behalf. *Woodfill of the Regulars* was published in 1929, but it was not a success. At the time of publication, Woodfill was working as a guard in a steel mill.

For the next 13 years, Woodfill guarded the time clocks and checked the trucks leaving and entering the lot at the Andrews Steel Company. He typically worked the 2:00 P.M. to 11:00 P.M. shift, and earned $115 a month. His obscurity during this time was almost complete.

On July 4, 1938, a reporter stopped in to check up on Sam Woodfill. The war hero had, in his own words, "cooled off." He thought there was still time for peace in Europe. "Humanity yearns for a square deal," he implored. "All that is necessary is a group of sane, unselfish men to bring about an international agreement." He was very much in favor of staying out of Europe, a common sentiment among those who'd gone over the first time. But he also believed that the only way to ensure peace was through a military buildup.

The reporter wrote: "There was no Fourth of July noise-making, no flag-waving, no bugle-blowing for Sergeant Woodfill. He passed the day quietly in his cool, green and yellow frame house." He remarked on his impressions of the attitude in America, but his drift seemed to come back to himself: "The old war wounds are gradually healing," he proclaimed, without specifying if he was speaking of his own emotional or physical wounds, or of wounds suffered by the nation. But he added, simply, "It is better to forget." As the reporter left, the aging veteran added a remark that suggested he still carried a reaction they called shell shock. "Isn't this a nice Fourth of July?" he said. "So few firecrackers."

There were only a few nice Independence Days, after he uttered those words, before the United States was back at war. But shortly after bombs fell on Pearl Harbor in 1941, Woodfill was preoccupied with developments at home. Lorena, after an apparently brief struggle with an illness not named in any of her obituaries, died in the hospital on March 26, 1942. Woodfill buried her in Falmouth, Kentucky, and went back to work at the mill. He continued to live on the farm they'd shared.

America's entry into the war probably prolonged the disheartened veteran's life by several years. In May of 1942, months after Woodfill had lost his wife, someone in the War Department thought it would be good for morale to reenlist sergeants York and Woodfill as majors in the army. "It was not known whether Major Woodfill would be sent to fight the Germans—a task he found quite simple in World War I," a Cincinnati reporter opined, "or to test his military efficiency against the Japs, but, in the words of army officers, it was encouraging to have him back in the army." As a morale booster, he started his job even before he packed his things to leave, supplying quotations like: "We will win if it takes every man and half the women in the country. Once trained, there is no finer soldier in the world than an American. We can't lose." Despite his optimism for the well-being of the country, he behaved as if he was leaving home for the last time. He sold his farm and auctioned off everything he owned.

The original plan was to put the aged heroes on the ground in charge of artillery units. But York failed the physical, and although Woodfill passed muster on most counts, he had to get a special clearance to gain admission because he didn't have the minimum number of teeth. It seemed a better idea at that point to assign Woodfill to a firearms training position. The newspapers were invited to witness his first time back on a rifle range, at Fort Benning, Georgia, after 18 years in civilian life. He reportedly hit "bull's-eye after bull's-eye."

But he was more than a show pony for the papers. He did some real training, always emphasizing knowledge of and proficiency with equipment, always challenging his trainees to follow orders, but also to think for themselves. He was truly back in his element. And he probably wished he could have stayed longer. But on his birthday in 1943, he hit the mandatory retirement age of 60.

After supporting his wife for over 20 years on a sergeant's pay and pension, he retired a major, with the attendant increase due to him. He had, however, to write a letter to correct an administrative oversight before he got any checks. The oversight was by then two years old, so he got it all in one lump sum. But he had no wife to support, no farm to invest in. He chose not to return to Fort Thomas, settling instead about 40 miles to the southwest, in Vevay, Indiana, directly across the Ohio River from Kentucky. He moved into an apartment, where he remained anonymous. His neighbors remembered him as a very pleasant man, but not someone who would go out of his way to see people.

When he died, in 1951, it was three days before someone reported the smell to the police, who had to break down his door when they arrived. He'd collapsed between the kitchen and bedroom. The neighbors didn't think it was strange that they hadn't seen him around. After all, he'd said something about going into Cincinnati for plumbing supplies.

Woodfill's body rested in Hebron Cemetery, between Madison, Indiana, and Vevay, until 1955, his plot marked by an eight- by ten-inch metal plate. He was survived by a brother and sister. His brother John had never resurfaced, even after all the appeals Sam had made during his moments of fame. Sam and Lorena had no children.

Once again, in 1955, an outpouring of support came Woodfill's way. A Madison reporter related his story in the local paper, which touched a nerve of national guilt. He was reburied in Arlington National Cemetery, in a plot carefully chosen: as close as regulations would allow to the grave of General Pershing. Full military honors accompanied this second funeral. Army chaplain Major Albert M. Shoemaker presided over a ceremony that included a procession with a black riderless horse, the empty boots turned backward. This highly symbolic honor was, and is, typically reserved for colonels and above. Shoemaker read a letter from Vice President Nixon, who assured the audience that President Eisenhower had been informed of Woodfill's heroic deeds. Shoemaker then quoted Wordsworth: "This is the happy warrior; this is he that every man in arms should wish to be."

The *Cincinnati Post* reviewed the ceremony, and the reporter was satisfied. "It was a final and lasting fame for the man. Never again will the name fall into obscurity as he, the man, so often did."

Return to Isolationism

The fierce combat that Sam Woodfill and other doughboys encountered during the Argonne offensive provides a sobering reminder that the killing on the battlefields of France continued at a brisk pace right through the final weeks of World War I. The American troops may have come late to the fray—they did not, in fact, become heavily involved in the fighting until the last six months of the war—but they still got there in time to catch plenty of action. And when it was all over, the U.S. death toll stood at 116,516.

Still, that figure must be viewed as modest compared to the appalling number of casualties sustained by the major European powers. France lost well over a million men, Britain close to a million, and Germany nearly 2 million. All told, more than 8 million combatants died in the war, and another 21 million were wounded. Those staggering numbers drive home the point that World War I was a senseless slaughter, a bloody carnage of monumental proportions.

What made it so horrifying was the long and deadly stalemate of trench warfare. Time and time again, ferocious battles were fought at close range—and at great cost—and, more often than not, all the winning side would have to show for its "victory" would be the few yards of territory gained in the struggle. That was the general pattern of the war—especially on the western front—from the fall of 1914, when the opposing forces first became mired in deadlock, until 1918, when the battered and exhausted armies finally agreed to an armistice.

Back in the days when we were engaged in Vietnam and the phrase "living-room war" came into vogue, an intriguing speculation began making the rounds. Impressed by the impact that television coverage of the fighting in Vietnam was having on viewers back home, some historians raised the question of what might have happened if cameras and correspondents had been on hand to record the slaughter in the trenches of World War I. They went on to assert that the visual images (buttressed by strong voice-over reporting) of what was truly taking place on those killing fields would have served as a powerful antidote to the steady flow of upbeat propaganda that was being dispatched through official channels. The inevitable conclusion was that outraged civilians throughout Europe would have put pressure on their respective governments to stop all the bloodshed, and the terrible war would have come to an end much, much sooner.

My reaction to that "what if?" scenario was influenced, of course, by what I do for a living. As a reporter who has worked in television since the medium was in its infancy, I could not help but be taken by the suggestion that TV journalism could have been responsible for saving millions of lives at a critical turning point in world history.

America entered World War I in a spirit of high optimism. When he appeared before Congress to ask for a declaration of war, President

Woodrow Wilson defined the U.S. mission in glowing and lofty terms. "The world must be made safe for democracy," he proclaimed. But the end of the war brought disillusion, a growing sense that the American sacrifices had been in vain. That soon hardened into a widespread belief that we had no business getting involved in the first place, and within months after the armistice, the country began to revert to the isolationism that had long been the cornerstone of U.S. foreign policy.

That would remain our posture over the next two decades, even after dangerous dictators and warlords rose to power in Germany and Japan. In 1937, Japanese aggression provoked a war with China, and in September 1939, Hitler's storm troopers marched into Poland, which marked the onset of World War II. Still we held back, clinging to the belief that the two large oceans on our borders would insulate us from all the upheavals in Europe and Asia. As late as 1941, the majority of Americans continued to believe that we could avoid becoming directly involved in another war on foreign soil. Then came the morning of December 7.

—MW

CHAPTER FIVE

David M. Shoup

WORLD WAR II

"Col. Shoup fearlessly exposed himself to the terrific and relentless artillery, machinegun, and rifle fire from hostile shore emplacements. Rallying his hesitant troops by his own inspiring heroism, he gallantly led them across the fringing reefs to charge the heavily fortified island and reinforce our hard-pressed, thinly held lines."

— MEDAL OF HONOR CITATION

THOSE WHO LIVED through the Cuban Missile Crisis in October 1962 will never forget the looming dread and the near certainty of a global nuclear exchange. Those who were close to the discussions and the man who would make the final call knew more than anyone at the time how real and frightening the situation had become. General David Shoup remembered distinctly how heavily the events of those 13 days weighed on the commander in chief he served: "I don't believe that I've ever seen a human being confronted with a decision, or confronted with the requirement to proceed on a half-way thwarted decision of such great importance as President Kennedy was confronted with at that time." Shoup was then commandant of the United States Marine Corps, a member of the Joint Chiefs of Staff, and so was a witness to and participant in this horrifying decision-making process.

Shoup was an Eisenhower appointee whose term continued into the Kennedy administration. Nominated and confirmed in 1959, he reported for duty on January 1, 1960. He was a steely-eyed man with a reputation for straight shooting and an aversion to politics. He was plucked from his post as commanding general of the Marine Corps Recruit Depot at Parris Island, with the rank of major general, and promoted to lieutenant general and Marine Corps Chief of Staff for a nominal period before assuming the post of commandant and the rank of general. During this rapid ascent in rank, he vaulted over five other lieutenant generals, all of whom resigned soon after he became commandant. But his appointment hardly made a stir on Capitol Hill, judging from the free pass he got at his Senate confirmation hearings. The senators seemed more impressed with his war record and the actions that earned him the Medal of Honor. Without these, it's doubtful he would have been selected over and above the five generals who ranked him.

He was, everyone knew, an apolitical man when it came to his job, which also may have been why Ike thought he was right for the job. He didn't come with a lot of baggage, he didn't owe a lot of favors. Shoup's career as commandant of the Marine Corps further proved his independence. One of the first things he did was criticize Eisenhower's plans for the Marines, as reflected in the proposed budget, even before the budget was announced. For a time, he refused to submit his speeches to the Kennedy administration for review. He reportedly even shouted down the new secretary of defense, Robert McNamara, shortly after McNamara came on board in 1961.

As the fate of the world pivoted on the decisions of Kennedy and Khrushchev during those 13 days in October 1962, the Joint Chiefs made plans based on a list of options Shoup called "a mile long." Few of the options were good. Shoup, who said that he opposed an invasion "from the start," felt that once the military was unleashed it had to go all the way. "And if that decision is made," he told Kennedy on October 19 during a meeting with the Joint Chiefs, "we must go in with plenty of insurance of a decisive success . . . as quick as possible." As Shoup spoke, his voice was recorded on a tape secretly made by Kennedy, one of thousands of utterances thus captured by the president from July 1962 until his death.

Shoup felt that limiting a military action to a surgical strike was a fantasy, considering that the U.S. Naval base at Guantanamo Bay would most certainly come under attack, and even the best defense would turn the base into little more than "a hunk of dirt that's taken a hell of a lot of people to hang on to." Escalation, once begun, was inevitable. "Someone's got to keep them from doing the goddamn thing piecemeal," he remarked to Curtis LeMay (who became the epitome of the hawk during the Vietnam era) after the October 19 meeting broke up and Kennedy had left the Cabinet Room. Unbeknownst to him, Kennedy had left the tape recorder on and caught Shoup cussing like a marine, something he didn't do in the presence of the president. "Do the son of a bitch and do it right, and quit friggin' around."

Shoup was a feared poker player, with eyes that to *Time* reporter Robert Sherrod looked like "two burn holes in a blanket." In military matters, however, he did not bluff. As the situation intensified in the days after the October 19 meeting, and all branches of the armed forces prepared for war, Shoup ordered assembled "one of the greatest assault teams in American history." Forty-five thousand marines, with another one hundred thousand ready to back them up, ready to invade Cuba. If the order came, Shoup would not have hesitated to send them in.

Bluffing isn't nearly as important to a poker player as calculating the odds and the cost. Once, at a time when, according to David Halberstam in his book *The Best and the Brightest*, "talk of invading Cuba was becoming fashionable," Shoup used a graphic depiction to communicate the odds and cost of invasion to the Joint Chiefs of Staff, who sometimes seemed to think invading a pipsqueak country like Cuba shouldn't be a problem. From an overhead projector, he cast a map of the United States on the wall. Over this he placed an enlarged map of Cuba. Suddenly, it didn't look so small as it stretched 800 miles from New York to Chicago. Then, over the map of Cuba, he placed a tiny red dot. This, he explained, represented the South Pacific island of Betio, 2.5 miles long, 600 yards across at the center, no more than 300 acres in all. And it took the Second Marine Division three days and a force of nineteen thousand men, on land, in ships, and in the air, to conquer it. His point was well taken. The Joint Chiefs of Staff knew that Betio is where Shoup earned the Medal of Honor under heavy fire in November 1943 and was credited with being "largely responsible for the final decisive defeat of the enemy," with his "indomitable fighting spirit."

In 1943, after the Japanese had, with a few thousand Korean laborers, shored up their defenses of Betio, their commander boasted loudly that 1 million Americans couldn't take the island in 100 years. His men had dug in with deadly seriousness. Their bombproof shelters were capped with 6 feet of concrete. Their blockhouses were 40 feet in diameter and 17 feet high. The island was dotted with 500 pillboxes and lined with tank traps. Around the entire shoreline, the defenders constructed a 4-foot-high sea-wall of palm trunks. The island, flat as a parking lot, bristled with guns: 70-millimeter howitzers, 75-millimeter mountain guns, 75-millimeter dual-purpose antiaircraft guns, antitank guns, 13-millimeter machine guns, grenade throwers, and tanks. Taking into account all the natural and constructed defenses, one writer asserted, "In the fall of 1943, it could have been the most heavily fortified place on earth." The 4,800 defenders, including 2,000 elite fighters known as *rikusentai*, which translated to one U.S. marine as "the best Tojo's got," finished their work and waited for the Americans.

Betio is an island in the Tarawa atoll, a hook-shaped group of islands

jutting from a coral reef. The atoll lies in the middle of the chain of islands known as the Gilberts, 2,600 miles from Pearl Harbor, 2,000 miles
south of Midway (where the United States had turned the tide of the oncoming Japanese navy by sinking four of their carriers in June 1942).
Nothing on this British colony would have been worth the life of a single
American if the Japanese invading force, after executing the British subjects, hadn't built an airstrip from which they could harass shipping lanes
almost anywhere in the South Pacific. Operation Galvanic, with the Gilberts as the target, became the first stage in the assault led by Admiral
Chester Nimitz, commander in chief of the Pacific Fleet, on Japan's con-
quests in the central Pacific. The operation also became a trial by fire for
the Marine Corps.

The intensity and concentration of the violence at Betio made it a
defining moment for the Marine Corps, the men who survived, and the
island itself. Tarawa, as the battle is now known, has reached the level of
Tripoli in Marine Corps lore. Twenty-five years later, inhabitants still
couldn't avoid finding human bones whenever they dug into the ground:
A reporter who talked to the head of the island's post and telecommuni-
cations department in 1968 learned that he'd recently dug up two arm
bones when he tried to gather some soil for his flowerpots.

Many battles lasted longer and took more lives, but nowhere else
would the fervor of Tarawa be matched. Fifty-eight hundred men—almost one thousand Americans and forty-eight hundred Japanese—died
on Betio's 300 acres in 72 hours. An additional 2,000 Americans were injured, giving the 7,000 marines who went into combat a casualty rate of
40 percent. The defenders, meanwhile, were almost all killed. They were
under orders to hold out until the Japanese fleet arrived and put a stop to
the invasion. In holding out, they were expected to take as many American lives as possible. Surrender was not an honorable option. The Japanese fleet never made it, and so only 17 Japanese combatants survived.

Shoup had, as a lieutenant colonel, been deeply involved in planning
the attack. He pored over intelligence and maps that made the island look

particularly uninviting. The man-made defenses were daunting, and the natural ones were a wild card. The south side of the island is pounded by surf while the north side of the island is ridged by a coral reef 800 yards out. The Japanese arranged most of their defenses to repel an attack from the south, so the Americans chose to brave the natural barrier of the reef.

Preparations were made from charts marked with ominous warnings—"Use these charts with caution," "This chart should be used with circumspection—the surveys are incomplete." Not merely incomplete, they were based on a survey done in 1841. On the ground, there wasn't a lot to survey—no mountains, ridges, or dense jungle—but the reef was another matter. It contained a shallow lagoon, beautiful to the eye, but a serious problem to Higgins boats. If they could get over the reef, the planners surmised, the boats would get close enough to shore to unload most of the marines in one piece. But only a high tide would make the reef passable.

Higgins boats draw about four feet of water. The high tide on Betio's D-Day, the morning of November 20, 1943, was supposed to leave five feet of water at the reef, according to some surveyors. Others disagreed. In the end, there simply wasn't enough information to predict the tides accurately. In fact, the abnormally low tides on the day of the invasion weren't scientifically explained until 1987.

Shoup, on his way to Tarawa aboard the flagship *Maryland* in 1943, knew the reef might be a problem. "What worries me more than anything is that our boats may not be able to get over that coral shelf . . . We may have to wade in."

As the day grew closer, Shoup's immediate superior, 20 years older, was removed from command. "It had become increasingly evident that [he] could not carry the ball," one officer wrote. General Julian Smith, commander of the Second Marine Division and Third Amphibious Force, was more blunt, saying that the colonel "broke down completely." D-Day was two weeks away, but they were prepared with a replacement. Shoup was promoted to colonel and thus went from commanding one segment of the invasion to commanding all American troops on the island. He had been an observer at Guadalcanal, the first island retaken (after months of fighting) in the American counteroffensive in 1942. In July 1943, he had been in combat at New Georgia, where he was wounded. That was the total of his combat experience, and he had never commanded a landing under fire, but he refused to be intimidated, and his confidence was evident to his marines. He was, according to reporter Robert Sherrod, a commander that men could "go to the well with."

Sherrod described him as "a squat, red-faced man with a bull neck, a hard-boiled, profane shouter of orders," and was surprised to learn that this growling, cursing beast had barely missed making Phi Beta Kappa at DePauw University. A comrade who'd known him longer called him the "brainiest, nerviest, best soldiering marine I ever met." In the final days before the battle, Colonel Shoup was putting that brainpower to work, finalizing blueprints for the landing, developing fall-back plans and redundancies, trying to think of everything. He knew that the reef might block the landing craft, but he had 125 amphibious tractors, or "amtracs." They looked like tracked troop transports, served as cargo carriers, and hadn't been proven in offensive warfare. But they could climb over the reef and keep going, possibly shuttling troops from reef to beach if the Higgins boats got stuck.

Shoup put only a little faith in the naval bombardment that preceded the November 20, 1943, attack. Although three battleships, four cruisers, nine destroyers, and waves of fighter-bombers and bombers delivered 3,500 tons of explosives to the island—over 100 pounds of bombs and shells per acre—Shoup estimated that if there were 3,000 troops on the island, maybe 700 would be dead after this hammering. The enemy knew how to dig in and hunker down. There would still be an awful fight. Only the reporters and a few marines were awed by the power of the bombing into thinking that they were about to walk onto a desert island. One marine put it succinctly in his diary: "This is to be a hell of a mess, and we will no doubt have our asses shot off." Indeed, the bombs and shells did little more than make Betio's sand bounce.

As the bombing and shelling drew to a close, 5,000 marines clambered down rope ladders into their boats and amtracs. They were heading toward an island that two historians later called "The most heavily defended atoll that would ever be invaded by Allied forces in the Pacific." They faced an uncertain tide. They only outnumbered the defenders by 1.66 to 1, a far cry from the dictum of 3 attackers to 1 defender. And their lives depended on Colonel Shoup, who had never done anything like this before.

Among the first into the boats was First Lieutenant William Deane Hawkins. Hawkins was covered with burn scars from an accident he'd had at age three, an accident from which his mother had nursed him back to a state of health the doctors thought he'd never reach. There was no question he was fit and capable, and he proved it at hard-labor jobs, but his body looked ravaged. The air force and navy both barred him for medical reasons. Determined to serve, he tried the marines, and got no complaints about his scars.

Hawkins's Higgins boat broke away from the others, and his squad of scout-snipers, joined by a squad of combat engineers headed by Lieutenant A. Gordon Leslie, made for the pier that stuck out from the center of the island past the reef, allowing ships to dock even at the lowest tide. The defenders had reinforced rather than demolished this structure, because it gave a clear line of fire into the lagoon. Hawkins and Leslie jumped together from the boat, and became the first to engage the enemy on Betio. They fought face-to-face with everything they had, including their knives. It became clear to the men in the boats, who had a full view of this melee as they headed toward the beach, that the battle would not be easily won.

The amtracs reached the reef, climbed over, and plowed through the lagoon toward the startled Japanese. But the Higgins boats did not follow. "Suddenly the craft jolted and came to a stop," one marine recalled. His boat had run aground on the reef. The shore looked miles away. "It was lodged there, solid. [The skipper] tried to back water, but the craft did not move . . . The hammer-blows of the machine guns rang now with increased tempo against the plating." The tide would not let any of the boats pass over the reef. The amtracs landed their men and ferried back, as planned, but their numbers dwindled as they took one direct hit after another. The Higgins boats that were stuck on the reef made plump targets, while others circled around aimlessly. Thousands of marines were forced to wade through 500 to 700 yards of chest-deep water, under dense fire.

Sherrod described the sensation of helplessness that came with this walk. It was slow going, and the adrenaline made everything seem slower and farther away. He said he was literally surrounded by bullets. He felt like he could reach out and grab hundreds of bullets. "Those who were not hit would always remember how the machine-gun bullets hissed into the water, inches to the right, inches to the left." He heard a marine moan, "Oh God, I'm scared. I've never been so scared in my life." He seconded the feeling: "I was scared as I had never been scared before." The closer they got to the beach, the more they were surrounded by bullets, and the more they were surrounded by dead and dying marines. One survivor remembered: "I kept as low as possible in the water and tried to pull my body up inside my helmet . . . I discovered the rows of marines along the beach weren't lying there waiting for orders to move. They were dead. There were dead all over. They appeared to outnumber the living."

The number of amtracs dwindled rapidly—90 of the original 125 were quickly lost—and more men were forced prematurely into the lagoon. When Lieutenant Colonel Herbert Amey's amtrac got stuck on a submerged wire, he jumped out to rally his men, flashing his pistol in the air like a cavalryman's sword. "Come on! Those bastards can't stop us!" With that, a swarm of bullets passed through his neck. Far above, an observation plane circled, with a pilot who later remarked, "The water seemed never clear of tiny men, their rifles held over their heads, slowly wading beachward. I wanted to cry."

Of the first wave, only one-third made it ashore. At one of three landing sectors, of the 880 men who were sent in, only 100 were in action as the morning dragged on. All along the beach the men huddled helplessly against the seawall; those who'd attempted to go over had immediately been cut down.

The Higgins boats and even the amtracs had failed the marines, but their commander felt this should not make a difference as to the final outcome. "No battle was ever won in a helicopter, amphibian tractor, or troop transport. Battles are won by marines with their feet on the ground." Shoup's first amtrac driver was killed by gunfire. He boarded another amtrac and his second driver was killed. "At that point I said, 'Let's get out of here,' moved my staff over the side, and waded to the pier."

His chances of getting ashore were the same as those of the men under his command. Leaving the amtrac, he waded toward the pier that provided the only cover this far out in the lagoon. Among the horrors around him, Shoup and his team came across a group of marines, shaken and unarmed, heading back. "'We can't get in,' one of them shouted, 'we're going back to the ship.'" Shoup tersely ordered them to "Pick up weapons from the dead and go in."

At 100 yards out, behind a Japanese vehicle stuck in the low tide, which was the last cover before the beach and the seawall, Shoup came across dozens of marines, shattered and trembling. His log, which he updated throughout the battle, describes the scene:

> Mortar shells getting closer as number of men grows larger. I say, "Is there an officer?" No one says. I turn up captain's bars. I unbutton my holster—Marine with fear and trembling and only head out of water pulls at my leg. I look into his face. He says "For God's sake, no, Colonel!" I button the holster . . . point to my eagles. "Are there any of you cowardly sons of bitches got the guts to follow a Colonel of the Marines?" I start through . . . turn later see about ten following—my heart beats big thumps. The marines are coming in and will be okay!

But the last 100 yards were the worst; the men who'd followed their commander very nearly saw his hand called. "Shell bursts. Man behind screams, flops forward on face, hands smack water at my side. Piece of something gets in my leg. Concussion puts me down in water . . . [Lieutenant Colonel Evans] Carlson comes out when he hears I'm down . . . I crawl closer, gather all I have and to my feet and to the beach."

Shoup was wounded in nine places as he approached the seawall. A ricocheting bullet bruised his neck. His runner was shot between the eyes while standing next to him. Shoup crouched at the seawall and attempted to establish communications, which would remain spotty throughout the day. Commanders on the *Maryland* received one desperate message after another from men on shore: "Have landed. Unusually heavy opposition. Casualties seventy percent. Can't hold." Shoup received a similar message from a commander not yet arrived: "Receiving heavy fire all along beach. Unable to land. Issue in doubt." Amid pessimistic exchanges like these, he sent Carlson back to the flagship: "You tell the general and the admiral we're going to stick and fight it out."

Sergeant William Bordelon had left his ship with a platoon of 22 men. At the seawall, he looked around at the five survivors. Then with a yell—"Cover me!"—he dove over the wall, ran to a pillbox, and jammed an explosive satchel in the slit. Bordelon repeated this two more times, returning to the seawall only after he'd run out of satchels. His shirt was soaked in blood. He grabbed more satchels and rose over the wall again. This time they were ready for him, and he became the focal point for a fusillade from three machine guns. He would posthumously receive the Medal of Honor.

Five thousand men boarded boats bound for Betio on November 20, and by nightfall fifteen hundred were dead or wounded. Those who'd made it ashore desperately clung to the tenuous positions they'd established. In the headquarters established 15 yards from shore and 500 yards from the headquarters of the Japanese commander, Rear Admiral Shibasaki, a reporter watched Shoup continuously improvising as his plans struck one obstacle after another. As he shouted orders into the radiophone, his hands shook. Darkness fell on a beachhead perimeter that Shoup called as jagged as a stock market graph.

Reinforcements came with daybreak, but the Americans were out of amtracs. The Japanese had established sniper and machine gun positions during the night. And the tide still refused to cover the reef. So even more blood was spilled in the lagoon on the second day of the battle. In full view of the marines on the beach, said one of their chaplains, "fire from enemy positions mowed them down as a scythe cuts through grass." As the Higgins boats on the reef dropped their ramps, the Japanese gunners, waiting for just that moment, would place a 75-millimeter shell directly into the crowded boat. Casualties quickly ran to 50 percent. Shoup's answer, seeing and sharing his troops' disgust and anger over the slaughter they watched from the beach, was an all-out attack over the seawall.

When Shoup called the assault, Hawkins and his group of scouts and snipers took the lead, as they had during the first day's landing. Hawkins made it about 75 yards in, ahead of all his men. He worked rapidly with grenades at point-blank range, putting an end to the destructive work of four pillboxes that were killing men still in the lagoon. One of his grenades, thrown back at him, filled his chest with shrapnel, but he continued to work. It was a sniper's bullet that finally stopped him. His men carried him back to headquarters, where he died within minutes, surrounded by marines who made no attempt to hide their tears. No one in his unit could recall his first name; they only knew him as "Hawk." Shoup, who was credited with winning this battle in his Medal of Honor citation, said of Hawkins, "It's not often that you can credit a first lieutenant with winning a battle, but Hawkins came as near to it as any man could. He was truly an inspiration." Hawkins posthumously received the Medal of Honor.

As Shoup's desperate offensive continued, he sent word back to the admiral: "Casualties: many. Percentage dead: unknown. Combat efficiency: *we are winning*." To Sherrod, he turned and confided, "I think we're winning, but the bastards have got a lot of bullets left." Shoup had a lot of men left, but their number was dropping by the minute.

Bullets poured out of the 17-foot-high bombproof shelter just to the east of Shoup's headquarters. Lieutenant Alexander Bonnyman had the option of staying safely on the shoreline, but he volunteered to visit this bloody section of the ongoing battle to see if he could help. Bonnyman, an engineer and former pro football player, had joined the marines as an enlisted man despite the fact that his ownership of a New Mexico copper mine (considered vital to the defense industry) cleared him from the draft. It didn't take an engineer to see how this bombproof structure would continue to take lives as long as it remained unconquered, but his engineering skills were vital in his analysis of its weaknesses. The team of fighters and engineers he hastily assembled was immediately dubbed "Forlorn Hope," borrowing the name of an assault team at Vicksburg in 1863 that faced similar odds. He rushed the mound with 21 men behind him.

Gaining the strategic high point of the bombproof mound, his men took out enough of the gunners inside to create an opportunity. Engineers went for the air vents with explosives and gasoline, and 150 Japanese fighters came pouring out. Those who weren't killed outright organized a counterattack on Bonnyman's position atop the mound. A marine lying next to him said that Bonnyman was killed by a single bullet as he called for more explosives. But by that time, the marines had gained the mound and repulsed the counterattack. Bonnyman's assault gave them an immediate gain of 400 yards and resulted in 150 enemy casualties. Somewhere along the line, his recommendation for a Medal of Honor was downgraded to a Navy Cross. The leadership of the Second Marine Division found this unacceptable, and after three years of bureaucratic wrangling, Bonnyman posthumously received the Medal of Honor.

The fighting slipped into a second night, and then a third horrific day. Even as the marines wrested control of the island, it seemed nowhere was safe. Dug-in enemy soldiers periodically sprang from hiding, determined to kill as many Americans as possible before they were themselves cut down. On the third night, the defenders commenced a series of suicidal but well-planned and strategic counterattacks, and as the marines fought them off, it seemed like the killing would never end. Dawn of the fourth day opened on a scene of horrors, but to the American survivors, it looked like most of the horrors were now in the past.

Shoup's last battle orders were for a concentrated assault on a pocket of defenders dug in near the beach on the west end of the island. They had been killing men in the lagoon for days, and turned out to be the most intractable of all. Only by surrounding and bombarding them at close range from all sides were they finally weakened and killed. The victors then discovered that many of them had died by their own hands. At noon, the first U.S. Navy plane landed on the airstrip, which was renamed Hawkins Airfield after the man who had first engaged the enemy, secured the pier, and broke the stalemate on the second day. Fighting continued sporadically throughout the day, but with this arrival, the battle was considered won.

The official casualty count, which would change several times, was weeks in getting back to the States, where Americans were learning of the atoll's existence for the first time in headlines and utterances like "Terrible Tarawa" or "Tarawa Fiasco." Representative Mike Mansfield of Montana stood on the House floor and pronounced that "we cannot afford to continue losses of this kind." The nation, it seems, was unprepared for the shock of the sudden death of 1,000 young men, and of the wounding of 2,100 more, over such a small and seemingly insignificant piece of real estate. But as the war continued and the marines moved on to Saipan, Peleliu, Iwo Jima, and Okinawa, Tarawa became a distant memory.

On June 15, 1944, Shoup witnessed the events of Betio replayed on a larger scale at Saipan, in the Mariana island chain. Once again, the intense pre-landing bombing did little to weaken the defenses. The 30,000 Japanese defenders on the jungle island fought the two American marine divisions and an army division for three weeks. Again, the defenders' last gasp came in the form of concentrated suicide attacks. This time, several thousand were killed. The remainder of the Japanese survivors on the island, including hundreds of civilians, threw themselves off a high cliff to their deaths.

After service during the invasion of nearby Tinian, Shoup was called back to the States and served out the end of the war at Marine Corps Headquarters, missing the Marine Corps' biggest moment, the landing at Iwo Jima. He served at HQ until 1947, then headed the Service Command, Fleet Marine Force, Pacific, for almost two years before taking over as the First Marine Division chief of staff in 1949.

Years after the war, he became a technical adviser to and performer in the film that fixed the wartime role of the marines in the public's imagination—*The Sands of Iwo Jima.* Before Sergeant John Stryker (played by John Wayne) got to Iwo Jima, he led his squad on Betio. Shoup played himself in the movie, shot on the much-adapted sands of Camp Pendleton, California, between July and August of 1949. The set, he said, "looks so real it scares me," and he interjected another dose of reality into the film by replacing the canned, overly dramatic dialogue in the script with something closer to what he had actually said during the battle. He attended the opening in San Francisco, and agreed with most of the critics: The battle scenes were terrifying. "It was a fearsome thing to look at because, having experienced the battle, goddamn, I didn't want to go through it again."

Shoup next served as commander of the Basic School in Quantico, then as acting fiscal director of the USMC, and then fiscal director. He was promoted to major general in 1955 and served as inspector general for recruit training (following the deaths of several marines during a training exercise), and then inspector general of the Marine Corps. He returned to command in 1957 with the First Marine Division and then the Third Marine Division on Okinawa. When he returned to the United States, in 1958, he was appointed commanding general of the Marine Corps Recruit Depot at Parris Island, South Carolina.

The Parris Island assignment had all the earmarks of a "sunset tour," the final plum assignment at the end of a distinguished career. So Shoup was shocked when word reached him at Parris Island in 1958 that he'd been tapped for commandant. "This is the first pot I ever won without having a hand in the game," he told a reporter.

He was still a little mystified by the time he met Eisenhower. Even a year later, as Ike prepared to leave office in January 1961, Shoup felt there was something incredible about how far he had come. During a farewell dinner, he and the outgoing president talked about cattle, "which most of us never get an opportunity to do, and particularly a farmer boy from Indiana who had spent many, many hours letting the concentrated dewdrops wet his overalls through miles and miles of cornrows. I felt rather proud of myself that I could sit and talk as a farmer boy with the President of the United States."

Shoup was born in 1904 on the struggling family farm near Battleground, Indiana. Like Sam Woodfill, David Shoup helped feed the family by hunting: "I used to make a little money in the winter hunting raccoon, muskrat, and skunk. Don't know how many times I got kicked out of school for showing up smelling of skunk." In spite of this, he kept his grades up in high school, and got into DePauw University as a math major with a serious commitment to athletics. He was a football player, a wrestler, and a marathon runner. He was also a waiter, dishwasher, and laborer in a cement factory, jobs that kept him barely ahead of his tuition, room, and board. But a huge boost—$9 a month—came from the ROTC. This sum was, Shoup told an interviewer, "exactly what I paid for my room rent, and in all truth, that was the only reason I signed for senior ROTC."

He had no plans for continuing a military career after college until a fellow cadet returned from an annual meeting of the National Society of Scabbard and Blade, an organization of ROTC cadets and alumni, in

1925: "And our representatives went to New Orleans, and the gentleman who gave the primary speech to these young gentlemen turned out to be General John A. Lejeune of the Marine Corps, then Major General Commandant . . ." The Marine Corps legend concluded his speech by inviting all ROTC honor students to write him a personal letter for a commission. This request was related back to Shoup at DePauw. "When I left my last class that afternoon, I went right home and got a pen and ink and a piece of paper . . ."

As his request was being processed, Shoup graduated and signed up for the Army Reserve Corps, again motivated by one thing: "my financial status, which hovered around the zero point all my life up to this point." He took as much active duty as he could, he said, "because I got good pay, more money than I ever saw in my life." When he wasn't on active duty, however, he was back at the farm, which is where the Marine Corps contacted him.

The first letter the Corps sent David Shoup, in 1925, started with the word "Please." He remembered that well. "Please report to First Lt. so and so . . ." So he went to Chicago for a physical, which he passed. The next letter he got from the marines didn't use the magic word. "So I told my mother, 'This thing doesn't say anything about *please*. This says *you will*.'" Maybe Shoup didn't realize at the time that that was their way of saying, Welcome to the USMC, and get used to it. Reporting for duty in Philadelphia in 1926, he got his first lesson in obedience. "Sir," he told his commanding officer when he learned that his first assignment would be on the sports team, "I didn't come in the Marine Corps to play football."

After standing at attention for at least 20 minutes and receiving a lecture—"From now on, the Marine Corps will tell you what to do, you're not going to tell us what to do"—Shoup was dismissed, and reported for football duty. Another assignment, however, was close at hand.

In 1925, British troops in Shanghai fired on demonstrating students, sparking the national revolution of 1925–1927. The attacks on foreigners prompted the European powers to deploy troops to defend their interests.

The American government sent in marines in 1926, but not to fight. It was a simple show of force—the American politicians wanted the Europeans to know America was there, and hoped that the very presence of the marines would discourage them from escalating their involvement and thus extending their influence to the point where they could squeeze out American business interests. Shoup, in summary, said their mission was "to outshine the troops of other nations."

He had plenty of time to think about this strange assignment, and came to believe that this was not an appropriate use of military might. "China has many Americans," he concluded, "or those who propose to be Americans, inhabiting her country and in many cases exploiting her peoples. Yet they [the Americans] claim their right to protection from the U.S. some 10,000 miles away."

The marines' duties largely involved polishing and repolishing helmets and boots. "Shina," the marines came to call the country where they'd been stationed. Shoup didn't see much of Shanghai that he liked—he found it crowded, dirty, and pestilent. He didn't have much good to say about the Chinese. Though he would later in life refer to them as "the great and wonderful Chinese people," in his China diary he repeatedly referred to their smell. He did not, however, excuse the British from their often brutal behavior.

Shoup was eventually sent home with a serious illness (that he later found out was influenza), and chewed over what he had seen. He came to believe that while the "American way," or the things that America professes to stand for, are worth protecting and dying for, it is pointless to force them on others.

Shoup would return to China in November 1934, after completing his training in Basic School (which had been interrupted by the China expedition), serving two years on a ship, and getting married. He wed his high school sweetheart, Zola De Haven, in September 1931. Zola had been a schoolteacher; to Shoup she became much more. When he was made commandant, Shoup broke into the following couplet: "One can attain a considerable height in this life / If he has an angel for a mother and an angel for a wife."

Near the end of his four-year term as commandant, Shoup told Kennedy he could not stay on for a second one. Kennedy and Shoup had seen some of the most trying years faced by a Cold War president. In April 1961, only a few months into the Kennedy administration, a tiny invasion force of Cuban exiles trained by the CIA landed on the shores of Cuba. Shoup probably knew more about amphibious invasions than anyone in the administration, but, he said, no one asked his opinion about the operation until it was too late. Then, in February 1962, Shoup locked horns with the senator from North Carolina, Strom Thurmond, over poor results on tests of the marines' knowledge of the evils of Communism, as administered by Thurmond's staff. The whole thing, Shoup insisted, was "rather ridiculous." Marines fight not because they hate Communists, but because of "Love of country, love of the Corps and its traditions, and love of the man to the right and to the left of you." The issue withered away under Shoup's widely publicized denunciation. Then, in October 1962, came the Cuban Missile Crisis and the threat of a third world war.

But it wasn't episodes like these that made Shoup want to leave his post. He told Kennedy that unless he left, a number of dedicated officers would never have a chance at the job. Kennedy asked him to stay, and since it wasn't a direct order, he refused. Shoup's last memory of the president was the good-bye following that exchange. "He didn't say good afternoon; he walked to where I was, then, facing the door, put his arm around me; and as we got to the door, he said, 'General, you were right, and I admire you for it.'" Rumors drifted through Washington that Shoup was being considered for the head of the CIA—an odd post for him, since he distrusted the agency ever since they used his equipment and one of his officers for their ill-fated invasion of Cuba—but before anything came of this talk, Kennedy was dead and Shoup was retired from the Marine Corps.

Shoup went to work for a life insurance company, but his name was still mentioned in the White House. President Johnson envisioned him as a silent ambassador during a time when he was trying to sell his policy on Vietnam. Johnson, who, like Kennedy, was also in the habit of taping his conversations, recommended Shoup to Defense Secretary Robert McNamara, who was preparing to visit Saigon in March, on February 20, 1964.

"From a psychological standpoint, and from a political standpoint," President Johnson said, "there's one man that I would have with me on that plane [to Saigon]—and that's Shoup . . . I'd have Shoup just go out there, and sit in on these meetings with [Chairman, Joint Chiefs of Staff, General Maxwell] Taylor, kinda ex officio." Johnson didn't see him as an adviser, really. More as a prop: "I think he's quiet enough and humble enough that he's not going to be bossing around and threatening any. He can sit in the back row. You don't have to mess with him." Johnson thought that Shoup's very presence would brighten the prospects of America's deepening involvement in Vietnam, and believed Shoup would loyally agree with his plans: "He's out, and he hasn't got anything to do, and he's got that medal on his breast."

The Medal of Honor creates a halo around the men who wear it, something not lost on politicians. Whether Shoup refused to accompany McNamara to Saigon or McNamara never made the request, the former commandant didn't make the trip. McNamara knew that Shoup wasn't the quiet type that Johnson assumed he was, and from his experience with Shoup during the Kennedy administration, he probably knew that Shoup wasn't eager to see marines fighting in those faraway jungles.

Shoup had traveled to Vietnam in 1961, after the Bay of Pigs, and like "so many of these people who go out there for three or four days," he joked, "I came back an expert." In his expert opinion, he had "no qualms whatever" about opposing intervention by American combat troops. He said that "every responsible military man" deemed a ground war in Southeast Asia "unnecessary and unwise." And yet, under Kennedy, the Vietnam conflict did escalate, with the introduction of helicopters, aircraft, napalm, and crop destruction. In the summer of 1963, Kennedy expanded the role of the advisers in Vietnam, and Shoup grew ever more skeptical. Meanwhile, one of Shoup's colonels, Edwin H. Simmons, who later related his story to history professor Howard Jablon, had been quietly angling for a role for the USMC in the operation. When he met with success, he took what he thought was good news to Shoup, who was both surprised and peeved, telling him, "We don't want to piss away our resources in that rat hole."

In the presence of Kennedy, however, Shoup never expressed opinions so bald: He was caught between his belief that his marines did not belong in Vietnam and his commander in chief's creeping insistence that there ought to be more. He limited his objections to how to do the job, staying away from policy. "Wherever the Commander in Chief sends us, our equipment, weapons, and training will stand us in good stead. Whether we go or not is none of my damned business." Which is probably why Johnson thought Shoup would quietly go along with whatever he had in mind.

Johnson, in fact, could not have judged the former commandant more wrongly. In the years following Johnson's phone conversation with McNamara, Shoup appears to have thought about what national loyalty meant to the retired soldier: "The courage of one's convictions and the willingness to speak the truth as one sees it for the good of his country is what patriotism really means—far more than flags and bands and the national anthem." Now that he was retired, he felt this call to duty grow ever stronger.

On May 14, 1966, General Shoup spoke his convictions at Pierce College in Woodland Hills, California. He held no position in the administration, and spoke only as a concerned citizen who happened to be a Medal of Honor recipient and former commandant of the Marine Corps. Shoup denounced the war in terms extreme even for a war protester, much less a former member of the Joint Chiefs of Staff. He told the students that all of Southeast Asia, "as related to the present and future safety and freedom of the people of this country," was not "worth the life or limb of a single American." He didn't stop there.

> I believe that if we had and would keep our dirty, bloody, dollar-crooked fingers out of the business of these nations so full of depressed, exploited people, they will arrive at a solution of their own.

Perhaps that solution wouldn't reflect American values, but at least it wouldn't be a solution "crammed down their throats by Americans." As for the domino theory, Shoup reflected on the fact that Vietnam was 8,000 miles away, and that only two men in history had ever walked on water (and Peter only made it a few steps). The American commitment to Vietnam was based on flimsy reasoning, fabricated threats, and a patriotism gone awry. The loud and accusatory speech went barely noticed beyond the campus of this small community college.

(As an aside, those who are shocked that a Medal of Honor recipient could speak this way about the United States' military activities should read the remarks of another marine and Medal of Honor recipient, who, incidentally, was commander of the Marine Expeditionary Force in China during the time Shoup was there. Smedley Butler's military career had taken him around the world, as he related: "I helped purify Nicaragua for the international banking house of Brown Brothers in 1909–1912. I helped make Mexico, and especially Tampico, safe for American oil interests in 1914. I helped make Haiti and Cuba a decent place for the National City [Bank] boys to collect revenue. I helped in the rape of half a dozen Central American republics for the benefit of Wall Street." General Butler, after criticizing strongly and publicly the American habit of interfering in elections in Haiti and Nicaragua, was passed over for the post of commandant in 1931. He retired the same year and became ever more radical. "In short," he said of his career, "I was a racketeer for capitalism." He died in 1940. Shoup and Butler were products of, in the words of a

Nation editorial, "an organization which has to be tougher when it fights than anyone else, and tougher also when it talks.")

Months after Shoup's Pierce College speech, President Johnson appointed him to the National Advisory Commission on Selective Service, in a year when the draft calls reached 400,000. The Commission, which submitted a report on January 1, 1967, and was praised by Johnson in his State of the Union address, recommended sweeping modernization and reform, including the abolition of the student deferment. The Chairman, Burke Marshall, felt that the Commission's work was sidelined and the recommendations never implemented. The Commission was disbanded a few months after it submitted its report.

Shoup had made his comments on Vietnam in a very small public forum. In February 1967, he chose to seek a wider audience. He gave the text of his speech to Rupert Vance Hartke, a senator from his home state and an early Vietnam dissenter. Hartke entered the entire "vital speech" into the Congressional Record, and called attention to the assertion by the general that the whole of Southeast Asia was not "worth the life or limb of a single American." The word was out; the growing antiwar chorus now had a Medal of Honor recipient among them.

As the bluntest quotations from Shoup's speech were printed and reprinted, he was repeatedly asked to speak at demonstrations. He repeatedly refused. But when ABC's *Scope* did a series about dissenters on Vietnam in summer 1967, he agreed to an interview to extend and clarify his position. The reporter read him the "dirty, bloody, dollar-crooked fingers" quote, and Shoup responded, "Right."

But he also made it clear that he was no pacifist. Just as he had insisted during the Cuban Missile Crisis when he spoke about the inevitable escalation following limited air strikes, he believed there was no sensible way to limit the war. Either America was in or it was out. For example, as long as U.S. troops were in Vietnam, U.S. bombs had to fall on North Vietnam, for the simple reason that "any bombing whatsoever that will increase the chance of success of those people on the ground that are bearing the brunt of this thing . . . must be continued. It must be continued. We cannot let those men down." America had to support the troops as long as we were there, he felt, but at the same time, we had no good reason to send them there.

"How do we get out of this?" the reporter asked. "I feel really ill at my stomach," Shoup answered. "It's very vomicating, so to speak, to think that there are many, many people today and a great many factions of our fourth estate that are mouthing the idea that negotiations are long since impossible." And without negotiations, "this whole thing could escalate until today's commitment could just be a baby's battle, compared to what we're going to get into."

Then, in December 1967, he made the clearest break possible from President Johnson. During an appearance on radio station WNYC in New York, U.S. Representative William F. Ryan, Democrat from New York, related President Johnson's view that the Vietnam War was in defense of America's vital national interest. Shoup didn't miss a beat, calling that view no more than "a bunch of pure, unadulterated poppycock." He'd already lost close friends among the marines; now he lost completely the goodwill of the Johnson administration. Shoup's activities were reported on by the FBI. His very patriotism was attacked in the media—something he'd probably never thought could come to pass as he waded onto Betio. But as he saw it, the stakes were far too high to worry over those considerations. He said that he was driven by the men who had given "the full measure of their devotion" in wars past: "Their presence may be unseen, but they shall not be unheard. Someone must speak for them."

His voice dripping with sarcasm, Shoup began his 1968 testimony before the Senate Committee on Foreign Relations (chaired by the same Senator Fulbright who had pushed through the 1964 Tonkin Gulf Resolution, which gave Johnson a free hand to escalate the war, without hearings) with an expression of how grateful he was. "Particularly," he said, "when you think that now an Indiana farm boy has been asked to come here and to talk about matters of great national interest and to give his views without any fear of reprisal whatsoever except being called a dissenter, a traitor, and being accused of giving aid and comfort to the enemy. That is all." In this forum, Shoup made explicit what he feared in an escalation in Vietnam. Any incursion into North Vietnam would lead to involvement by China. The only way to defeat China would be with nuclear weapons. But what was most frustrating to Shoup, a man accustomed to clear objectives, was the lack of any mission in Vietnam: "Our actions are limited to unlimited escalation in the South Vietnam area, because we have no objective, as far as I know, to defeat the armed forces of the enemy." The only way to defeat the armed forces of the enemy would be on the ground in the north, and there the United States was back again, looking at an escalation against China that no one wanted.

Committee Member Stuart Symington—senator from Missouri, World War I veteran, secretary of war for air during World War II, first secretary of the air force under Truman—worried about the financial repercussions of such an escalation, which he saw as catastrophic. "Can you imagine anything which would be a greater disservice to the American people than spending to the point where, in major fashion, you reduced the value of the dollar and thereby reduced heavily the value of life insurance, of pension plans, of retirement funds, and of social security itself?" Shoup sardonically replied to this distinguished questioner, "Senator, nothing could have a greater impact on America and its future except a nuclear exchange and, of course, that solves insurance problems, real estate mortgages and you can start from the bottom again."

But what got most people's attention was his answer to how many troops it would take in the south to pacify South Vietnam. "I think you can just pull any figure you wanted out of the hat and that would not be enough." It seemed incredible. South Vietnam, a tiny country, could absorb any number of troops without end in sight? Yes, Shoup felt, because, again, there was no plan to defeat the forces of the enemy. We would be fighting there endlessly until we pulled out.

By 1969, Shoup had become convinced that it wasn't enough to speak against what he saw as the facts of the war, and he, with another military man as co-author, went after the causes of the war in an *Atlantic Monthly* article, "The New American Militarism." Here he challenged the very notion that America is a peace-loving nation. He accused the military of wasting lives and resources to simply perpetuate its own existence. He accused the military chiefs of "racing to build up combat strength" simply to outdo each other. He saw the defense contractors manipulating policy for profit. The entire process was horrifically self-perpetuating. "Somewhat like a religion, the basic appeals of anticommunism, national defense, and patriotism provide the foundation for a powerful creed upon which the defense establishment can build, grow, and justify its cost." Where he had once advocated a negotiated settlement in Vietnam, as he'd expressed on ABC's *Scope*, he now called for a unilateral pullout.

Shoup's article marked the culmination of his developing criticism of the American military. It couldn't have been easy for a man who had lived his entire life serving his country in the military to reach this conclusion. But now the antiwar movement had gained so much momentum that Shoup's voice was rarely heard. He lent his moral support to the actions of the Vietnam Veterans Against the War, but he didn't march with them or speak at their rallies. His speaking and writing dwindled away before America finally pulled out of Vietnam in 1973. The remainder of his life was quiet and out of the public eye. He died in 1983.

CHAPTER SIX

Maynard H. Smith

WORLD WAR II

"The airplane was hit several times by antiaircraft fire and cannon shells of the fighter airplanes . . . The situation became so acute that three of the crew bailed out . . . Sgt. Smith, then on his first combat mission, elected to fight the fire by himself."

— MEDAL OF HONOR CITATION

HIS WAS THE FIRST Medal of Honor ceremony to take place in the European theater—even though the United States had been in the war for over a year—so the army made sure the presentation to Maynard Smith in July 1943 would make history. The Medal of Honor was partially born of a desire to boost morale, and here the planners made every effort to ensure that the deeds of Sergeant Smith, B-17 gunner, would be known to every man in uniform and everyone on the home front.

Maynard Smith was the first Air Corps enlisted man to receive the medal, and the first in that theater who'd survived to receive it personally.

Early in the war, Army Chief of Staff (the Air Corps was under the army until 1947, when the National Defense Act created the air force as we know it today) General George Marshall had ordered a streamlined process for awards, hoping to avoid the situation in the First World War where medals were frequently tied up in red tape, sometimes years after Armistice Day. The esprit de corps that swirled around medals became especially important in the famous Eighth Air Force, where flyers were well aware of their slim chances for survival, a knowledge that grew deeper with each mission as they watched comrades' planes drop from the sky. Airmen were 14 times more likely to be given some kind of decoration than the average infantryman, but when it came to medals for valor, the army was restrained. Of the half million medals showered on the Eighth Air Force between 1942 and 1945, only 14 were Medals of Honor.

The first Medal of Honor earned in the European theater was that of First Lieutenant Jack Mathis, whose medal was approved the same day as Smith's, even though Smith had earned his in May 1943 and Mathis earned his in March 1943. Mathis was the leading bombardier of his squadron on a mission over Vegesack, Germany, assigned to take out a vital U-boat yard. The antiaircraft batteries ringing the base were manned by some of Germany's best, and one of them managed to place a round directly in Mathis's bomber. The explosion shattered his arm, tore into his abdomen, and sent him flying to the rear of the plane. He knew that the other planes were waiting for his cues, and so, according to his citation, "1st Lt. Mathis, by sheer determination and willpower, though mortally wounded, dragged himself back to his sights, released his bombs, then died at his post of duty." The bombs were dead-on. Two other bombers were lost on that mission. It had been six months since the Americans joined the Royal Air Force's strategic bombing campaign, but it was already clear that in this war there would be many more difficult missions. In a quiet ceremony at an airfield in Texas on September 21, 1943, an army general presented the Medal of Honor to Mathis's mother.

But the travel plans of Secretary of War Henry L. Stimson meant that

Smith would receive a much larger ceremony, months before Mathis. Stimson was days away from making his first trip to England, where the Eighth Air Force was based, when Smith was approved for the medal on July 12, 1943, just six weeks after his action, which occurred on his very first mission. As the hurried preparations for a fanfare-filled ceremony drew to completion, someone realized, on the eve of Stimson's departure, that they would, after all, need to produce a medal. There was not a one in the entire European theater. They cabled Washington and found a medal, and it fell to Stimson himself to carry the hastily procured decoration in his coat pocket. Then, on the day of the ceremony, July 15, someone realized that they would have to produce the hero to wear the medal. He was still alive and well, but special dispensations had to be made for Smith to attend his own ceremony. He had been assigned to KP for a week—punishment for arriving late at a briefing.

So on that day, instead of scraping leftovers off of the metal plates that his fellow airmen messed from, the B-17 gunner received praise such as the following from General Ira C. Eaker, commander of the Eighth Air Force: "Sgt. Smith not only performed his duty, he carried on after others—more experienced than he—had given up. Through his presence of mind, determination and bravery, he saved the lives of six of his crewmates and the Fortress in which he flew." Smith stood before seven saluting generals, 25 Air Corps officers, technicians from two radio networks, a brass band, a busload of newspaper reporters, and the secretary of war. As his squadron of 18 bombers flew 100 feet over his head, the five foot four, 130-pound hero tried to, in the words of one reporter, "dispel his usually glum expression with one of pleasant sternness," as he stepped up to the microphone. There was silence and anticipation, with the reporters' pencils poised above their pads. Then Smith, who during his time in the army had been given the moniker "Snuffy," after the comic strip character, made their note-taking simple by muttering only, "Thank you," before stepping back.

The reporters later took turns trying to pry something more quotable from Snuffy's tight lips. Many were pleased over how his stint on KP would add color to an otherwise prepackaged story, and one asked with some sarcasm what he planned to do to celebrate, expecting him to answer that he would be forced back into peeling potatoes or slopping discarded food. Snuffy surprised them with the assertion that "I haven't got a pass for tonight, but I think I can arrange for one." Another reporter was looking for a man as humble as Sam Woodfill, the World War I recipient profiled in Chapter Four. So the reporter asked the leading and convoluted question: "Isn't meeting the secretary of war and facing all the reporters' questions worse than the experience you had putting out the fire on board the Flying Fortress?" Smith fixed the reporter with a quizzical stare and said simply, "No." He was then released into the arms of his fellow flyers, who hoisted him above their shoulders for a cheer-filled run around the base.

These scenes were witnessed by Andy Rooney, who was then a reporter for the armed forces newspaper *Stars and Stripes*, and who had first reported the story of Sergeant Smith's heroic act. He'd done quite a bit of work on Smith, and really wasn't surprised at the fact that this unlikely hero had landed himself on KP. "From the time he entered the Air Force he had been in some kind of trouble over one petty matter or another. 'Snuffy' was, in fact, known by the fourteen other inhabitants of his Nissen hut by an Army phrase for which there is no socially acceptable replacement. He was a real fuckup."

Another reporter who worked with the "Mighty Eighth" phrased his description more delicately, calling Smith a real "character." Indeed, he didn't quite fit in with most of the airmen with whom he served. For one thing, he was 32, "practically senile," in the words of one observer, compared to the 21-year-old officers who took the Flying Fortresses into battle. For another, he took to more serious pursuits than the chase after women and liquor that occupied most of his comrades' off-duty time. He was an avid reader, and could range across topics like, as described by a *New Yorker* reporter who spent some time with him after the ceremony, "electricity, religion, politics, endocrinology, golf, energy in a pure state, Army life, England, swans, dogs, flowers, Michigan in the winter, Florida in the summer, the British form of government, and the effect on mankind of the Flying Fortress."

Whenever he had a pass, he could be found down at the local pub, trying to convince the patrons that the presence of America in this war would cause the demise of the British class system and even the House of Lords, or defending some other equally controversial and weighty thesis. This is how he got busted to KP, coming back to base late after one of these nights, only to find that he'd missed a mission briefing and that another gunner had had to go in his place. The *New York Times* perhaps phrased it best: "As a fighter, he is a stayer. When he gets a pass and a night off, he is an overstayer." To some, he seemed highbrow. To others, he simply appeared arrogant and lazy. But Snuffy Smith himself really didn't seem to care.

Arrogant or not, no one doubted his heroism on the day he saved the lives of six men on his first mission. Smith himself was fairly self-assured that he deserved the Medal of Honor, and he wasn't one of those types who tried to deflect praise or reject the hero's mantle. But he'd been reading a book called *Glands Regulating Personality*, and had become convinced that the secret to heroism wasn't breeding or patriotism or the quest for glory. It was all about adrenaline. He had a story handy for the people who asked him how he did it:

There was a fellow who was an apprentice seaman in the British Navy. A kid. He got torpedoed and his hands were horribly burned. Just the same, he somehow managed to get into a lifeboat and he took his regular place and rowed. In the morning, his shipmates discovered that the flesh had been burned off his fingers and that he was literally rowing with the bones of his hands. This was probably heroism. But I'm not sure that a bombardier who gets a terrific stomachache just as he's aiming his bombs and nevertheless gets them off isn't a greater hero. You never know. In either case, you can be sure, there was plenty of adrenaline being pumped into the bloodstream.

As a Congressional Medal of Honor recipient, Smith began signing his letters "Sgt. Maynard Smith, C.M.H." He gained, or just took, the privilege of sleeping well past reveille into mid-morning. He got into the habit of hopping into a jeep and having an MP cart him around base. He always seemed to have an extra supply of cigarettes. He once got caught cooking Spam in his barracks at night, and when he looked up from his strictly forbidden snack at the officer who'd followed the smell, his superior grumbled, "Oh, it's you," and walked away. As he looked back years later, he said, "The Medal of Honor opened doors then and it still does, from the Pentagon to the White House. I don't abuse it, but if it is necessary, I will use it."

Smith went on five more missions, and shot down a Focke-Wulf on the last one, but then he was grounded. His wife, whom he married a year after the Medal of Honor action, says he was pulled off flights to do publicity for the army—to make recruiting appearances, sell war bonds, and boost morale. The rest of the time, he worked at a desk job.

But according to many accounts, his arrogant behavior around base is what got him grounded. "As he goes about his business at the station," one reporter wrote, "he hands out autographs with the pleased, cooperative air of a brand-new picture star and on occasion he gives bits of advice to gunners who have just arrived from America or have never seen action. His fame has spread throughout the Eighth Air Force." Smith had gone from being a character to being a "difficult character," in the words of another reporter. Remarked a third, "It was just that the crews decided that his medal had gone to his head." The reason for the grounding, as given by these witnesses, was that the crews no longer trusted him.

But there is another explanation, given by Smith himself in a 1980 interview: He simply broke down. This was not an uncommon event.

The B-17 was a sturdy, reliable aircraft, but German defenses sent them plummeting to the ground at an astounding rate. The intensity of even a short and simple bombing run was one that the strongest mind found difficult to absorb. Drs. Donald W. Hastings, David G. Wright, and Bernard C. Glueck concluded a study just months after Smith's heroic act, and published their findings in *Psychiatric Experiences of the Eighth Air Force*. They found everything from trauma to psychotic episodes in their subjects, and tied it to the continuous pounding of flak and the continuous death of comrades.

One pilot in the study who had watched the plane in front of him explode was, according to the report, close to the breaking point. An object, which turned out to be a man, flew from the wreckage into his propeller. He had to scrape the frozen blood and bone fragments off the windshield with his knife. A tail gunner they interviewed for the study had been trapped at his post as his damaged Fortress screeched toward the ground. Of all the crew, only he and one other were able to bail out. The tail gunner had to kick his way out. Suspended by his parachute 1,000 feet above the ground, he watched his plane turn into a ball of fire at impact. He'd been claustrophobic ever since, and the wind, as it whistled through the trees, or the barracks, or just about anything, reminded him of the air sailing through his cramped quarters during those seconds of sheer panic and terror when he was sure he was going to die.

What most airmen had in common, however, was a sense of helplessness. They were required to stay the course for hundreds of miles toward a specific target—usually something as specific as a single factory. They had to stay the course even as they were peppered by flak and strafed by fighters. The bombers were really just big targets, flying in visible formations, and the crews knew it. They typically became "very conscious of their anxiety . . . and feeling quite hopeless about their chance of survival" after just four or five missions of the required twenty-five. Smith had joined the Eighth Air Force in England at a time of heightened loss. In May 1943, when Smith flew his first mission, the casualty rate was 82 percent. From May to October 1943, the pool of airmen was diminished by a third each month, for a total turnover of 200 percent. In actual numbers, 6,300 men were killed or captured during this short time.

Smith may have suffered a breakdown caused by the pressures of the air war. He told one reporter, much later in his life, that he had been walking through an English village in late October 1943, when suddenly "I just forgot where I was." In this version of events, he was grounded only after he had been hospitalized for several weeks for battle fatigue. Then he was assigned to clerical duties. This account runs against what writers who were with the Eighth reported. His wife didn't know about it. The story may have been dressed up by the army to prevent an inevitable drag on morale, or it may have been invented by Smith himself. Like some other details of his life, this detail, sadly, has been obscured from our view. We do know that he stayed in England, worked a desk job, and married an Englishwoman.

Mary Rayner was a hostess at a USO club in Bedford, England, where Glenn Miller was a frequent performer and Smith was a frequent customer. She remembers his intelligence and his *joie de vivre*, but she doesn't remember him bragging about the medal. She also remembers that while he was a average dancer, he was a magnificent ham when he got out on the floor.

On July 15, 1944, one year after the Medal of Honor ceremony, they married in Bedford's register office. Her parents were present, and Smith selected as best man the bride's uncle, Captain O. P. Rayner of the Royal Army Fire Service. It was Smith's second marriage; his first, which had produced a son, had ended in acrimony before he joined the army. His hometown paper reported the nuptials, but there was little fanfare at the ceremony. Smith returned to his desk job as the Allies advanced across Europe.

Just short of one year later, Smith was discharged under a new rule allowing Medal of Honor recipients to seek early release. As he discovered after he'd applied, he already had enough points to seek a discharge even without the new rule. His hometown paper, which had been covering his every move since he'd performed the action that got national attention, let a headline scream, using the nickname he'd somehow been assigned in childhood: 'HOKIE' SMITH IS GIVEN DISCHARGE. Caro, Michigan, a town that had barely made the map, got ready for the return of its native son.

Caro's townsfolk had been miffed ever since the radio broadcasts had mistakenly claimed that Smith hailed from Cairo, Illinois (they were probably just following the army's citation, as did the two major reference works on Medal of Honor recipients, which made a similar mistake). From the moment he announced that he would return to Caro "for a few days," they started measuring windows for bunting and making plans that would assure the ceremony would take place in Caro, and not in Detroit, where Smith was landing. The hero rode in an open car down State Street with his mother and Governor Harry F. Kelly to a wildly cheering crowd. A day of speeches and celebration followed, with a U.S. senator singing Smith's praises, three bands blasting, and twenty air corps planes flying low enough to add their engine noise to the merriment. Smith was at his most modest, saying in his speech that there were "a lot of fellows" who deserved the medal as much as he, admitting, "I've made some mistakes in my life," and acknowledging that but for the grace of God, he would be "at the bottom of the Bay of Biscay right now," referring to the bay to the west of France over which Smith's bomber flew. Finally, he thanked the town and told them how glad he was that the "affair" took place in Caro instead of in "New York or any other place."

What no one knew was that the "affair" was something he'd stated as a requirement for him to ever return to the little town. Back in 1942, as the newly enlisted Smith rode the bus out of Caro with the other recruits, he remarked to one that he hated Caro and would never return "unless they lined the streets and cheered him." What no one mentioned during the celebrations was that young "Hokie" had almost been more than the town could handle.

During his childhood, Smith had been "a little spoiled," according to his son, Maynard Jr. "My dad was never really made to do anything . . . He always had pretty much what he wanted or wished." Snuffy's father had been Henry Ford's lawyer for a time, so the family sailed through the Depression in style. Maynard got used to getting what he wanted, and if what he wanted was trouble, he got away with it. By the time he was old enough to cause a serious ruckus, his father was a circuit court judge with no tolerance for the policeman or prosecutor brave enough to drag his boy into court.

After the "congressional medal deal," as Smith liked to call it, a reporter asked Smith about his early years. He claimed that he could not recall a single significant event growing up in Caro. The residents of that tucked-away town, however, could recall quite a few. Like the time he rode his horse into the drugstore because he wanted an ice-cream cone and they hadn't provided a drive-up window. Or the time he chased a cop down the street and up a lamppost on his new motorcycle. Then there was the story of how he came flying downhill into town at 65 miles per hour in his new 12-cylinder roadster and took a horse clear off its harness, leaving the farmer sitting in the cart, dazed and still holding the reins. By the time he returned as a war hero, this story had been cleaned up and retold as an example of his quick reflexes (he missed the cart, didn't he?), reflexes that served him well on that day in the flaming B-17.

We don't know if it was in order to straighten him out, but the teenage Maynard was sent to a military academy to finish school, an experience he reportedly loved. When he was done, he still had no idea of what he wanted out of life. He became an income tax field agent for the Treasury Department in Detroit, and then assistant receiver for the Michigan State Banking Commission. His father died in 1934 and left him a bit of money—not enough to last a lifetime, but enough, Smith felt, to "retire" for the time being.

His mother at least quietly approved of his choice, and the pair spent summers in Michigan and winters in Florida. When a reporter prodded him about these idle years, which lasted until the day he went into the army, his explanation was simple: He could afford to, so why shouldn't he? Besides, it allowed him to get a monumental amount of reading done. He focused first on psychology, then phrenology, then endocrinology, then the history of religion. He never subscribed to an organized faith, but he was no materialist either: "The earth is a combination of molecules, and a molecule is a combination of atoms, and an atom is a combination of ions. But this means nothing. Who made the first ion?"

The war didn't shake Smith's repose until the draft came. He wasn't the volunteering type, and wasn't "particularly pugilistically inclined." But Smith had been married and then divorced, and then had fallen behind on child support. He never said much about this first marriage, and his nonsupport may have been an objection to continued support after his ex-wife remarried. Or he may have just been negligent. In either case, he was arrested and the judge gave him a choice: army or jail. He went into the army, perhaps knowing that he was about to be drafted anyway. He claimed later that he beat the draft by 20 minutes. The fellow Caro resident who heard him say that he would never return to Caro without a parade remembered clearly the day Smith signed up: "When I went into the army a group of thirty of us assembled on the courthouse steps for a picture. While we were lining up the sheriff came down the steps with Maynard 'Hokie' 'Snuffy' Smith beside him in handcuffs."

He hated basic training, and, being unaccustomed to being told what to do, he hated being a private. But he heard that volunteer gunners for the Air Corps were automatically made sergeants, and he figured being in a plane might be better than marching through the muck. He trained at Harlingen, Texas, and in spring 1943 was stationed in England as a B-17 waist gunner. Nothing in his life thus far had suggested to his bunkmates, his superiors, or, most important, his crew that he would ever distinguish himself. But, as perhaps all the proof we will ever need that heroism turns up in the strangest places, he did.

The B-17 Flying Fortress flew with a crew of ten very cramped men. The nose of the plane had barely enough room to contain the navigator and the bombardier in sitting positions. Behind and slightly above them sat the pilot and copilot, looking out over the top of the nose. Just behind and again slightly above them was the top turret gunner/engineer, who had a 360-degree field of fire. A bulkhead separated the top turret gunner from the bomb bay, and another bulkhead separated the bomb bay from the radio operator, who sat in a tiny compartment over the wings. Another bulkhead separated the radio operator from the next compartment, which contained the left and right waist gunners (the position Smith had trained for) and the ball turret gunner, who sat in what airmen called the suicide position.

The ball turret was a Plexiglas sphere that protruded from the belly of the B-17 and was rotated by the gunner's foot pedals. Sticking out of the ball were two .50 caliber machine guns, providing the only defense to the B-17's underside. The ball gunner had the clearest view in the plane, meaning he was also the most vulnerable.

The final position in the plane was the tail gun, the most isolated and cramped station in the plane. The tail gunner worked in a kneeling position against fighters that attempted to creep up on the formation from behind for an easy kill. This team of ten often trained together and flew most of their flights together. Smith stepped into a plane full of veterans, and assumed the role of low man on the totem pole.

At the last minute before his first mission, Smith was reassigned to man the ball turret. This plastic protrusion on the underbelly of the plane was a tight fit for most men, but the slight Sergeant Smith fit easily into the compartment as Flying Fortress 649 took off to bomb the U-boat base at St. Nazaire, France, on the Bay of Biscay. The antiaircraft fire was heavy, as expected for a place known as "flak city," and Smith, who had managed to enjoy the ride across the channel in his bubble—"It was just like you were floating in the air"—learned immediately to dislike flak. These 20-pound shells, each set to explode at a certain altitude and spread 1,500 chunks of shrapnel over a 20-yard radius, were slung up routinely by about 900,000 German gunners stationed at strategic points throughout the country. Even though the Luftwaffe, Germany's air force, brought down more bombers than the gunners on the ground, most bomber crews named flak as their most hated enemy. The fighters you could shoot at. Flak you just had to take.

Smith described his first encounter with flak with the detached air of a scientist: "There are three distinct impressions you get from flak if you are in the bottom turret, and there are only two if you are in the waist. First you hear a tremendous whoosh, then the bits of shrapnel patter against the sides of the turret, then you see the smoke. The one you don't get in the waist is the pattering sound." Smith's natural curiosity and his inclination toward detached observation proved to be a strong tonic against the fear that most men experienced on their first mission. Instead of panicking when the flak started to explode, he found it interesting.

The flight plan traced, roughly, a quadrangle across the English Channel and back. Starting from the base north of London, the bomber group crossed the English Channel, turned east shortly after making landfall near the Normandy-Picardy border, and flew toward the target at St. Nazaire. The cloud cover was 70 percent, not too much to obscure the target, but enough to hide from the fighters.

To the surprise of Smith's pilot—L. P. Johnson, a veteran on the last of his 25 missions—the fighters didn't come up until after the bombs were away. He followed the lead plane into the clouds, managed to shake them, and remarked to his copilot that this had been too easy. There was one little flak hole in the left wing, but the plane was intact, and they were on their way home. When they popped out of the clouds and began their descent toward the shoreline ahead, remembered copilot Bob McCallum, Johnson joked that "he ought to ditch the plane just off the coast to make a dramatic story he could tell his children." His children got their story.

Disoriented in the clouds, the lead navigator in the lead plane made a tragically wrong turn. He thought he was coming up on the English shoreline, but he was actually taking the bombing group into a descent on the heavily fortified German-occupied town of Brest, at the westernmost tip of France. They passed over at 2,000 feet and were unaware of the error until the guns opened fire. Smith watched one Fortress fall to earth, then another. His pilot struggled to get the plane out of range, then "took it to the deck"—just hundreds of feet above the ground—when the fighters came in at six o'clock. "The slugs came all around us," McCallum remembered. "The whole ship shook and kind of bonged like a sound effect in a Walt Disney movie." Smith was firing when he could, but the fighters had the advantage. They were over the English Channel. "I was watching the tracers from a Jerry fighter come puffing by our tail, when suddenly there was a terrific explosion," recalled Smith. "*Whoomp,* just like that. Boy it was a pip." His intercom was dead, and his electrical controls were gone. There was no reason to stay in the immobilized turret, so he cranked the hand controls, opened the hatch and climbed out.

The enemy had scored a hit that ruptured the gasoline tanks, which set a blazing fire, and the oxygen tanks, which gave the flames all the fuel they needed. The entire midsection, the bomb bay and the radio room, was ablaze, and the fire cut Smith off from the men in the front section of the plane.

Up front, the pilot sent the top turret gunner/engineer back to help however he could. He opened the door to be greeted by a wall of flame, and reported back to the pilot that there would be no leaving the plane by that route. So the pilot, copilot, top turret gunner/engineer, bombardier, and navigator were trapped. The pilot, however, stayed calm, despite the creeping feeling that the fire would only be extinguished when they crashed into the sea.

In the midsection, just as Smith climbed out of the ball turret, the radio man came running from his station, where the fire had started and was at its worst. "He made a run for the left waist door and dove out. Dove right out." He jumped high, and failed to clear the horizontal stabilizer. "He must have broken into a dozen pieces," Smith surmised, but his parachute opened, allowing him a soft landing in the frigid English

Channel, where he presumably drowned. The young man was on his 21st mission, just four missions short of a ticket home.

Both waist gunners took the same jump, but one got hooked going out the window. Smith grabbed him and shouted in his face a remark that Andy Rooney called "Snuffy at his best and worst." "I asked him if the heat was too much for him, but all he did was stare at me and say, 'I'm getting out of here.'" Smith helped him clear the door. None of the men who jumped were ever seen again. Smith looked around the compartment—and he was alone. He wrapped a sweater around his face and grabbed a fire extinguisher.

The tail gunner joined him moments later, crawling and groaning and in no shape to help. Smith saw that he'd been shot in the back with a 20-millimeter shell. His lung was punctured and he was falling into shock. Smith rotated him on his side, wounded side down, so the blood wouldn't drain into his one good lung, gave him first aid and a shot of morphine. He then turned back to the fire.

Smith was suddenly interrupted by a German fighter swooping in from 11 o'clock. He manned the left waist gun, let loose as the plane passed overhead, and then switched to the right waist gun to let him have another burst as he left. He didn't hit the plane, but he convinced its pilot that this Flying Fortress, though smoking and flying erratically, still had some fight left.

Inside, Smith returned to the radio room, where the blaze had burned a man-sized hole in the fuselage. That was bad for the plane, but handy for Smith's immediate needs. He tossed out pieces of burning equipment, shielding his hands only with the sleeves of his flight uniform. When the boxes of ammunition started to explode, he threw those out too. At this point, he found his parachute too cumbersome, so he tossed it aside. "I was glad I hadn't taken it off sooner," he remarked later, "because I found a fifty-caliber bullet halfway through it. It would have gone all the way through me."

The severely wounded tail gunner again needed his attention, briefly, and then once again the fighters were back. "You have to show these babies you mean business or they are supposed to finish you off real quick," Smith would later tell a reporter. There wasn't much ammunition left, but there was enough to make a statement. He fired accurately, and the fighters broke off. They didn't make another attempt on the crippled plane. Up front, the pilot couldn't figure out why they were still in the air, but he concentrated on keeping them straight and level, avoiding any maneuvering that might stretch the now fragile fuselage to its breaking point.

Smith saw they were approaching land, the pilot trying for the nearest airstrip. By now all the extinguishers were used up, and still the fire persisted in tearing holes in the side of the plane. He emptied all the water bottles he could get his hands on, and then he fought the fire with all he had left: "I was plenty mad. I pissed on the fire and beat on it with my hands and feet until my clothes began to smoke." When he noticed that the plane was tail-heavy, he tossed out everything in sight: "Guns, ammunition, clothes, everything. I really had a time with the ammunition cases. They weigh ninety-eight pounds and I weigh one thirty."

Smith fought the fire for 90 minutes as it ate through the plane. He finally put out the last flickering flame as they touched down hard, without a rear wheel. Moments later, the plane broke apart, as if it had been straining to hold itself together this entire time and now sought only rest. "All I know," Smith said to wrap up one interview, "is that it was a miracle that the ship didn't break in two in the air, and I wish I could shake hands personally with the people who built her. They sure did a wonderful job, and we owe our lives to them."

Inside the plane, the fire had melted the metal of the camera, radio, and gun mounts. The fire had gutted the entire radio and tail-wheel section. The control cables and the oxygen system were shot to pieces. One of the propellers was shattered; the interphone, radio, and ball-turret controls were out; the flaps had been raked by cannon shell; and the left wing's gas tank was destroyed. Only the engines were salvaged. The nose had been smashed open by flak, and there were about 3,500 holes in the plane from projectiles of various caliber. Smith found two bullet holes in his airman's silk scarf, a scarf he kept as a memento with his Medal of Honor. Juxtaposed, the two made a strong statement—the one honoring his heroism, the other reminding him that he escaped by the narrowest of margins.

Seven bombers of the twenty-nine that went to target didn't make it back. Seventy-three men went down, presumed killed or captured. Two planes returned with a dead man on board. Seventeen were wounded. But three days later, unbeknownst to any of the survivors or any of their commanders, the grand admiral of the German navy reported that "the towns of St. Nazaire and Lorient have been rubbed out as main submarine bases." The long Atlantic crossing, during which thousands of American troops were torpedoed, was made that much safer because of the airmen's sacrifice.

Smith was immediately recommended for an award by his pilot, who wrote that when he first heard about the fires he thought that mission would be his last deed on earth. He claimed that Smith had performed "acts which, by the will of God alone, did not cost him his life, performed in complete self-sacrifice and the utmost efficiency and which were solely responsible for the return of the aircraft and the lives of everyone aboard." Thanks to the *Stars and Stripes* article by Andy Rooney, soon everyone had a chance to fall in love with the short sergeant whose most prominent feature was his bulging Adam's apple and who answered to Snuffy. He became "soldier of the week" on a nationwide radio broadcast. After the Medal of Honor award ceremony and the discovery of Snuffy on KP, the *New York Times* chimed in with a glowing editorial on the "Peeler-Bomber" (even though he wasn't actually peeling potatoes while on kitchen duty) and referred to him in their news coverage as the "diminutive, fire-eating Staff Sergeant Maynard H. Smith."

As the war in Europe proceeded, new heroes came to the forefront, and Smith's celebrity faded. His marriage and his triumphant return home in 1945 were covered heavily in the Caro papers, but after the celebrations were over, he chose not to live in the town where he was known, and now, suddenly, loved.

After a short time in Albany, New York, where several members of Mary's family lived, the pair settled in Washington, D.C., where Smith took a comfortable job with the IRS. But he was once more behind on money owed to his ex-wife and their child, leaving him open to arrest if he ever crossed the Michigan state line. In 1946, she came to D.C. for her day in court. She had remarried, then divorced, and now sought the $15 a month her divorce from Smith originally guaranteed. But this time, the judge sided with Smith, blocking an extradition attempt until it was made clear how much of that money would go to the child and how much to the ex-wife. Smith only owed her alimony if she was unable to support herself, and the judge felt she lacked proof of her needs.

Still, money for child support was owed, and the government job wasn't going to return Smith to the lifestyle he'd enjoyed before the war. To earn some extra cash, he dabbled in over-the-counter, hard-to-find, specialized medications for particular ailments. That's how he caught the eye of another government agency, the FDA.

Smith was selling a topical cream that he'd imported from suppliers in England, and the FDA felt it was mislabeled. Indeed, its claims were fantastic: Based on an ancient Chinese formula, the "hormone cream" was supposed to provide "rejuvenation" and restore "lost manhood." That is, it was supposed to do the same thing that Viagra does, but this magical salve went by the far more colorful and descriptive name "Firmo." When the U.S. Marshals visited Smith's home, they confiscated 62 jars of the stuff, executing a warrant written on the Pure Food, Drug and Cosmetic Act, something relatively novel at the time.

That was in 1947. In the next year, he pleaded guilty to a violation of federal law in selling "misbranded" cream. The only victim of the crime who came forward was an elderly Arlington man, whom Smith repaid. The war hero was then released on his personal bond and a promise to never do it again. He lost his jars of Firmo and got some bad publicity in his local and home state papers, but he walked away unshaken and only a little poorer.

Smith left his IRS job the same year. They told him that if he wanted to advance to the next level, he would have to take an exam. He told them what they could do with their exam and walked out the door. In 1952, he was again facing cash problems. He'd become a salesman for George's Radio and Television Company in the District, and moved out of town to suburban northern Virginia. He had four children now, including the one back in Michigan. He was sure that television would take off, and he was feeding his second passion—politics—by working part-time for the District Veterans for Ike Committee. He seemed ready to turn this sideline into a full-time pursuit, but a tight wallet kept him from taking the leap.

In May 1952, while Smith was living in Falls Church, Virginia, and commuting to Washington, D.C., the Washington *Evening Star* ran a "Where are they today?" feature headlined: MEDAL OF HONOR MEN ANONYMOUS NOW. Emphasizing just how anonymous Smith was these days, he wasn't selected for the article. He was short on funds, with a wife and four kids to support, and the years after the Caro parade had not been the most kind.

It was at this juncture that Smith's life took one of the strangest possible turns, forcing him again to take up the hero's mantle. As he told the *Evening Star*, he was sitting alone on the afternoon of July 31, 1952, just a few months after the same paper ran its "Where are they now" story: "I was on the floor above having a soft drink in the USO lounge [located in the YWCA building]. I looked out the window and saw a woman climbing [out from] the floor below." He said he saw a crowd gather, and so he asked someone what was going on. The woman looked ready to jump, so he went down to the ninth floor, removed a screen from a window, and went out on the ledge on his hands and knees.

As I got near her, my hand touched hers and she drew further away. I started talking to her. I asked her why she wanted to jump. She said she had lost her baby last week and was also having financial difficulties and didn't want to live anymore. I asked her if she had any more kids and she told me about two others at home. I told her it wasn't right to leave them for somebody else to take care of, that they needed her and that no matter what she thought, nobody else could give them the same care she could. A policeman crawled out on the ledge behind me. She saw him and became frightened. I shouted back over my shoulder for him to go back. Finally I edged up to her real slow and got hold of her arm and pulled her back to the window, where firemen and police grabbed her . . . I think it was my talk about her responsibility to her children that turned the trick.

MEDAL OF HONOR MAN SAVES YOUNG MOTHER FROM SUICIDE PLUNGE, the headline read. The news traveled across the country, and the Michigan papers returned the hero to their pages, detailing how Mrs. Lucille Whomble, 22, had been saved "from certain death as hundreds of rush-hour passersby watched the tense drama from the street below." The fire chief gave all credit to Smith, who alternated between lecturing the reporters and ingratiating himself to them.

The players in stories like these typically fall quickly from public view. The saved presumably go on to live happy, normal lives; the saviors settle back into a routine. But in this case, both were on the front page in a matter of days, along with a third who had apparently been there, but went unnoticed. This time, on August 5, the headline read: ONE OF PAIR ACCUSED OF SUICIDE TRY HOAX SURRENDERS TO POLICE.

The man who surrendered was Roland M. Bennett, 26, of Washington, D.C. Ex-boyfriend of Mrs. Whomble, he worked in the TV shop with Smith. His name had come up during Whomble's psychiatric examination at Gallinger Hospital, after, she said, she decided to come clean. One night, she claimed, Smith and Bennett visited the home in Southeast Washington where she lived with her husband, and her ex-boyfriend asked her for a favor: "'I want you to commit suicide,' he said, then laughed. 'Not really, just to fake it.' He told me there was five hundred dollars in it for me, and said, 'I guarantee you five hundred dollars.'"

She asked the obvious question—why?—and Bennett explained to her that this publicity would be perfect to help launch Maynard Smith's Virginia gubernatorial campaign. The nationwide attention would make Mrs. Whomble "famous," he continued, and gifts of sympathy for the infant she had recently lost were sure to pour in. The fruits of this scheme, he insisted, were guaranteed, because her ersatz savior was a recipient of the Congressional Medal of Honor.

She took the idea to her husband, a cab driver who struggled to support their two children. He stood against it strongly, but she finally persuaded him to "cover" for her. The following day, she claimed she went out driving with Smith and Bennett, scouting Washington for tall buildings. She immediately ruled out the idea of the 14th Street Bridge as too dangerous, and they ruled out the National Press Building, probably too brazen a location for a publicity stunt. They finally settled on the YWCA, which had a conveniently high ledge and stood at a bustling intersection.

"Roland told me to hang over the side of the ledge," Whomble told reporters, "and then when Smitty came there to let him grab hold of me and kind of slip. They wanted me to stay on the ledge for two or three hours and yell at the people [below]." She never took seriously the thought of thus heightening this drama, and in fact, as soon as she got out on the ledge, she wanted to back down. But Smith was already right behind her. "People heard [Smith] saying 'Don't, don't!' A photographer was there and took a picture just then. But he was saying, 'Don't come back in.'" As she reached this part of the story, the *Evening Star* reported, "Mrs.

Whomble smiled briefly at the recollection, but for the most part she was a grim-faced woman as she sat beside her husband." She finally admitted that she was wrong to take part in the affair, and now just wanted it behind her: "I'm glad it's over. I'm tired, I'm hungry, I want a bath, I want to go home."

Bennett, who had turned himself in and was released on $300 bond, stood accused of masterminding the plot. The prosecutor said he harbored dreams of being the "man behind the man" as his war-hero friend rose to power. This, and almost everything else in Whomble's story, he flatly denied. Both he and Smith claimed that they had no political aspirations whatsoever, and Smith pointed out that he was still a new resident of Virginia, not yet eligible to run for governor. He had never met Mrs. Whomble before he saw her on the ledge, he continued, and proclaimed confusion over why she would accuse him so. "That woman is a good actor," he said. "If that is an example of her best work, she should be in Hollywood."

Bennett and Smith were charged with filing false reports, but because this was a misdemeanor, the hands of the D.C. police were tied as long as Smith stayed in Virginia and didn't cross into D.C. Then he disappeared. "The whereabouts of Maynard H. (Snuffy) Smith was almost as baffling to police today as the suicide hoax he is charged with arranging with another man and a young mother," was the lead of an August 6 news report. In fact, Smith had taken his family for an outing along scenic Skyline Drive, he said, and took some time to think things over. He wasn't running from the police, his wife said—he was shielding the family from reporters. The next day, he showed up at a D.C. precinct and "surrendered."

There was some question as to whether any crime was actually committed. The charge was for filing a false report, but neither Smith nor Bennett had actually filed a police report or made official statements— there was no need, since police and firemen had witnessed the whole thing. So Smith's lawyer tried to get the charges dismissed based on the fact that the prosecution had failed to address this point. The judge took the motion under review, and returned the following day, August 28, with a stern harbinger of how this trial would turn out for Smith: "The whole object of the defendants' scheme was to attract attention and it succeeded. One is under a duty to foresee the normal and logical consequences flowing from his act—and certainly here it was within the normal purview that the attention sought to be attracted was bound to result to calls to the Police and Fire Departments."

The prosecution wasn't about to let this one go. They called to the stand Whomble, her husband, and her sister, all of whom were witnesses to the alleged pre-hoax visit by Smith and Bennett. The trial was closely detailed in the papers, and handled with gravity. Smith's defense lacked anything beyond repeated denial. The idea of running for governor, Smith said to reporters, was "so damned ridiculous it isn't worth talking about." The woman was obviously under a lot of "pressure . . . from some source." And besides, he continued, "Where would I get five hundred dollars?"

The prosecuting counsel confronted Smith's denial that he had political aspirations. "Isn't it a fact," he earnestly questioned, "that you attended a national political convention?" Well, yes, Smith admitted, he had been invited to the Republican convention, probably something to do with his medal. Then, looking at the reporters in the room, he added as an afterthought that he had one political aspiration: "I am interested to see the Democratic Party removed as a whole." This statement was particularly odd considering that Snuffy later became a devout Democrat.

The judge quickly convicted the pair of making false reports (even though they made no official reports), but seemed more puzzled than condemning of this "very strange story spun out here," and punishment fell far short of the $300 fine he could have imposed. Bennett, as the "moving party in these activities," was hit with a $75 fine or ten days in jail. He paid and walked. The court told Smith that it "has in mind the good war record which every man has the right to be proud of and which makes it even more difficult to understand this silly scheme." He was then fined $50 or ten days. Smith's attorney pleaded with the court for 48 hours to come up with the cash, but Smith's war record didn't help him here. The prosecution objected, and he was led away to jail.

The next year, 1953, Smith's mother passed away, leaving him a decent amount of money. He was humiliated by the hoax incident and saddened over his mother, but the financial problems now weren't so pressing. Smith tried to put this whole sad chapter in his life behind him, never mentioning it to his children, and leaving, in 1954, for Albany, New York, with his family. There, he underwent his conversion to the Democratic Party. It was Kennedy, who he met at the White House, who solidified his newfound commitment to the party he once wanted removed as a whole. In Albany, he discovered his gifts as a lobbyist and grassroots organizer, actively campaigning for the New York State Lottery. Maynard Jr. remembers that he got 375,000 signatures in favor of the lottery, to the surprise of most in the state government: "The legislature never took him seriously until he walked in with all those signatures. They put it in a bill and bang, it passed."

But even as Smith stayed to the straight and narrow, he and his wife began a series of separations that would lead to divorce in the late sixties. Maynard Jr. remembers his father, who never lost his son's admiration, crying on the phone as the situation spun out of his control. "My dad loved my mom until the day he died," the son emphasizes.

By the early seventies, Maynard Smith had a series of failed business ventures behind him, most recently an alarm and security company that was in the wrong place at the wrong time. The money his mother left wasn't enough to take him where he wanted to go. As Snuffy put it, "My father told me you should be either so rich you could afford to go fishing all the time or be so poor that you had to go. I decided to go with the former." In New York City, he finally hit on a winning formula that was not only legal, but had a strong association with the law. The *Police Officer's*

Journal was a free paper founded in 1970 that by 1972, Maynard Jr. says, was "as big as the *Village Voice.*"

Smith and son ran the business together, sharing all the duties of selling advertising space, writing articles, and getting the paper distributed. "We gave it out to every single precinct in all five boroughs," recalled Maynard Jr., in his early 20s at the time. The transit police, the housing authorities, every cop in any agency had a chance to pick up a free copy of the paper, which covered community and law enforcement issues. The father and founder admitted that he had nothing but an idea when he started: "I didn't know anything about publishing a newspaper, but I knew how to sell advertising and I knew human nature, psychology, and sales. And if you have that much under your belt, you don't have that much to worry about."

They sold the paper in 1976 "for a fortune," says the son, and finally, Smith could move permanently to Florida. He bought a home in St. Petersburg and a boat and settled back into the retirement he'd left behind in 1942. This included lots of fishing, of course, but also a massive amount of reading. "I cannot remember a time when my father was sitting and did not have a book in front of him. A thousand times," said Maynard Jr., who moved to Florida at the same time, "I've taken his glasses off and laid his book to the side" after he'd fallen asleep.

Smith continued his exploration of the world's religions, but, according to his son, "He was not an over-spiritual guy. He was not a very heavy-duty religious person, although he had a strong feeling of what was right and what was wrong." In his later years, he also became very interested in the Yeti, a.k.a. the Abominable Snowman. He didn't necessarily believe it was out there—he remained undecided and unconvinced—but he gravitated to the subject. It was, after all, either the most elaborate hoax or potentially the greatest scientific discovery of the time.

Adding one more diversion to his list, Smith picked up the game of pool from the man who'd played Minnesota Fats in *The Hustler*. He met

Jackie Gleason at a convention, and the two hit it off, bounding about town before Gleason left. Smith was a quick study and, as his son relates, became a notorious trick shot—the kind of guy who would leave his opponents shaking their heads and muttering, "I lost, but it was worth it." "Every VFW [Veterans of Foreign Wars lodge] in the St. Petersburg area knew Snuffy Smith," Maynard Jr. says. "And they all knew, if they could beat Snuffy just one time, they had bragging rights."

Maybe some people who knew Snuffy Smith back in the glory days during the "congressional medal deal" would be surprised, but Maynard Jr. insisted that his father wasn't much of a braggart: "In his older years, he was very mellow, very sweet. My dad would drive a hundred miles to pull a thorn out of a dog's paw . . . He was a very quiet man unless he was asked his opinion. He didn't impose on anybody, he didn't force his opinion on anybody."

Sometimes, in the presence of reporters, Smith couldn't resist a little boast. When he was 67, Smith recounted the Medal of Honor story in a 1979 interview with events out of sequence, and the extra element of giving first aid to the pilot and copilot. He also said, "I think I remembered I repaired six wires" that controlled the tail flaps. It had been almost 40 years, and he may have truly forgotten. Then, at a later date, the story became wildly, outrageously embellished—with Snuffy pulling the pilot out of his seat and flying the plane to a safe landing. In 1980 he told this embellished story to reporters for a local Florida paper. This more dramatic version has since been repeated in several articles and books, but it was never told at home. Maynard, Jr. never heard those more inventive versions. "What he did was enough. He didn't have to prove anything to anybody." Snuffy always put it down to discipline: "I did what I was trained to do," and nothing more.

Even if he stretched the truth in later retellings, six lives were saved by his actions. Snuffy, whether he was arrogant or simply was smarter than everyone around him—whether he was a "fuckup" or just a character— lived a life that reminds us that heroes can be flawed and still be heroes.

As the editorial pages of the *New York Times* pointed out the day after he was decorated, "He is a man his mother, his State and his country can't be too proud of. Some of us will like him all the more because he isn't too good for human nature's daily food."

Smith's second ex-wife and daughter flew in from Hawaii to join his other children when they heard that he was hospitalized for what looked like the last time. They said their good-byes, and Maynard "Hokie" "Snuffy" "Smitty" Smith died of heart failure on May 11, 1984, at the age of 72.

On May 23, his hometown paper, the *Tuscola County Advertiser*, ran an obituary that left out those less-than-flattering Firmo and hoax incidents. The town with which he'd had such a rocky relationship until he returned as a conquering hero sent him off in style by detailing a most colorful version of his heroics, a version that one can find duplicated in various books and articles written after his death. The 98-pound ammo crates became 250 pounds each. The pilot and copilot were collapsed in their seats, and the plane was out of control by the time Smith put out the fires. Smith pulled the pilot from his seat and flew the plane to England, despite having no previous flight experience. Finally, "He landed the plane before it gave out." He was a certainly a hero, but this obituary made him a giant.

CHAPTER SEVEN

Vernon Baker

WORLD WAR II

"Second Lieutenant Baker demonstrated outstanding courage and leadership in destroying enemy installations, personnel and equipment during his company's attack against a strongly entrenched enemy in mountainous terrain."

— MEDAL OF HONOR CITATION

THEY FOUGHT IN DIFFERENT WARS, but their Medal of Honor actions are remarkably similar. They both crept up on dangerous enemy positions with the stealth of hunters. They were both deadly marksmen. They both were army men before the nation was called to war. Sam Woodfill's and Vernon Baker's actions—Woodfill's in World War I, Baker's in World War II—began in a remarkably similar fashion. Vernon Baker, a second lieutenant fighting in northern Italy, led his men in a head-on attack. Moving ahead alone, as Woodfill had done years before, Vernon Baker took out multiple enemy positions single-handedly. From there, Baker's action continued throughout a horrific day of bloodletting. But Vernon Baker served in a segregated army unit composed entirely of black men commanded by a white captain. And Vernon Baker was, at first, awarded the Distinguished Service Cross, not the Medal of Honor.

Not a single African American who fought in the First World War received the Medal of Honor until 1991, when it was presented to Freddie Stowers's surviving sisters. Not a single African American who fought in the Second World War received the Medal of Honor until 1997, 52 years after the end of the war.

African Americans were excluded from the Medal of Honor roll for nearly half of the twentieth century. Alphonse Girandy, a black native of the West Indies and U.S. Navy volunteer, was awarded the medal in 1902 for "heroism and gallantry; fearlessly exposing his own life to danger for the saving of others" during a fire on board the USS *Petrel* on March 22, 1902. He was the last man of African descent so decorated for 49 years, until the award was given to Private William Thompson for actions in the Korean War. Three hundred and sixty thousand African Americans served in the First World War, 40,000 of those in combat roles. Five hundred thousand African Americans served overseas in strictly segregated units during the Second World War. And yet, the complete and total lack of black veterans of those conflicts in possession of the Medal of Honor escaped official notice for nearly a half century.

Vernon Baker was given his medal in person on January 13, 1997, with an apology. Six other African Americans were awarded the medal posthumously. Three had died performing their heroic deeds, and three had passed away in the intervening years. Baker said he did not then, nor had he ever, asked for the recognition the medal gave: "I did not seek this final chapter to my life," he wrote in his autobiography.

For a while, it seems everyone took notice of Vernon Baker: Colin Powell called him "a national inspiration, a national role model." Secretary of Defense William Cohen quoted him in a speech at the Air Force Academy in June 1997: "Give respect before you expect it; treat people the way you would want to be treated; remember the mission; set the example; and keep going." The networks turned his private home, Baker says, "into a TV studio." The more humble he appeared, and the more he resisted the "hero" label, the more the media wanted him. But he wasn't just acting humble, he was resisting the attempts made to glorify his heroism. "After the first combat death splattered blood across my face," he wrote, "I realized there is no glory." But rather than dwell on that and other traumas, he says he spent years "of trying to forget, of regretting many deaths." The recognition that came with the Medal of Honor was, in the end, a mixed blessing.

From 1864, when the medal was established, to 1902, when Alphonse Girandy received his medal, 55 black men received the Medal of Honor. Even as an average of four blacks a week were lynched in the Deep South during the 1890s, 18 received this highest of military honors. But in the 20th century, the American armed forces erected more obstacles to black enlistment, and by 1940, there were fewer than 5,000 blacks in military service. Vernon Baker became one of those few in 1941, seven months before Pearl Harbor.

Vernon Baker was born on December 17, 1919, and raised in Cheyenne, Wyoming. The town was home to 11 black families in a population of 20,000. In a railroad hub like Cheyenne, a man like Baker's granddad could always find work on the Union Pacific. The boardinghouse Baker's grandparents ran, however, made its money as the only place in town that would harbor the men and women of color who passed through. This boardinghouse was where Vernon Baker grew up.

The last thing he remembers about his parents is their funeral. His grandparents explained that there had been a car accident. Vernon, four years old, and his two older sisters, Cass and Irma, immediately fell under the wing of their mother's parents. Vernon grew up trying to stay out of his grandmother's mile-wide mean streak and trying to live up to his grandfather's mile-high standards. She was stricken with rheumatoid arthritis, wheelchair bound, and in almost perpetual pain. He was a quiet man of immense size who kept his conversations short. He taught by example, by exhibiting a quiet strength, and, on many occasions, by taking off his belt.

Other lessons he taught by offering experience. Vernon Baker never took up smoking, even during the war when soldiers were burning through cigarettes as fast as they could light them. This he owed to the day his grandfather caught him smoking—or pretending to smoke without really inhaling—out back in a rotting car at age eight. He sat him down on the porch and thrust a pipe full of Granger Rough-Cut tobacco in his face. And he made sure he inhaled, telling him, "There you are, boy, that's real smoking." Vernon was sick for days, and for decades even the smell of tobacco nauseated him.

His older sister Cass taught him to read—and he learned well enough to be able to skip a grade. The fall that Vernon was almost 12, his grandfather took him out and taught him to hunt. His first lesson was with a double-barrel 12-gauge shotgun, and it turned out to be more of a lesson in respect for firearms than in how to shoot them. After listening patiently to his grandfather's explanation, Vernon put the stock to his shoulder, aimed quickly, and let go with both barrels. His grandfather was laughing as he got back on his feet. Vernon learned to calm down and fire one barrel at a time.

His grandfather decided that his pupil had learned his lessons well, and presented Vernon with a .22 Remington that Christmas, shortly after his 12th birthday. He'd been generous with the rifle, but he was tight with the cartridges. He ordered Vernon to return an empty shell for each cartridge, and to procure a dead critter as well. He sent him off with the words, "If you can't make the shot count, don't make it."

Just like fellow Medal of Honor recipients Sam Woodfill and David Shoup, he wasn't out in the forest just to terrorize rodents. Their meat was a regular part of their diet. To Vernon, the fact that he could come home from a walk down Crow Creek with fresh-killed game slung over his back didn't just mean that he was a good shot. He was a provider, a man of the house. He was also spending more time away from home, in the quiet of the forest, without anyone asking where he was or coming after him. He learned to cherish this solitude.

When Vernon was 15, he graduated to the deer hunt, and bagged a four-point mule deer from 150 yards with one shot. His grandfather, at his side, said simply, "Good shot, boy," which were the sweetest words the youngster could hear. But when he wasn't hunting, Vernon was hanging with a group of angry, culpable older kids, and he knew that in time, he would be caught up in trouble. After meeting a resident of Father Flanagan's Boys' Home, Vernon saw a chance to get out of Cheyenne and stay out of trouble. He spent grades six through eight at Boys' Home in Omaha, Nebraska, holding one short conversation with the legend himself, and returned home for good following his grandmother's death and his grandfather's remarriage. With this second wife, it seemed to Vernon, came tighter budgets. He didn't return to the boarding school after eighth grade. It was free to orphans, but Vernon's grandfather had an opinion on that: Vernon may not have had parents, but he wasn't an orphan.

Today, Baker admits that it sounds like a line from a novel, but his first job was shining shoes. He didn't return to school, following instead his grandfather's footsteps by working at the railroad. After a year as a baggage carrier and porter, he and his grandfather attended a relative's funeral in Iowa. Before long, he decided he wanted to go back to school in Iowa, away from the rising tensions between him and his step-grandmother, and get his diploma. He succeeded, and excelled, graduating with honors and a letter in every sport. But then it was back to Cheyenne and the railroads. As his life sought direction, his grandfather, mentor, and guide passed away. They buried him on Christmas Day, 1939. Baker had just turned twenty.

Baker vaguely yearned for something more, but it was a young woman's insistence on a "man of means" for a husband that got him actively looking for a good job. The army, he heard, had comfortable, good-paying jobs for people who worked as quartermasters. A friend of his on the railroad told him that this was a foolish thing to do, but he succeeded in talking another friend into going down to the recruiting office with him. One glance was all they got from the officer, who told them point-blank that the army didn't have any quotas for "you people." A month later, he made his way back, where a different officer gladly helped him fill out the papers. The smiling officer guided the course of Vernon's life by writing *infantry* where Vernon had requested *quartermaster*. Vernon noticed, but didn't mind; he was about to become a man of means. He married the day before he went off to basic training, boarding a Texas-bound train on June 26, 1941.

Having grown up in a small northern town, Baker didn't understand why they asked him and another black passenger to move to the front car, closer to the noise and exhaust of the locomotive, shortly after the train crossed into Texas. Boarding the empty bus for Camp Wolters, he tossed his bag down and moved into the first seat behind the driver—his first mistake in the segregated South. The driver spun around with words uglier than Baker had ever heard: "Hey, nigger, get up and get to the back of the bus *where you belong.*" Baker's fists clenched as a friendly hand touched him on his arm and led him to the back of the bus. The old man who'd intervened, and possibly saved Baker's life, gave him a quick education in Jim Crow. He'd been close. Stronger men had been lynched for less.

Because he could read and write, Baker was made company clerk, and then promoted to supply sergeant. So when Congress declared war against Japan on December 8, 1941, he was in a position to become a staff sergeant. Most of the men in his company were poor southerners "with nothing to lose," and a few of them resented Baker's rise in rank. They caught him alone in a dark corner and delivered a beating while asking him if he thought he was a "smart nigger."

His white regimental commander called him in one day in spring 1942 and said, without fanfare or congratulations, "Baker, you are applying for Officer Candidate School." Baker was relieved to leave, until he got to Georgia for Officer Candidate School. To his astonishment, the racism was even worse than in Texas, and wearing officer's bars didn't exempt him. White enlisted men openly expressed their disgust with Baker, while the black enlisted refused to salute him. But Baker learned to lead, and the men under his command in the segregated units came to respect him. As long as he served in a segregated army, however, the white soldiers—whether officers or enlisted men—he could do nothing about.

In 1998, during one of his then frequent guest visits to an elementary school, Vernon Baker took questions from his young audience. They quizzed him on how long he was in the army, how old he was, and when the war started. One curious youngster asked him how he got into the war, and he answered, "I went down and raised my hand and said 'I will.' That's how I got into the war." Of course, he and other black soldiers had been raising their hands for years. It wasn't until summer 1944 that the army finally decided that they too could fight, or, in the memorable words of one commander, "All these years, our white boys have been going over there and getting killed. Well, now it's time for you black boys to go get killed."

Baker, a second lieutenant, had the job of carrying out the orders of his white commanders, who regarded the segregated "Buffalo Soldiers," named after the black Cavalry units of the late 19th century, as "too worthless" to lead themselves. "The army decided we needed supervision from white Southerners, as if war was plantation work and fighting Germans was picking cotton," Baker remembered. He was sent to Italy as a platoon leader with the 370th Infantry Regiment, Company C, assigned to the First Armored Division. They landed in Naples in July 1944 and made their way up the peninsula, fighting sporadically, as the Germans fell back to the treacherous Gothic Line, a series of strongpoints and defenses that ran across northern Italy. Here the Germans hoped that they could slam the door on Fortress Europe, leaving the Allies out in the cold. Baker and his men were sent in to achieve in a few months a position that, Baker recalled, "more experienced troops had not been able to accomplish in a year." The 370th was reassigned from the First Armored to the 92nd in October 1944, bringing them to the brunt of this battle.

Even though racism was evident everywhere, on the front and back at home, and even though the assignment seemed impossible, Baker today doesn't feel that his platoon was used simply as cannon fodder: "I really couldn't say that we were sent to do things that some of the white troops couldn't do," he said in an interview for this chapter. "Everybody's over there fighting a war and everybody was given a mission to accomplish . . . whether they were black, white, green, or red, it had to be done." Baker felt his main job was keeping his men alive.

He watched two of his men die in the dark in an ambush in the fall of 1944, and he wondered if there was any way he could have seen the ambush coming. He knew that the enemy could have easily wiped out his entire patrol. That they slowly withdrew instead was inexplicable luck. Only two, he thought to himself.

Not long after, he watched three men die while marching up a slope where a camouflaged machine gun was waiting for them. He'd sent them there.

Under orders to take a German-held house in October 1944, he ordered his men up a path while he and a capable sergeant snuck around back. They took the house, but three of his men on the path were killed. He called his orders his "lethal stupidity." He felt responsible, and then nauseated. He was himself shot in the forearm, put out of action for two months. He was back at the front December 26, 1944. By that time his men were approaching the Gothic Line.

Castle Aghinolfi, set into a naturally strong position and occupied by various armies since the fifth century, was one corner of what the Italian freedom fighters despairingly called the "triangle of death." The three hills below the castle were less dramatically named X, Y, and Z by the Americans, and nowhere else in this section of the Gothic Line, on the western coast north of Pisa and south of Genoa, did American blood flow more freely. Six weeks after his return, and with his battalion in reserve, Baker watched one of several assaults on the hills that ended in disaster: "My sense of helplessness slipped in and my self-control snapped," as the hidden and dug-in German weapons blew up or mowed down the advancing Americans. "I cried, pounding my fist against the wall of the observation post until my hand was raw and my arm ached." He also knew, as he watched this attack fail, that he and his men would be next. It wasn't long before he saw his regiment sucked dry of morale. One soldier reflected the mood of the men with the resigned comment, "Might as well write that last letter home."

Making matters even worse was the introduction of new commanders, new troops, and a reorganization of the surviving officers. Baker was demoted from executive officer to platoon leader and put in command of troops he didn't know, men who didn't know him or his abilities. The one bright spot was the arrival of the 442nd Regimental Combat Team and the 100th Infantry Battalion. Both comprised Japanese Americans who volunteered directly from the internment camps established throughout the West to contain the "Japanese threat" on the West Coast. These were men determined to prove their loyalty, and their superiors gave them every chance, shipping them from one hot spot to another.

On April 5, 1945, as Baker's men prepared themselves at his company's jumping-off point, from where they were expected to take Hill X and then keep moving another 300 yards to the castle, Baker felt a rush of invincibility. "Today," he told them, "we're going to do it." He still has no idea where his words came from. When he rose that morning, he put on his dress uniform because "the day spelled death. I wanted to go up sharp." He left his helmet behind. It restricted his hearing, and he felt it didn't do a thing against shrapnel.

The platoon moved slowly up the terraced hill in the pre-dawn darkness. Baker should have been commanding 36 men that day, but the engagements up the coast had left him with 25, two rifle squads and one mortar squad. Ahead, Baker spotted two figures crouched in a menacing and well-camouflaged machine gun nest. Creeping forward, he got into position and fired. They "dropped like deer," and he motioned his men forward. Still in the vanguard, he overcame a second position, with two more enemy soldiers, with two more shots. The third position he only noticed because of an irregularity in the hillside. He aimed for the bunker's slit and emptied his clip. As before, artillery fire covered the crack of his rifle. He crept up and peered inside to find one man still alive. Dropping a grenade in the slit, he fell back as it exploded. The position turned out to be an observation post, "as lethal as machine guns or mortar rounds" to soldiers still creeping up through the valley.

They were far enough up the hill to turn east to meet up with the castle itself. Walking at the head of his file in the twilight, Baker suddenly stopped and braced himself for "serious fire" from a .50 caliber machine gun nest, camouflaged so well he might have stepped right into it. The rounds never came. The crew was eating breakfast. Baker fired from the hip. Then he took a moment to reflect on his incredible luck. He was 300 yards from the castle, closer than anyone had gotten before, much closer than anyone expected. His mortar teams were missing, but he assumed they'd catch up. Encouraged but wary, he met up with his captain, who'd come up in the rear.

Captain Runyon had been part of the shake-up among the ranks that preceded this attack, and according to Baker was yet another white commander among many who seemed to not care at all for the black troops. Twenty-five yards away, a German soldier came into the clearing, just as surprised as the two Americans. He acted first, lobbing a grenade that landed squarely at their feet. Runyon, Baker says, made a panicked dash with his arms thrown wide. One of those arms knocked Baker's rifle from his grip. Catching it on the way down, Baker leveled it at the German, who had now turned tail. Baker hit him twice, and he went down. His grenade failed to explode.

Runyon was gone, a fact that Baker cursed under his breath. Baker's anger was intensified by the momentary loss of his rifle. Because of those lost seconds, he had been forced to "adopt enough cowardice to shoot another soldier in the back."

The German's sudden appearance suggested more nearby. Baker consulted with his squad leader, traded his M-1 for a submachine gun, and set off alone. He found a trail in a ravine, worked his way forward, and found a dugout protected by a steel door. A grenade fit cleanly under the door, and after the explosion, a soldier emerged, confused and injured. Baker killed him and rushed the open door, tossing a second grenade and then spraying submachine gun fire. In the clearing smoke he found three dead soldiers and their scattered breakfast.

By the time Baker got back to his men, the mortar squad was still unaccounted for. The enemy had detected the Americans in their very midst, and then, Baker recalled, "came chaos." Mortar shells flew so thick that one of his men at first mistook them for a flock of birds. Bullets hummed everywhere. His men were falling quickly. His radioman was trying to convince the commanders back at headquarters of their position, but no one in the rear believed they had penetrated three miles past the front lines. Once swayed, American artillery started to fall. Baker knew that "the margin of error between our position and the German position was negligible," and was relieved as American shells rained on the enemy's lines instead of their own. The relief lasted only a moment.

Baker was close enough to hear the command, "Feuer!" shouted from the enemy lines. He knew that on the heels of this order to fire would come another barrage of mortar shells. He desperately kept his men moving from position to position, always just one step ahead of the explosions. Or sometimes not ahead at all. "Men dropped. A few pitched forward, others went bulleting backwards, as if struck by a freight train . . . An hour before, charged with adrenaline, I'd felt born to do combat. I'd known I was an invincible giant. This slaughter jarred my immortality."

He went looking for his captain. One of his men pointed him to a nearby stone house, where the captain had taken refuge ever since the grenade attack. "Runyon was sitting on the dirt floor, knees pulled up to his chest, his arms wrapped around his legs. His face was translucent, the color of bleached parchment." Their conversation was brief and left Baker even more enraged. The captain, according to Baker, asked if he was planning on holding the position. "I couldn't believe the question. We had accomplished something four other attempts hadn't matched. And we were within conquering distance of the castle. 'We're staying,' I replied. 'We can do this.'"

Runyon's reply, Baker continues, was that he would leave for reinforcements. "Reinforcements? A captain going for reinforcements? Wasn't this the task of a sergeant and a couple of privates? . . . 'All right, captain. We'll be here when you get back,' I said, hoping my stare told him what my mouth hadn't." Runyon feebly announced his departure to the crouching men. Baker says he learned later that Runyon had gotten back to base and advised against reinforcements, claiming that the men left behind would never survive.

Baker formed a perimeter and started collecting dog tags from the dead. Then the enemy began their counterattack with renewed determination. They would let loose with mortars, then spray with machine guns, then attack with soldiers who appeared "from nowhere." After several waves, Baker's men still held their improvised fortifications. Then a small group of Germans moved in, carrying a stretcher. Baker saw the red cross on their helmets and on their flag and calmed his men's twitching trigger fingers. But when the team was within 50 yards, they pulled a machine gun off the stretcher and tried to quickly set it up. Baker's men opened fire.

Out of the 25 he'd started with, Baker had 8 men left. They were down to their last bullets. "They crouched along our perimeter and stared at me. I can still see their faces—I see them every day, in my mind." Baker looked downhill to see if there was any sign of the promised reinforcements, a messenger, anything. "It finally came to me. Our commanders hadn't believed we made it three miles behind enemy lines. We held this ridge for nothing." He ordered a withdrawal.

The men stuck together during their trip back down Hill X, even when they came under sniper fire, even after they came under galling fire from two machine guns they'd missed on their way up (which they took out), even after they lost two more of their number, including their medic. Baker's men dispatched a tank they discovered dug deeply into the hillside. Then they broke into a run down the hill, still under fire, until they reached their own lines, which were a confusing buzz of men and machines. Only Baker and six others had made it out alive. In a cruel vagary of war, months later, after there was peace in Europe, three of those six would lose their lives in a freak explosion as they danced at a USO club.

Back at base, Baker dismissed his men. Then, "I turned, lowered myself to the side of the road, hung my head between my knees, and heaved my guts out." He recovered, checked his watch, and was surprised to see that early evening had crept up on him. He and his men had spent an entire day under fire. He had watched 19 of his men die on that day. He felt most of these deaths were preventable. He felt he was responsible. He'd lost track of the number of Germans he killed.

Baker was debriefed by a white lieutenant colonel, who complimented him and his men on their "damn fine work." The man shook his head when he heard how many Americans had been killed. Baker was surprised: It seemed that this white officer actually cared about the black lives lost in the maw of Hill X. But Baker's next stop, at Regimental HQ to drop off the 19 dog tags weighing heavy in his pocket, wasn't as cordial. A colonel gave him "one of the better ass chewings I ever received in the army" because he had refused to wear a helmet. He also informed him that the next day, he would be going back up the hill as guide for a fresh company.

At daybreak of the second day, the guns were silent as Baker served as guide to an all-white company that retraced his platoon's steps. The hill was speckled with dead soldiers. All the dead Americans were barefoot, their boots appropriated by the enemy. As the company reached the ridge, the fight resumed in Baker's mind. He saw his men dying a second time. He saw the Germans he'd killed fall to the dust again.

> We proved we could go up and fight and die. We had cleared the way for this all-white company to go all the way to the castle without hearing a shot. We had made an ass out of everyone who said we couldn't do it. This was some success. Yet, I still wanted respect and the acknowledgement that we were good. Our thanks was an ass chewing and an assignment to scout for white soldiers. It was a way of life for my men. It made me furious.

Baker pointed the way, but he could stay on the ridge no longer. Alone, he walked back down the hill and came across the tank his men had disabled the day before. He found inside the bodies of "two young German boys, too young to grow whiskers." His sense of responsibility, that he carried for each man under his command, expanded when he saw the faces of the dead. "If I had arrived sixty seconds sooner, I could have prevented this. We could have captured these lads instead of killing them. These two days had impressed me more with the futility of war than the previous eight months of combat." He spend the remainder of the day digging up land mines. Even that was futile. After the war, it took 15 months to remove the mines from these three hills.

The day he fought on Hill X was Baker's last day in combat. His company marched north as the Germans fled. Events unfolded quickly after the Americans broke through the line at Bologna on April 19. The Italian Resistance shot Mussolini as he attempted to escape to Switzerland on April 28. Baker saw the bodies of the Italian fascist and his mistress in Milan. Two days later, Hitler committed suicide. Baker's unit fell back to the area of Castle Aghinolfi, and stayed in nearby Viareggio, where there was now an eerie quiet. They were told they would be sent to the Pacific to take part in the assault on Japan. "I had enough combat time to avoid it, but I wanted to go. I rationalized it by telling myself I was born to be a warrior." As they waited, Baker was promoted to first lieutenant.

Vernon Baker received the Distinguished Service Cross on July 4, 1945. During the same ceremony, Major General Edward Almond, commander of the 92nd Infantry Division, had oak leaf clusters added to his Silver Star, and Captain Runyon, who, Baker maintains, had abandoned their platoon on the hill, received the Silver Star. Baker stood next to Runyon, his bitterness growing when Almond took the place of honor, typically reserved for the highest-decorated soldier.

> I'd had a job. I'd done it. I didn't want a medal for it. I wanted one
> of those commanders to verbally acknowledge we had far exceed-
> ed their expectations, that they were sorry for the scurrilous lies
> they had told about the performance of black soldiers in combat,
> and that they regretted the loss of my men at the castle. A sentence
> or two of contrition for failing to provide reinforcements would
> also be welcome.

The first atom bomb fell on Japan just one month later. In 1947, Baker returned from the war after an extended service in occupied Italy that mostly consisted of guard duty. He toyed with the idea of entering college, but realized that there still wasn't much for him on the outside.

Hero Sam Woodfill faced a tight job market and his own lack of skills. Vernon Baker faced that and more: "I stayed in the army because in those days a young black man couldn't find a decent job."

Baker will never forget the day when a white colonel approached him on the street in Fayetteville, North Carolina, with some serious doubts about the medal on his chest: "Ain't no nigger I ever saw deserved no Distinguished Service Cross." Baker refused to remove it, the first direct order he ever disobeyed. "That was an order I could not follow," he reflected during an interview. "I made it plain to him that I earned it and I'm wearing it, and not he or anyone else is going to take it off of me." The colonel,

Baker supposes, went away to check Baker's record, and he never heard from him or saw him again.

Baker was lucky compared to other black veterans who, in the years following World War II, had it much, much worse. In Taylor County, Georgia, a black veteran who had committed the "crime" of voting in 1946 was forced from his home and shot. Two days later, a white mob attacked two veterans and their wives as they drove through Monroe, Georgia. Sixty bullet holes were found in their bodies. President Truman learned of another incident involving black veterans, and said, "My stomach turned over when I heard that Negro soldiers, recently returned from overseas, had been dumped from a bus and beat. I shall fight until that evil is eliminated."

As commander in chief, there was one step he could take immediately—desegregation of the armed forces. He had the support of only 6 percent of the nation, but still issued Executive Order number 9981 on July 26, 1948: "It is hereby declared to be the policy of the President that there shall be equality of treatment and opportunity for all persons in the armed services without regard to race, color, religion, or national origin." It asked for expediency, but conceded to those who felt it would take time to make adjustments for morale. Powerful men in the armed forces took this allowance as license to dig in their heels. Eisenhower vocally opposed the move on the grounds of national security. War hero and chairman of the Joint Chiefs of Staff General Omar Bradley insisted that the army was not a place for "social experiments." It wasn't until 1951 that desegregation of the armed forces was a reality.

Those who honestly thought desegregation would crush morale could have looked back to the integrated United States Navy that fought in the Civil War. Despite efforts early in the war to limit the enlistment of blacks, the navy was a magnet for escaped slaves and free northern blacks who chose to heed the words of Frederick Douglass: "Who would be free themselves must strike the blow." Blacks in the navy were not allowed to rise to the rank of petty officer, but they served in all stations below, including gunner, landsman, and pilot. The impracticality of segregating the navy forced whites and blacks to work, eat, and sleep side by side. Three black men were on the *Monitor*, the Union's first ironclad vessel, when it sank. Casual surveys of crew rosters late in the war revealed that African Americans often comprised a quarter or more of crews on most ships. Hardly any crews were all white.

Usher Parsons, a naval surgeon, said, "There seemed to be an entire absence of prejudice against the blacks as messmates among the crew." Admiral Dupont wrote that the "contrabands"—escaped slaves—should receive equal pay, as they were "skillful and competent." On land, where blacks served in segregated army units, their skill and competence was often questioned. The fact that two dozen black men received the Medal of Honor in the years during and immediately following the Civil War didn't convince everyone of their loyalty or worth as soldiers. Some insisted that those awards were politically tainted. But in the cases of the several medals earned at sea, there could be no such attempt to detract from the accomplishments of the recipients. In those cases, recommendations for honors were often submitted without any mention of race attached.

John Lawson was one of the navy awardees. Lawson seemed destined for distinction ever since the day his Virginia slave owner threatened to beat him for a slightly tardy breakfast. "If you beat me today," Lawson replied, "we will both eat our breakfast in Hell." At the Battle of Mobile Bay, August 5, 1864, while Admiral Farragut hung from the rigging of the flagship *Hartford* and shouted, "Damn the torpedoes," Lawson was down below manning the shell whip, the mechanism that delivered ammunition to the cannons above. The Confederate *Tennessee* fired an exploding shell into his station at point-blank range, and Lawson was slammed against the bulkhead, grievously wounded. Four of the six men who operated the shell whip were dead or immobilized. When Lawson came to, he and another man, Wilson Brown, rose from the bloody deck and, despite the fact that their blood was still flowing, refused to leave their posts, instead working triple time to fill the shoes of six men and supply the ship's guns with ammunition. Both received the Medal of Honor after they were recommended by their captain, who made no mention of their race, only of their heroism.

In fact, Wilson Brown wasn't recognized as an African American by historians for over 100 years. Wilson was former slave from Mississippi who'd escaped to a Union ship in a skiff. He died in Mississippi in 1900, owning nothing but a home on an acre of land worth $40.

Joachim Pease received the Medal of Honor for his handling of the number-one gun aboard the USS *Kearsage* during its famous engagement with the *Alabama* on June 19, 1864, off the coast of France. His recommendation by Captain Winslow similarly and appropriately ignored his race and focused on his exhibition of "marked coolness and good conduct." Captain Winslow called him "one of the best men in the ship."

But by 1901, navy recruiters were refusing to enlist black men for shipboard jobs. The few blacks on navy ships were relegated to positions like cook, steward, or cabin boy, and their numbers dwindled. By 1919, the navy was completely segregated.

After a very short stint in the Signal Corps doing photography, a hobby he'd picked up in Italy after "liberating" a camera from a dead German soldier, Vernon Baker decided to join the Airborne Division for the sole purpose of netting an extra $50 a month. It certainly wasn't for the thrill of jumping out of planes. On his first jump, he says, "I looked out the door and asked, 'What the hell am I doing up here?'"

Baker volunteered for combat duty in Korea in 1950, but found that the still segregated army wanted to keep him safe from harm. With that Distinguished Service Cross, the army could always point to him as an example of how fair-minded they were. So, he says, they wanted to keep him alive. When asked why he would want to go when he had already done more than his fair share in Italy, he explained that everyone else was being sent over, so why not him? "It kind of pissed me off," he said, "It kind of diminished my role, because how could I stand up and tell people 'This is your duty' when the higher-ups were keeping me from doing my duty?"

In Korea, desegregation was being tested, as was a new generation of black soldiers. But in the 24th Infantry Regiment, the old rules were still in place. The 24th was the last segregated regiment in the army, and was a frequent scapegoat. Private William Thompson of the 24th was near Haman, South Korea, on August 6, 1950, when his unit was hit by a surprise attack. He quickly established a machine gun position and held back the attackers momentarily while his unit pulled back. In the darkness, his fire was so accurate and deadly that he alone was able to hold back an onslaught of emboldened, overpowering troops. Even as he absorbed hit after hit from rifle and shrapnel, he refused evacuation. He was killed on that dark field, and in June 1951, General Omar Bradley, who had denounced desegregation in 1947, personally presented the Medal of Honor to his mother. Thompson became the first black man to receive one since 1902.

Sergeant Cornelius H. Charlton, son of a West Virginia coal miner, took over when his white commander was wounded on June 2, 1951, in an intense firefight at Chipo-ri, near the 38th parallel in Korea. Like Vernon Baker, he led his men up a dangerous hill and took out several enemy positions on his own. His leadership and example rallied his unit three times, and on the third attempt, they took the hill. Charlton took a severe chest wound. From the crest of the hill, he saw a surviving and deadly enemy position, which he charged. A grenade exploded at his feet, but he lived long enough to shower the enemy position with bullets, killing or scattering the defenders. His parents received his Medal of Honor from the secretary of the army. He was the second and last African-American Medal of Honor recipient in Korea.

On the morning of September 11, 1951, Vernon Baker walked into his new office in Fort Campbell, Kentucky. The date marked the first day of the completely desegregated U.S. Army, so Baker was, as of this day, the equal of others in his rank, white or black, and for the first time in his career, as a company commander, in command of white troops. In his new office he found a white second lieutenant who didn't realize he was sitting at Baker's new desk. His feet were up on the desk and he was ready to dismiss the black man who strode in with unusual confidence. Baker ordered him to get up; the desk was his now.

Baker said that the men under his command adjusted quickly. When they defied his orders, they were written up. "I tried not to let my already ample anger agitate the situation," Baker recalled. After all the concerns about morale and the supposed impossibility of black and white troops ever working side by side, the transition, according to Baker, looked easy and sensible. "It didn't take long, maybe two or three weeks," he said when asked about how long it took to gain the respect of white troops. "Most of the troops at that time were not in the army their entire lives. It was a new army. They thought, what the hell, I'm a soldier, he's a soldier, regardless of whether he's black, green, or red. We've got a job to do and we might as well do it." People, he said, began "to know one another, and began to talk to each other instead of at one another."

Meanwhile, outside the gates of the desegregated base in Kentucky, Baker was in an America that acted like it didn't want him. He says he didn't go off base much, didn't cross the lines that whites had drawn across the civilian world. But it was impossible to avoid. When he was trying to buy a home in California near Fort Ord, where he transferred in the mid-1950s, he got the too-common line from a real-estate agent, "I'm sorry, the house is sold," as soon as he met the man face to face.

Desegregation in the military brought him into the world of white officers—the politics, the cocktail parties, the back scratching and jockeying for favors. This was one unexpected piece of serving in a combined army that Baker wasn't ready for, and an environment he didn't suspect he would thrive in. He left Airborne and reenlisted with the Signal Corps as a photographer after the Korean War, even though this meant he would again be a sergeant.

When he moved to Ford Ord, near Monterey, California, he was accompanied by his wife, Fern. This was his third marriage, and his first successful one. Leola, his first wife, the one who'd set him on his path to make himself a "man of means," had moved in with her former boyfriend the day Baker left for the army. Baker's sister Cass let him know in a letter. Leola later suffered an alcohol-related death. Baker met his second wife while in Officer Candidate School. Not long after they met, she was in tears; she said she'd been wronged by a man who left her pregnant. She would lose her job as a teacher. Baker saw a chance to make a rescue, married her, and started sending her checks. She moved to Chicago and stopped writing while Baker was in Italy. An army friend pointed out that maybe she loved the allowance more than she loved him. They later divorced.

When Fern met Vernon, she was supporting two children on her pay as a swimming instructor, but she wasn't begging for help. She was being harassed by her ex, but she wasn't asking Vernon for protection. One day, he ended up giving it to her anyway, during a violent confrontation during which the ex pulled a handgun that went off during the ensuing struggle. The ex left, beaten and bloodied, and stopped coming around.

Fern and Vernon married in June 1953 and had a daughter together, making a family of five. They might have stayed five if Baker hadn't been transferred to Korea in the late 1950s, well after the end of the Korean War. Orphans, many of them the offspring of American soldiers, were everywhere. Almost as soon as he found out that Baker was a family man, an American doctor practically insisted that he adopt. Baker's heart went out to these children, and his wife and girls back home were unanimously for it, so he brought home a daughter, nine years old, half black and half Korean. When he returned to Fort Ord, he took stock of his family and became "amazed at how lucky we were, amazed at how lucky I was." They settled into a routine, until he got a chance to end his career in the army with a "European adventure."

Baker's last assignment was in Germany, where he moved in 1967 and found an army he hardly recognized. His troops were dangerously strung out on drugs, he said, temperamental, uncontrollable, and violent. To someone who didn't smoke or drink, it was inconceivable that a young man would put poison like that in his body. He hated what his job had become: "I would get up in the morning and I had to strap on my forty-five because I realized somebody's going to kill me or I'll have to kill somebody. I didn't want my career to end like that." He left the army in 1968.

But before he slipped into retirement, he took a job with the Red Cross as a counselor to military families. He was sent to Vietnam and once again was back in a war zone. His day on Hill X came back to him in nightmares. "I worked to shake it, to bury the memories of the nineteen men," he would write in his autobiography. At the same time, he was scratching his head over the conflict that raged around him. "I thought it was a bunch of crap. I don't know why we were there. I couldn't see us accomplishing anything by fighting this war. What do we have over there that we have to fight for? . . . I couldn't understand why we were there and what we accomplished. We didn't accomplish a thing." In between nightmares, however, he had dreams of stalking elk, dreams that took him back to his childhood in Wyoming.

Fern was hospitalized for a heart attack in 1986, and passed away soon after. The children had left home, and Vernon decided to buy a small piece of land in Idaho and a cabin that was, he says, conveniently located next to nothing except elk. There he began what he thought would be the final chapter of his life, but he was in for two surprises. First, in 1989, at age 69, he met a woman at the Spokane airport. She was younger, German, and living on the East Coast, but they started seeing each other and married in a small chapel in 1993. Second, the army wasn't done with him yet. In the early 1990s, he became a focus of what Baker called "its own self-examination."

In 1992, Acting Secretary of the Army John Shannon, in agreement with pressure applied by the Congressional Black Caucus, started an independent investigation into why no black Americans had been awarded the Medal of Honor for service during World War II. Rather than let the army check on itself, Shannon asked for proposals on conducting an investigation from historians. Shaw University professor Daniel Gibran submitted the winning proposal.

Gibran and his team of academics, historians, and veterans combed the National Archives for evidence of unprocessed applications, and months later came up empty-handed. That meant that the path to the nation's highest honor wasn't blocked at a high level, but it also made it tougher to award a medal to anyone they now found who might be deserving. If the government and the military made an exception for an African-American veteran, if it bent or broke the rules to put a medal on his chest, it could be seen simply as a political move. The meaning of that award would be diminished. The accusation that the medal had been cheapened by political correctness would inevitably be leveled. Gibran decided that all his recommendations had to follow established precedent.

Finally, after scouring the National Archives, he found one. After the First World War, frustrated that, because of slow paperwork, only four veterans had been awarded the Medal of Honor before the armistice, General Pershing ordered a review of Distinguished Service Cross awards. Seventy-eight of these were upgraded to Medal of Honor awards. Similarly, General Eisenhower ordered a review after noticing a dearth of medals for actions in the Mediterranean. The result was four upgrades to the Medal of Honor. It followed that if the army was in the habit of reviewing awards to correct administrative inefficiency or a geographical imbalance, it could review awards to correct a racial disparity that could only be due to discrimination.

Gibran quickly found ten cases that seemed to beg for review. Nine had received the Distinguished Service Cross, and one—Ruben Rivers—had received the Silver Star. These went before a review board of four senior army officers and one enlisted man. All were combat veterans. One was himself a Medal of Honor recipient. Three were white and two were black. The cases they reviewed had been heavily disguised, with all references to location, unit, and timeframe removed. These ten cases were then mixed in with the citations of ten white men who had actually received the Medal of Honor, and submitted to the review board, which had been told they would review and make recommendations on twenty cases. This sort of "double blind" approach would, Gibran hoped, place their decisions above the slings of anyone who wanted to accuse them of playing politics.

The board recommended all of those who had already received the medal, and seven of the ten who had been passed by—Ruben Rivers, George Watson, Charles Thomas, Edward Carter, Willy James, John Fox, and Vernon Baker.

Ruben Rivers was with the all-black 761st Tank Battalion, which joined Patton's army in October 1944. Patton was desperate for replacements in the French Saar Basin, and told them, "I don't care what color you are, so long as you go up there and kill those Kraut sonsabitches." Staff Sergeant Ruben Rivers was directly responsible for killing over 300 in the short distance between Hampont and Guebling, France. On November 16, outside of Guebling, a land mine disabled his tank and shredded his leg to the bone. He refused a morphine shot, took command of another tank, and led the way into Guebling the next day. On November 19, he engaged a column of enemy tanks, radioing back, "I see 'em. We'll fight 'em." During the battle, he was decapitated by an enemy shell. He posthumously received the Silver Star. The 761st fought all the way to Austria, where they joined the celebrated closing of the eastern and western fronts on April 25, 1945. One of Eisenhower's former aides recommended them for a Distinguished Unit Citation, but theirs alone, among twelve such recommendations, went unsigned by Eisenhower.

Private George Watson was on a troop ship near Porlock Harbor, New Guinea, that was going down. He ferried soldiers to life rafts until he was exhausted. When the ship went down, he was pulled under. Major Charles L. Thomas of Detroit, while serving as a decoy, was struck in the chest, legs, and left arm outside of Climbach, France, but he refused to be evacuated until his men had established their position. Staff Sergeant Edward Carter Jr. advanced alone on a warehouse that concealed a number of German soldiers with a bazooka and submachine guns. Carter was hit three times in his left arm, one in his left leg, and once through his left hand, but killed six and captured two. Private First Class Willy F. James Jr. scouted ahead across the Weser River. He was pinned down by enemy fire for more than an hour, but he wasn't idle. By drawing the enemy's fire, he established the location of their positions. Once he was sure he knew their strength and location he returned across an open field of more than 300 yards to report. He then volunteered to lead the assault on their key position, and was killed while rushing to his commander's aid. These men, all African Americans, received the Distinguished Service Cross, the same medal received by Baker.

So did First Lieutenant John R. Fox, who fought in Sommocolonia, Italy, not far from where Vernon Baker saw his fiercest action. On Boxing Day, 1944, Fox volunteered to cover the withdrawal of his comrades from the town as the Germans fiercely attacked. As they swarmed through the streets, he directed artillery fire. Finally, he ordered a barrage on a set of coordinates that caused the commander to protest: "Fox, that will be on you!" The last words that came over the radio were "Fire it! There's more of them than there are of us. Give them hell!" The Americans successfully withdrew, and when they retook the town, they found Fox's body among those of over a hundred German soldiers.

When the review was done, only one man—Vernon Baker—was still alive. Gibran's team continued research on his select seven, finding through witnesses and records that four of them, including Baker, had actually been recommended for the Medal of Honor. When they contacted

Baker, explaining that they were trying to find out why and how no blacks had received the Medal of Honor for actions during World War II, he was incredulous: "Brilliant, I thought. Next there would be a study to determine why southern states with large populations of impoverished blacks levied poll taxes. From there, perhaps a group of academics could investigate whether Ku Klux Klan founder Nathan Bedford Forest was racist."

No one had ever told Baker he had been recommended for the Medal of Honor. A warrant officer recalled doing the paperwork, but his superiors never followed the regulations that required them to pass the recommendation up to the Department of War. Instead, they got Baker the Distinguished Service Cross. Other recommendations had been similarly blocked, Gibran found.

As Baker learned the facts that had been obscured from him in Italy, the old soldier had the sensation that the past he had escaped by moving to Idaho was creeping back up. He had put aside the anger, he had almost forgotten the bloodshed. He was no longer in possession of his Distinguished Service Cross, the one thing that brought Gibran to his door. After his grandson had discovered it in a box and deemed it "cool," he told him to keep it, with the secret hope that he was "giving away the memories as well as the medal." Now another medal was about to replace it.

Baker cried during the widely broadcast Medal of Honor ceremony at the White House, where his award was presented by President Clinton. He remembers thinking about all the men he lost up on that hill. He remembers how the networks turned his home into "a TV studio," and how little the attention meant to him. But one reporter, who had been there before the medal and stayed after the hubbub died down, got to take part in something most journalists would envy.

One day, while they were talking and eating lunch, Baker asked Ken Olson, who'd written a series on Baker for Spokane, Washington's *Spokesman-Review*, "'Hey Ken, do you plan on writing a book?' And he looked up at me and smiled and said, 'I wondered when you were going to ask me.'" The result was *Lasting Valor,* an account of Baker's Italy ordeal and a powerful telling of his life before and after.

As Baker has met other Medal of Honor recipients, he's found they have something in common: "We don't like to talk about it." He's found that they also carry a sense of responsibility that reaches further than their abilities, and that's something they are unable to let go. "I cannot forget the faces of the men who died beside me," he wrote, "nor can I stop wondering if, as their platoon leader, I am responsible for their deaths." At one point in their march up the peninsula, they learned of a horrific German massacre of civilians at Sant'Anna. Some men were so jaded the news hardly registered. Others were angered and swore to help wipe fascism off the face of the earth. But Baker wondered if he could have prevented it. "Couldn't we have moved faster up the coast and stopped this? Did this happen because of the days we spent on make-work and perfunctory marching, waiting for orders to move into combat?" And then, on the hillside, there was that moment when he thought, "Sixty seconds," believing that's all it would have taken to save two German teenagers from the grenades of his own men.

Valor may be closely tied to adrenaline or to patriotism, but in Baker's case, it seems to be more closely linked to responsibility, a sense of responsibility he learned from his grandfather. He still has plenty to be angry about, but he would rather not, when he's out speaking at a school or being interviewed, focus on that. "Down through the years I've realized," he says in order to explain what happened to his anger, "that we as a population have come to talk to one another instead of at one another. And I think by that, my feeling is, that we as a country have matured. We've grown up a little bit more."

Uneasy Peace

The last three stories of heroism speak to the remarkable scope and diversity that characterized our role in World War II. Tarawa, where David Shoup so bravely led his men under fire, ranks next to Iwo Jima as the bloodiest battle the U.S. Marines fought as they slogged their way across the Pacific. On the other side of the world, Snuffy Smith and his valorous comrades in the Eighth Air Force lived in constant peril during their long struggle to wrest command of the skies over Europe from the Luftwaffe. And the story of Vernon Baker strongly underscores the point that G.I. Joe—that mythic model of the American fighting man—came in many guises, not all of them white.

Let me take a moment to dwell on the missions of the Eighth Air Force. Even though I served in the Pacific Theater during the war, I can't help but feel a certain kinship with those bombing raids launched from English air bases. And that's because of the close professional connections I've enjoyed over the years with two longtime CBS colleagues who, as young journalists, covered the Eighth Air Force. One of them is Andy Rooney, who (as Allen Mikaelian notes) was then working for

Stars and Stripes, and the other is Walter Cronkite, who was then a reporter for the United Press.

From them and other colleagues I've heard stories about how difficult it was to cover that air war, especially during the bleak early months of 1943 when the Luftwaffe was still a very formidable foe. On any given day, 20 planes might take off across the English Channel, and only 12 or so would make it back. Cronkite said that he and the other reporters assigned to the beat had to learn to steel themselves against the temptation of getting too close to the young American fliers. One could form a friendship with a pilot one day, only to lose him the next.

Nevertheless, that did not prevent Andy and Walter from pestering the Air Force brass for permission to accompany the flight crews on a mission. (One of the senior officers they appealed to for help on that request was none other than Lieutenant Colonel Tex McCrary, who later did so much to promote the Medal of Honor Society. Yes, it is a small world.) Permission was reluctantly granted, but only on the condition that the correspondents undergo rigorous training. This included learning how to fire 50-millimeter machine guns, for they were told they would be expected to shoot at any enemy aircraft they encountered on the way over or back. Rooney, Cronkite, and four other reporters signed on for the raid, during which they were indeed ordered to open fire on the swarms of Folke-Wulfes and Messerschmitts that zoomed in on them. And blast away they did, as though their very lives depended on their prowess as machine gunners—which may well have been the case.

Andy and Walter went on from there to other wartime adventures in Europe, which included such milestone events as the invasion of

Normandy and the Battle of the Bulge. They certainly saw a lot more action than I did, which is something that Rooney in particular is not loath to remind me.

As for the 52-year snub that Vernon Baker had to endure, that is a sad and all too familiar story. There is, of course, no denying that the segregated army he served in was an accurate reflection of American society in general. At the time of his heroic deeds in Italy, Jim Crow laws and customs still prevailed throughout the South, and in major league baseball—our so-called national pastime—which was still restricted to white players. The world had not yet heard of Jackie Robinson, much less of Martin Luther King Jr. and the other leaders of the social revolution that transformed America in the fifties and sixties.

I covered certain aspects of the civil rights movement, and had the privilege of interviewing Dr. King on numerous occasions. As I have written elsewhere, I admired him more deeply than any other public figure of that era. One of his sterling qualities was an extraordinary forbearance, which, I suspect, stemmed from his profound religious faith. "Justice delayed," he once said, "is better than no justice at all." I couldn't help but recall that remark as I read about Vernon Baker.

America emerged from World War II stronger than ever, and this time there was no nostalgic push for a return to the "good old days" of isolationism. We had become a global power, the undisputed leader of the free world, and it wasn't long before we had to meet the challenge of a new and different kind of conflict, one that became known as the Cold War. Less than a year after the war in Europe ended, Winston Churchill delivered the famous speech in which he warned that "an iron curtain has descended across the Continent." Among our reactions to the spread of Soviet-controlled Communism in Eastern Europe were the Marshall Plan, the Berlin airlift, and the formation of NATO. But there was nothing we could do to prevent the Russians from exploding an atomic bomb and thus becoming the world's second nuclear power.

Developments in Asia were no less ominous. In 1949, our allies in China were driven out of power by Communist revolutionaries, and in June 1950 Communist forces from North Korea attacked the pro-Western government of South Korea. To counter that aggression, U.S. troops were dispatched to Korea. And so, less than five years after we defeated Japan, Americans were once again involved in a shooting war in Asia.

—MW

CHAPTER EIGHT

Hiroshi "Hershey" Miyamura

KOREAN WAR

*"When the intensity of the attack necessitated the withdrawal of
the company Cpl. Miyamura ordered his men to fall back while
he remained to cover their movement . . . When last seen, he was
fighting ferociously against an overwhelming number of enemy
soldiers."*

— MEDAL OF HONOR CITATION

ANYONE WHO TALKS TO Medal of Honor recipients, or who reads
their citations, will begin to wonder what he or she would do in their
shoes. One may never wish for that kind of test, may shudder at the
thought of the split-second decisions these men faced, but the question
remains. We admire them, we praise them, and we wonder if we have
even a germ of the stuff they have.

Hiroshi Miyamura, who earned his Medal of Honor in Korea, questioned himself in exactly this way during the Second World War. Miyamura's heroes were the men of the 442nd Regimental Combat Team and

the 100th Infantry Battalion, the Japanese-American units that fought during the Second World War. The "four-four-two," which incorporated the 100th Infantry Battalion in June of 1944, was the most heavily decorated unit in the war. But only one Japanese American received the Medal of Honor in the years following the Second World War. The award came only because of great pressure from the unit's public relations officer.

The recipient was Sadao Munemori, born in Los Angeles, California. Near Seravezza, Italy, quite literally on Vernon Baker's right flank, Private First Class Munemori took the initiative when his squad leader was wounded and his comrades were pinned down on a hillside by machine gun fire. Alone, he broke the line the only way it could be broken—with a frontal assault. His one-man grenade attacks took out two machine gun nests, which left an opening in the defenses but left Munemori out in the open. He flew for a shell hole, waved in by two of his squad members, as the entire hillside poured their fire on him. It looked, however, like he was actually going to make it. And he probably would have, but for the grenade that bounced off his helmet. Still unexploded, it landed directly in front of the two other men in the shell hole. Before they could react, Munemori threw himself directly on the grenade.

Sadao Munemori's parents were still confined in the Manzanar Relocation Center, California, when they received a letter from the War Department, informing them of their son's death. Their son had volunteered to serve directly from the camp.

When Hiroshi Miyamura questioned himself in 1944, while in basic training in Florida with the 442nd, wondering if he too could display courage and patriotism on a par with the men he met there, he wasn't however, thinking about throwing himself on grenades. He saw courage and resolve in their very decision to serve, to serve despite the fact that they and their families had been imprisoned by the United States government. Like those he met, he was Nisei—second-generation Japanese–American—but unlike many of those, he had never felt the sting of racism or the combination of insult and fear that came from being forced into a relocation camp.

"That's where I learned about patriotism," Miyamura said of his time in basic training with the 442nd. "They told me . . . that they were sent to these camps and then they *volunteered* for service. That was hard for me to understand. I said, 'Gee, I don't know if I could do that.' Or would have done that if I were in that situation. But they felt they had to prove their loyalty. This was the only way the community could do it. And I could see and understand then that was something they had to do."

Miyamura had grown up in an small, accepting New Mexico community with a few, but not many, Japanese-American families. "I naturally assumed I was an American. I didn't have to prove myself. I didn't know anything about my mother country. My dad never talked about it, so all I knew was what the other Americans knew, and I grew up that way." Miyamura's experience with the men who volunteered out of the camps taught him that he had been taking his freedom for granted. "I learned a lot from them about patriotism."

Miyamura had been born in 1925 and raised by his father in Gallup, New Mexico, a place few of the Nisei of the 442nd had heard of. The town, which grew to a population of 8,000 by the mid-1930s, when Hiroshi was a schoolboy, had two things going for it: proximity to Route 66 (which later gave it a place in the song of the same name) and a coal mine. The mine managed to draw immigrants from both sides of the globe, including Hiroshi's aunt, who established a boardinghouse in one of the mining camps. As the town grew, it became ever more mixed.

About 20 Japanese families called Gallup home when Hiroshi was growing up, but he didn't limit his association to these families alone. The immigrant families of Italians, Slavs, Irish, Greeks, and Germans were all, according to Miyamura, "more or less in the same boat," and so fairly free of prejudice. The Mexican, Anglo, and Navajo populations in and around Gallup had been living side by side and intermarrying for generations. There were episodes of ugliness—Hiroshi says that Chinese people had

been unwelcome in the town ever since one had been accused of rape—
but for the most part the isolation of Gallup bred fellowship.

Hiroshi's father first came to America around the turn of the century,
and made his way to his sister's boardinghouse. He didn't stay long before
heading back to Japan to marry Hiroshi's mother. He would have come
back sooner, after the birth of their first child, but he was drafted into the
Japanese army, where he served two years.

It wasn't until 1906 that he returned to Gallup for good and got a job
weighing the coal as it came out of the mines. After a year, he'd saved
enough to get a start as a restaurateur in town. His and his wife's first establishment fell somewhere between a hamburger stand and a diner, but
they advanced before long to a large restaurant in the center of town.

Their fare was always all-American—not a single Japanese dish found
a place on the menu. Hiroshi's father spoke only broken English, but insisted that his children, all but the oldest of whom were American-born,
grow up speaking only the language of their adopted home. Hiroshi says
he knew a few written Japanese characters, but knows nothing of the spoken language. He was raised, with some deliberate forethought on his father's part, to be completely American. And the kids Hiroshi grew up
with, whether the children of new arrivals or established families, cooper-
ated with his father's efforts, enlisting the young Nisei in games of kick
the can, marbles, baseball, football, and basketball. A grade-school
teacher who found his Japanese name difficult to pronounce substituted
the symbolically American "Hershey," and it stuck, even to this day.

His father was avid about fishing, and the young Hiroshi joined him
on the many nearby lakes and rivers. But when his father pulled out his
fly fishing equipment, his son backed away: "Fly fishing was not for me.
It was too much like work." Casting, which he preferred, was work
enough. Likewise, he stayed away from the horseback riding that was
more than just amusement in this corner of the country: "I didn't like the
aftereffects."

Miyamura says the building where his father established his restaurant still stands, but the lease has changed hands many times. His father, despite his success, had to relocate to a smaller, more manageable location after his mother died. By that time, Hiroshi, 11 years old and the middle child, had five sisters and a brother, and it got ever harder to feed these many mouths after the eldest sister married and left town. Any extra money he had he earned himself, first by shining shoes, then by selling newspapers. When he turned 15, his cousin took him under his wing to train him as an auto mechanic.

In high school, Hershey followed a desire to "be one of the top" in athletics. As he was too small for the football team, he turned to boxing as an outlet for the aggression he'd felt since his mother died. He became a very good boxer, and he knew it: " I wouldn't call myself a bully, but a lot of people did call me that. I just wasn't one to back down . . . I was so cocky I used to wear boxing gloves around my neck and go looking for guys to box."

But he never had any ambition to get into the ring as a pro, or even in amateur competitions. He saw himself staying in Gallup, fixing cars, living a life he knew. He was 16 when the war broke out in 1941. It was then that he joined the ROTC. The draft almost immediately cleared out the mechanics in the Ford garage where Hiroshi had been training without pay, an unexpected boon to his career, but one that he was ready to leave behind when his birthday arrived and his number came up.

Like every other community in the country, large or small, Gallup tightened its belt for the war effort and braced itself for the tragedies ahead. But unlike other places where Japanese Americans concentrated, Gallup left all its citizens in place and in step with their neighbors. Hiroshi says he wasn't even aware of what was happening to the Japanese and Japanese Americans outside of his small town until one day when a train pulled in. The blinds were drawn, and no one but the rail workers got off. But he heard it was full of detainees being sent off to the camps. "I just couldn't understand why they were doing that," he remarked. He credits the people of Gallup, who he says signed a petition, with keeping the

Japanese families out of the camps. "They liked the Japanese," he said, adding that most of the Japanese were, like his father, entrepreneurs who ran key businesses, "and they didn't want to lose them."

Coming of age after the War Department opened the military to Japanese Americans in early 1943, Miyamura was drafted almost immediately. When he got to training camp, he found that being around so many other Nisei was something completely strange. "It was something new to me, and I rather looked forward to meeting more of my kind, and see how they lived . . . I found that most of the boys were from California, and they were brought up entirely different from [me]. Most of them knew how to speak Japanese. They ate more Japanese food than I ever did." He was a little wary at first, thinking of himself as a "country bumpkin," but he formed close friendships, and found that his people had made homes across the United States.

The first order of business for this set of recruits, who were to replace the heavy casualties suffered during the 442nd's Italian engagements in fall 1943, was to clean up their disused section of Camp Blanding, Florida. "When we arrived at the camp it was so covered with weeds that it was like it hadn't been used since World War I. We had to clean up the whole area. There were five-men huts at that time, and all the huts needed to be repaired. So we spent a lot of time doing that before we could even begin training."

Across the street were units of white trainees, separated from the Japanese Americans except when they were off-duty. "That was mostly when the trouble started," Miyamura explained. He didn't see it firsthand, since he didn't drink and preferred to stay close to base, but his comrades would fall into frequent brawls with the white troops, who, they claimed, usually started it off with a series of taunts. Tensions were high. To the white troops, filled with anger over Pearl Harbor and the ongoing slaughter in the Pacific, the men of the 442nd were a legitimate target. The insults and physical attacks, however, only seemed to strengthen the resolve of the Nisei in training.

Miyamura was still 18 when they changed the rules in 1943, allowing only those 19 and over to ship overseas. So his unit left without him, and he was sent to Camp Shelby, Mississippi, for heavy machine gun training. After his birthday, he was attached to a Japanese-American unit on its way to Europe, but was diagnosed with a hernia and separated for rehabilitation. "I didn't even know I had a hernia. Apparently it was just beginning . . . So I went and got my operation, and by the time I went through convalescing, all I had to do was wait a week until the next group was ready to leave. I joined them, and we got aboard ship at Norfolk, Virginia. Anyway, we were on ship and five days out of Naples when we heard that the war in Europe was over." They landed anyway, and Miyamura's job would be to guard medical supply depots and German prisoners being held in Italy.

He was neither disappointed nor relieved, but he did wonder what the men he'd trained with had gone through. The fact that the 442nd was the most highly decorated unit in the war wasn't highly publicized. Nor was the fact that they had broken the German line to reach the "Lost Battalion," a group of white Americans trapped and hammered by German troops near Bruyeres, France, for several days. Certainly not widely circulated was the comment of one of the rescued lieutenants of the Lost Battalion: "We men who came off that hill know that the Nisei aren't just as good as the average soldier—they're better." Even in the Japanese-American community, the awards and deeds of the four-four-two were not widely known. But Miyamura talked to them, and learned about what happened while he was still 18 and stuck back in the States, about how one of the friends he'd made in basic training died, and how another man he'd trained with, George "Joe" Sakato, earned the Distinguished Service Cross.

Sakato was a Californian who was baffled after the army classified him "4C"—enemy alien—when he tried to join the U.S. Army Air Corps. Then he was angered when they sent him and his family to a relocation camp. In 1943, however, when the War Department started recruiting Nisei directly out of the camps, Sakato signed up and became one of those volunteers that Miyamura met who were determined to prove their loyalty. On October 29, 1944, Sakato's all-Japanese unit was surrounded at the base of Hill 617 near Biffontaine, France. As he saw enemy troops take position above him, he yelled for his men to get down, but one of them, a close friend of his and Miyamura's, stood up. He was instantly shot through the head and died in Sakato's arms.

Sakato was blinded by rage and, grabbing a machine gun and a German pistol he'd found, charged the hill alone, determined to find and kill the man who'd shot his friend. He killed twelve and wounded four, but more important, the rest of a freshly inspired team soon joined him, and took the hill. Sakato never expected or wanted a medal for an incident he today compares to a fit of "road rage." Nonetheless, he was decorated with the DSC shortly after his action. The Japanese-American veterans, like the African-American veterans, would have to wait before their heroes were truly recognized by a review similar to and inspired by the review of Distinguished Services Cross awards received by African Americans, described in the previous chapter. In 2000, the review was complete. Sakato and 21 others received the Medal of Honor for their actions in the Second World War.

Once in Italy, Miyamura succumbed to the charms of an Italian girl, who he says he almost married. He found out from the chaplain that the army would only consent if both sets of parents agreed to the union. Once he secured a three-day pass, he made his way to Rome, wearing his best dress uniform and hoping nervously that he could win over her parents and brothers. He did (and the fact that he was Japanese-American never was an issue with these Italians) but winning over his own father turned out unexpectedly to be another matter: "My father said, why don't you come home and think about it? Her parents said it was all right . . . but my father said no, come home and think about it, so that's what I did."

In late 1946 he shipped back to the States, his war service amounting to little more than a work-abroad program. When he got back, he realized that the distance between him and his Italian girlfriend couldn't be made up. "There were so many things in my mind at the time," he says of the weeks after his return, "that I didn't know what I was going to do."

He was interested in studying air-conditioning repair and entered a technical school under the GI Bill. But when he came back to Gallup on vacation six months later, he learned that his cousin was opening a garage there. Miyamura decided to stay in Gallup and work for his cousin. Then he started dating a young woman he'd met before he'd gone off to technical school. After a six-month courtship, they married in June of 1948. She'd been born in Arizona to Japanese immigrant parents, who had moved to Gallup while Miyamura was in Italy. "She was so easy to talk to and get along with that I felt this was the girl for me."

Few things about Gallup had changed, but it had been hit hard by the war. "A lot of my friends went," Miyamura remembers, "a lot of them didn't come back . . . A lot of my classmates left Gallup, and a lot of my friends got killed over there." However, all of Gallup's Nisei who were able—about seven—had served in the 442nd, and all of them made it back. Another of Miyamura's school chums returned with a commendation for his actions as a tail gunner with the Air Corps. The story that had attached itself to Maynard "Snuffy" Smith, the one which had him pulling the pilot out of the seat and landing the plane, was actually lived out by this airman from Gallup. After his commander was injured, he took the controls and helped land the bomber. As Miyamura learned what had befallen his classmates and friends, however, he felt neither upset nor relieved that he had avoided combat. "I wasn't happy or sad . . . I felt there must have been a reason for me not to."

The Korean War was unfinished business from the end of the Second World War. Vanquished Japan left Korea in 1945 to the Russians and the Americans, who divided the administration of the country along the 38th parallel, with the United States caring for the South and the Soviets managing the North. But when the discussions started for an independent Korean state, the Americans and the Soviets naturally disagreed. The UN supported free elections, as did the U.S., but the UN Commission for Free Elections was prohibited from entering the North. Elections were held in the South in August 1948, and the Korean communists in the North founded the People's Republic of North Korea in September. Both governments claimed to govern all of the Korean peninsula. The Russians and the Americans went home.

The surprise attack by the North Korean People's Army (NKPA) came on June 25, 1950. Washington was caught unawares. Many predicted the North Korean troops coming across the 38th parallel were the beginning of the Third World War. The United Nations voted to ask member nations to intervene on June 27, and American troops were on the ground and engaged on July 5. America found herself back at war before she'd reached the fifth anniversary of the Japanese surrender that ended World War II. Only this time, it was called a police action.

Miyamura was called up from the reserves and sent to Japan to train with his new unit. His comrades were fresh out of the reserves, and so his short time in Italy gave him seniority. He was promoted to corporal and put in charge of a machine gun squad. He was too focused on training when he was in Japan to explore his father's homeland. "All I did was stay up in the mountains and train, and that was it. We didn't go out of the compound, although some of us did sneak out and go to the village and drink some beer. That's about the extent of my seeing Japan."

While Miyamura was finishing his training in Japan, General MacArthur, who had received the Medal of Honor in World War II for his command of the retreating troops in the Philippines after the Japanese invasion on December 22, 1941, was driving the NKPA back from their near-total conquest of the Korean Peninsula. His September 15, 1950, amphibious landing at Inchon, about 20 miles from Seoul and hundreds of miles behind enemy lines, was one of the greatest gambles in military history. In a matter of weeks, his men were chasing the remaining NKPA troops to the Chinese border. In some places on the front, the UN troops were looking directly across the Yalu River, which separated North Korea from China. Across that river, China had assembled an army of 300,000. But no one, especially not MacArthur, expected the Chinese to cross over and risk massive U.S. retaliation.

"When they crossed over, they came over real fast," Miyamura said of the Chinese assault that started the day after Thanksgiving, November 25, 1950. "So I was given the order to withdraw from my position and re-assemble down the road." He was so far up on the front that he almost came under attack by the U.S. Navy Air Corps. But he and his troops succeeded in falling back. MacArthur had nearly won the war with one brilliant move, but the Chinese counterattack made it a whole new game.

Miyamura fell back to a position adjacent to the Chosin Reservoir, site of some of the worst fighting in the war. The Chinese kept coming, and Miyamura received orders to pull out before the Chinese engaged them. "When they started straight for my position," he remembered, "I got the order for my men to get down off the hill, fast." The waist-deep snow kept them from moving as fast as they would have liked, and when they got to the road, they found it "jam-packed with all kinds of troops and North Korean people." Nevertheless, Miyamura was part of "an orderly withdrawal," the longest retreat ever undertaken by an American army. He was incredibly lucky—to the west, the Eighth Army was nearly wiped out in the attack. And he was also lucky to be on the east side of the Chosin Reservoir.

The Fifth and Seventh Marine Regiments, assigned to the UN X Corps—led by the same General Edward Almond under whom Vernon Baker served in Italy—were isolated on the west side of the reservoir when the Chinese attacked. While most of the army and Marine Corps troops on the east side made it easily to the port of Hungnam, where they were evacuated by ship, the 8,000 trapped marines had to fight for every step of their 80-mile retreat through mile-high mountain passes. It all began on November 27, when the X Corps was savaged by the waves of Chinese troops.

Marine Corps Captain William Barber was ordered to hold the Tok-tong Pass until the slowly moving column of marines were on the eastern side. He assembled his company of 240 men on a rise above the highway, had them fashion an entrenched position out of the frozen ground, and waited. A Chinese regiment attacked that night, and when they pulled back, they left Barber's force diminished by 22 men. Barber reported his situation by radio, and was ordered to retreat. Barber requested permission to stay. He knew that leaving this pass to the Chinese would spell the end of the 8,000 men making their way up to his position, would lessen the chances of the 3,000 waiting farther down the road for the additional reinforcements to fight their way out, and would sacrifice the wounded in his own company. Barber and his men stayed. After five days of fighting, they were relieved, but by that time, only 72 of Barber's men were able to walk off the mountain. Barber himself had been shot in the groin, but had continued to command from a stretcher carried up and down the tenuous and constantly tested line. The evacuating troops of Barber's company left behind over 1,000 enemy dead. He received the Medal of Honor in 1952.

"During the time we were there," Miyamura says of his part of the retreat, "the weather was so cold, and in the snow, you couldn't get around too well. I think it was really bad for both sides." They were also very hungry—the UN forces had advanced so far, so fast, that the supply lines had been drawn out. So he, along with most of the other soldiers in and around the Chosin Reservoir, were cold, hungry, and bitter to know that they were retreating when they had been, just days before, so close to complete victory.

Meanwhile, Marine Corps Captain Carl Sitter was dispatched from Koto-ri, about 20 air miles south of the reservoir, with a convoy of eight tanks and 100 supply trucks to replenish the underfed marines making their way down the Toktong pass, southwest of the reservoir. The assignment became a running battle as they were attacked from all sides by Chinese. Sitter fought alongside his men and moved up and down the hastily improvised line on the sideboard of a jeep, directing and inspiring their every movement through a series of attacks that made casualties of 25 percent of his men. They delivered their supplies, but found themselves in the middle of an ongoing battle for East Hill, one in which another commander, Major Reginald Myers, earned his Medal of Honor.

Meanwhile, Miyamura, in Hungnam, found that all the privation he and others had suffered in the hills was unnecessary. "All the time I was in North Korea, we never got enough food. And when we got to Hungnan, there was nothing but rations for miles, and that got all of us madder than hell, because those rations never got to us." The UN forces, Miyamura said, were set to destroy them so they wouldn't fall into Chinese hands after the evacuation. A few of the men got to go through the rations before they were destroyed, and went away with armfuls for their units.

Marine Corps Major Reginald Myers, acting under orders to retake the East Hill from the Chinese, said he gathered together a patchwork of an assault team, "the cooks and the candlestick makers and whatnot," numbering about 250. He knew, he added, "everybody was just absolutely frightened to death about the whole thing." For a good reason—they were taking on a force estimated at 4,000. Myer was on the line throughout the advance, barking, making threats, pushing his men forward. As the Chinese saw the advance, they panicked, thinking it was the forefront of a much larger onslaught, and they abandoned the ridge. The Americans had the hill, but now they had to hold it. Myers's men held the position through 14 hours of nonstop combat, during which 170 men were lost. Myers lost most of his own staff during an intense hand-to-hand fight after the enemy broke through the perimeter, and was wounded himself, but held the position with 70 men, inflicting 1,100 casualties before Sitter reinforced him. Sitter was himself wounded during the continued battle by a hand grenade that landed directly in the command post, but he refused evacuation until the enemy, suffering casualties of 50 percent, pulled back. Sitter and Myers both received the Medal of Honor on October 29, 1951.

All the while, Miyamura continued to serve with the force, setting up defenses around the port of Hungnam. "We were given orders to defend Hungnam. We were going to be the last to leave North Korea." As they waited for the trapped marines, news and stories about their progress trickled in.

Miyamura was close to, but always just outside of, the most intense fighting during this retreat. But he had many examples of extreme self-sacrifice close at hand. The American troops, though defeated and sometimes demoralized by the fact that they were retreating, pulled together to make sure no one was left behind. When the marines of the Fifth and Seventh filed into Hungnam, their final goal, they entered a heavily guarded city fully capable of repelling a Chinese attack. But the attack never came and the U.S. commanders saw no strategic value in holding a beachhead at this northern port. Although the American troops were under no pressure, the city was abandoned by the UN on Christmas Eve, 1950.

Miyamura, on the last ship to leave the harbor, watched the explosions that destroyed the last of the ammunition and supplies left behind. The entire city was set afire as the rear guard was loaded up. Then the docks themselves were blown up. As he sailed out of the harbor, it never crossed his mind that this long retreat, and the most severe drumming received by the United States in this century, meant the war was lost. "We were just going to another area. We got off the ship and immediately got re-equipped and headed back up north [to the front lines]. Didn't think anything of it."

As with all machine gun squads, Corporal Miyamura's team was shuffled around from position to position. He never stayed long enough to form strong bonds with other soldiers, and often was left commanding teams of complete strangers. As a result, he got used to being disoriented. "I never really knew where I was at, the whole time I was there. Never cared to know." His unit crossed over the 38th parallel in April 1951, but was forced back, and then fell back again. Finally, he was with the Third Infantry about 30 miles north of Seoul, near the junction of the Imjin and Hantan rivers, at one of the most strategic points along the UN lines. Here, near the end of April, his men braced for an all-out Chinese drive on Seoul. Many of the troops were new arrivals who had seen so many skirmishes and so few outright battles that they didn't take this threat seriously. Miyamura, who had watched the troops build up their forces on the Chinese side of the Yalu River and saw their attacks at the Chosin Reservoir, certainly did.

> I was assigned four riflemen to my squad. Never did get their names. I was given orders to hold that position as long as I could. That was the last time I saw my platoon sergeant. He told me where the CP [command post] was and that was it. That's when they hit us, on the night of the twenty-fourth.

Official Medal of Honor citations do not always match the recipient's memory of the event. The citations are often combinations of the memories of several witnesses, memories that may not match each other, much less that of the actual recipient. No witness can be as close to the action as the recipient himself; but many recipients don't fully remember their own actions, actions often undertaken without thought or planning.

Hiroshi Miyamura isn't sure about the accuracy of his citation, but he can't really say it's wrong either. "I can't remember much about what I did that night. I just reacted." He isn't at all sure about what he calls "the number," that is, the number of enemy soldiers he killed that night. He supposes that the citation is "fairly accurate," but added, "I don't know if they gave the right number I bayoneted." According to his citation, "he killed more than fifty of the enemy before his ammunition was depleted and he was severely wounded." Further, it says he added "approximately ten" to that number "in close hand-to-hand combat."

"I guessed it to be about midnight. We were lit up with flares on the base of the mountain, but that night just before they attacked, you could hear [the Chinese forces] making all kinds of racket, blowing bugles, whistles, banging on pots and pans, then it got quiet and the next thing we knew, we started hearing rifle fire on one side or the other. Then they started hitting my position. And the gunner on the heavy machine gun said it was getting too hot for him, so he wanted another position. That's when I just got madder than hell at him, and I told him to get out, and that's when I went to the gun. I didn't think about what the others were doing or anything. I just felt I had to get to that gun. And start firing."

He says that he wasn't, at that moment, driven by patriotism or by the desire to prove himself as the men of the 442nd had done, but rather by his temper: "I was mad. Even as a young boy, when I got mad I lost control. And I did a lot of things I wouldn't have done if I were not in that state of mind . . . You just don't care. You don't think about what's going to happen afterwards. You just do it because that's the way you think and feel at that time." He referred back to his days when he walked around Gallup with boxing gloves draped around his neck, looking for a fight. "I never was one to back down."

When the machine gun jammed, he turned to the men in his charge and told them to get out. He crawled to the other gun, showed them the way back to the command post, and started firing as they began their trek to the rear. Once his gun was empty, he turned to the advancing enemy with all he had left. "I had an M-1 [rifle], a carbine, and a pistol, so I was just using whatever I could, and throwing grenades, two cases of hand grenades, until I got rid of them all . . . Once I got started, then I lost all sense of time and everything else. I didn't know what the other squad members were doing at all. It was just as if I was in the war by myself." As reported in his citation, "When last seen, he was fighting ferociously against an overwhelming number of enemy soldiers."

Others had abandoned their hillside positions in the face of the Chinese, who were by then well beyond what had been Miyamura's perimeter. But it wasn't the fact that he was surrounded that brought Miyamura to his senses. "What woke me up was our white phosphorus bombs falling around my position. I figured they must think I'm off [the hill]. So I thought I better get off." As he made his way down, he came face-to-face with an enemy soldier. They both reacted at the same time—Miyamura with his bayonet and the other with a grenade. "I felt something hit my leg, I kicked at it, and it went off." He fell backward, but, as he says, "everything happened so fast" he didn't know he had been peppered with shrapnel. He thought he ended up on his back because of the momentum gained by pulling his bayonet out of the torso of the enemy.

When he got to the bottom of the mountain, he realized just how alone he was. He spotted and made for a friendly tank, but ran directly into a tangle of barbed wire concealed by darkness. He waved desperately at the tank as it drove away. His hands bleeding from gashes made by the barbed wire, his leg cut open by shrapnel, and his spirits crushed by having missed the tank, he still made one more attempt to push on. "I crawled and ran another fifty yards or so and dropped. I couldn't go any more. Fell facedown."

He lay prone in the pre-dawn light, until he heard footsteps. "The next thing you know, the sound disappeared, so I started to get up, and in the same instant I heard a voice saying, 'Get up. You are my prisoner. We have a lenient policy, we won't harm you.'"

The Chinese soldier who captured Miyamura was referring to his government's new "Lenient Policy," an attempt at reform of the prisoner-of-war camps. Most of the American POWs were captured in the early months of the war and were sent to camps run by the North Koreans, where they died by the score. At one camp, prisoners had completely lost the will to live by the time the Chinese took over administration from the North Koreans in early 1951, and around 20 were dying every day. The first British captured in January 1951 were sent to this camp and witnessed mass burials of over 1,500 prisoners of all nationalities. The Lenient Policy was supposed to change that—no more forced labor, no more brutal indoctrination. Prisoners of war were to be treated as well—or as poorly—as felons in China.

The Lenient Policy still fell short of the Geneva Conventions of 1949, which had not yet been ratified by China, North Korea, or America. But it probably saved Miyamura's life. Well over 5,000 Americans were captured during the war; only 3,746 were exchanged at the end. Most of those deaths pre-dated the Lenient Policy.

Still, POWs were not exactly lavished with medical supplies in the camps or on the field, and those who were too wounded to walk were left behind. As Miyamura walked forward with a rifle pointed at his back, he tried to conceal his wounded leg as best he could with a determined hobble.

On another part of the now quiet battlefield, a friend of Miyamura's had also been wounded, but he was being ignored. The Chinese abandoned him and ten others, leaving them to fend for themselves on the cold mountainside. The American soldier later told Miyamura how he and the other ten, injured past the point of walking, had lived off the land for ten days while waiting for their rescue.

In the late morning of April 25, Miyamura was concentrated with the other prisoners, surrounded by Chinese riflemen. "We helped each other trying to get bandaged up and fixed up as best we could," he remembered. They knew that they couldn't expect help from their captors, and that a long walk lay ahead. "This one guy who was in the group with us, Joe, couldn't walk too well . . . he was in pain. I was helping him, he had his arm over my shoulder, and I was hobbling. Finally he says, 'I can't make it any more.' I put him under a tree, hoping the Chinese wouldn't even bother with him. And they didn't . . . They just left him there." The soldier miraculously survived, and was able to thank Miyamura later.

During the early part of the forced march, more prisoners joined them until they were 400. Then, over the next 30 days, as they marched all the way to Camp One, Changsong, near the Yalu River and the Chinese-Korea border, their numbers began to dwindle. "They gave us some rations," Miyamura explained, "what they called their magic emergency rations. It was a powder, finely ground rice, millet, barley. And I mean very fine. Almost like a flour. Well, they said you grab some of it in your hands and put it in your mouth and get some water and swallow it. When it gets into your stomach, it swells and makes you feel like you had some food. That was pretty hard to do." Some men wouldn't eat it. They were the first to waste away to their deaths. "They started getting thinner and thinner as we marched," Miyamura remembered, "and we lost a lot of them on the way." Many of these were young men, 17- and 18-year-olds. Miyamura, at the mature age of 24, took it upon himself to convince them that they had to take this food, even if it was both disgusting and an insult. "They said they just wouldn't eat it. After they realized they were dying, they tried to eat it, but it was just too late."

Others took the rations with well water and developed dysentery. Those who took the rations dry, as Miyamura did, barely hung on. Those who were sick or wounded were badly off, but those who were strong and healthy had their own problems: "A lot of the real big fellows lost so much weight, we lost some of them, because they needed so much more to keep them going."

Cold, hungry, demoralized, and in many cases sick or wounded, this miserable column moved north, reminded along the way that as bad as things were, they could always get worse. Miyamura recalls how they were repeatedly mistaken for enemy troops and strafed by their own planes. "So they made us walk only at night, and that was pretty hard to do, but we had to make so many kilometers a day."

Miyamura was, of course, an oddity among the mostly white Americans, though he says that neither his comrades nor his captors singled him out: "The only time I felt uncomfortable was when we went into the villages." The Japanese had occupied the Korean peninsula from 1905 to 1945, and the villages had suffered more than their share. "The local people gathered around me . . . they would gather around me and be pointing fingers and the guards would have to come and surround me, more or less. And that went on from almost village to village." One villager was a profound exception: "I got to a point where I almost was ready to give up, and when we pulled into the village that night—I can't speak Japanese very well, in fact I can't carry on a conversation—but I could in my broken Japanese get across to this Korean lady that I needed some food bad. And she understood and gave me what little she had. That gave me enough strength to keep going."

On the other side of the lines, Miyamura had been listed as missing in action and recommended for the Medal of Honor. His citation was written as an open question, not stating if he had survived the action, only describing how he had last been seen. And it was kept secret even from his wife and parents, who had nothing but the notification that he had disappeared during battle. His medal and attendant papers were locked in a "Top Secret" Pentagon security vault, out of fear that his captors would punish or kill him if they found out what he had done. His status as a POW wasn't even released to the U.S. government until a year after his capture.

Some of the men on the long march to Camp One had nothing to keep them going except the hope that their rations might improve, but each day brought nothing but more ground millet. Real food seemed a distant memory. And when they arrived in the camp, they found they were to be fed nothing but a watery broth for meals. As Miyamura recalls, "We were assigned to nine-man huts, so we had to live and eat and all in that hut. But the way we ate was we were all issued a bowl, a little shallow bowl with a spoon, and a wash basin for one of the nine men to go out after the soup, and come back and ladle that out to the others . . . Never got any rice, it was maybe barley. We would get just a bowl of that, that's it. And I'm saying that those bowls weren't very large bowls. They were *shallow* bowls."

Testing their very sanity was, once again, an American bomber that strafed the camp every night the first few nights they were there. Then the strafing became less frequent, but the planes still flew overhead every day, so the prisoners hid in makeshift bomb shelters. After about six months, the bombers stopped flying over altogether. "Apparently they notified our government that there was a camp there," Miyamura related, "but it took a while to get that across to them, I guess."

After work detail, which was mercifully short and consisted of dragging firewood back to the camp, the prisoners were sent to "discussion groups" for reeducation. The Lenient Policy was supposed to prevent harsher attempts at brainwashing and indoctrination, but in this camp the Chinese communists still felt they had to take a shot at their captive audience. The "teacher" would speak through an interpreter, and here, as the captives would take turns arguing with the interpreter, their attempts broke down. "[The interpreter] started agreeing with us . . . so they would replace the interpreter. And that went on and on. Pretty soon they just gave up. And we didn't have to go hold these discussions anymore. I guess they figured it was no use, they couldn't convert us."

The prisoners' morale was precarious. The younger ones, who had no families of their own, were often the worst off, and most often succumbed to a wasting demise that couldn't always be explained. "But I felt I had to get back," Miyamura decided. "I said, 'I'm going to try to make it back.' I would see some of my fellow soldiers injured a lot worse than I was, and they were still going . . . and I figured if they could keep going, I could keep going." Miyamura's own shrapnel wounds had healed as well as possible under the circumstances. Here again, he was one of the lucky ones. "Many men died from their wounds because of a lack of medical attention and malnutrition."

Home was always one of the topics of choice in the huts at night, but nothing kept the conversation rolling like descriptions of home cooking. "We swapped a lot of recipes. I had a list of all different kinds of food. Italian, Greek, all different kinds of food. That really helped. A lot of fellows enjoyed talking about things like that . . . We had to keep our minds working and try to stay as active as possible. Even though I was on my back a lot of times, I did try to keep my spirits up." Miyamura feels that living through the march and then the camp took more courage, bravery, and fortitude than his Medal of Honor action. "I found out how much the human body can withstand. Basically, it can take a lot of punishment. And I found that your mind plays a very important role in whether you can survive or not. If you give up, you have no hope of making it. You have to have something, a will to live."

The men faced another attempt at indoctrination when the Panmunjon talks resumed, after several deadlocks, in March 1953. Loudspeakers blared the day's news across the camps, always blaming any setbacks on the UN. The men may not have believed the propaganda, but some started to believe that peace and freedom were very far away.

The Panmunjon Agreement, which set the military demarcation line, established protocols for the exchange of prisoners, and ended hostilities, was signed on July 27, 1953. Days later, the flow of prisoners started and didn't stop until December 23, 1953. Many sick and wounded had been exchanged during Operation Little Switch between April 20 and May 3, 1953, but Miyamura had not been among the 684 UN troops repatriated during that optimistic time of the peace talks. Operation Big Switch, which started on August 5, returned 12,773 UN troops. Miyamura's camp was among the first. He could hardly believe that he was going home until he saw the American flag flying on the other side of the demarcation line that August. "It was hard to imagine that we were actually crossing over to our side." The secret war hero was in the last group to leave his camp. They were trucked to a train station, and then walked across a bridge to Freedom Village, one of two villages allowed to remain occupied in the demilitarized zone. As they went over the bridge, no one in the group made a sound.

We were all in a state of shock. It didn't really hit you until we shed our clothes, they deloused us, and we took a shower and all, got

clean clothing and tried to lie down on a cot. And then it finally
hit you that you are finally back. But I do remember the one sight
I saw—the flag flying over the camp, the tents. It was one of the
most beautiful sights. I remember looking at it for a long time.
Crossing over [the bridge], that's about the only thing I can
remember looking at.

As he was trying to adjust and convince himself that he was free, a non-
com instructed him to report to the camp's brigadier general. A thought
crossed Miyamura's mind: Could he be court-martialed for failing to control his men that night on the hill? With that, he walked into a tent where
the general sat with a small group of officers and men from the press.
Miyamura saluted, and the general reached out to shake his hand. "All I
can remember is that when he told me I'd won the Medal of Honor for
the action of the night of April twenty-fourth and the morning of April
twenty-fifth, all I could say was 'What?'"

Given the option of flying home in August 1953 or spending 19 days on
a ship to San Francisco, Miyamura curiously chose the longer trip. His
two years and four months as a prisoner of war had made him so thin that
he didn't want to make a homecoming until he'd had a chance to gain
back some weight. "But I was seasick almost the entire way," he said with
a laugh. "Eleven days I was in that bunk; I couldn't get out of it." He was
slowly discovering his special status as a Medal of Honor recipient, like
when he was allowed to be the first one off the ship in San Francisco. To
his surprise, his wife, father, and two of his sisters were waiting for him.
He spent a few days in Los Angeles with his mother-in-law and had a
chance to further recuperate. His hometown used those days to complete
plans for a surprise parade.

As he pulled into Gallup, a crowd gathered around Miyamura's train.
Each face was a familiar one. Jets flew overhead, prominent citizens made

speeches, the school kids got the afternoon off. A local doctor loaned him his convertible, which took Miyamura through the streets to his doorstep. The crowd respectfully dispersed, and "Hershey" was home. "I just knew I was very happy to be home, to be in Gallup. I missed Gallup when I was gone. I always felt I was a good representative for Gallup, because everywhere I went I told people how friendly the people in Gallup were. I guess that's what makes a town more than anything."

When President Eisenhower draped the medal on Hiroshi Miyamura on October 27, 1953, Miyamura became the only living Japanese-American Medal of Honor recipient. At the time, Miyamura focused on the honor of the medal itself. Truman had signed his citation, and Eisenhower presented the medal. Being honored by two of his heroes filled Miyamura with pride.

It took time, but Miyamura finally decided what he would do in his small town. He'd taken the fact that his mechanic's tools had been stolen as a sign that he should try something else. He worked briefly at an auto parts store, and when his boss decided to open his own store, he offered Miyamura a job selling household and automotive items. "Next thing you know I was there seven years. Had three kids in the meantime." He'd forgotten about applying to schools or trying something new, determined now to let his children have those options: "My goal was to be able to send them to school, college, further their education . . . Fortunately, they did try to better themselves and they all went to college."

The next opportunity came from a friend and veteran of the Bataan March. He had a few things in common with Miyamura, in that both were veterans and former POWs. The Bataan March followed the surrender of U.S. and Filipino forces on the Bataan Peninsula in the Philippines on April 9, 1942, and went on for six days and 60 miles. Between 5,000 and 11,000 men died or were killed, including 2,300 Americans. After the war, this survivor worked as a distributor for an auto company. Miyamura was given the chance to run the company's first service station in Gallup in 1960, and he did so for the next 25 years. He made enough to send his kids to college, but only because he worked backbreaking hours. "I wasn't really selling enough gas," he explained, "but to keep the company happy, I was buying most of my parts and accessories from them." The repair side of his business, the part that took the most time, had to make up for the fact that Interstate 40 bypassed his station. "So the only people who were really helping me were the local people." The police station sent in their cruisers, as did the state police. The local contractors brought in their trucks and equipment during the Interstate construction. "So I kept awful busy," he concludes.

He hadn't planned on retiring in 1984, but the company that owned his store "reconsidered" their western locations and suddenly he was out of work. With an unexpected amount of free time suddenly before him, Miyamura realized that there had all along been another reason he'd kept himself so busy. "When I had more time, it seemed like I thought more about the war than I did while I was working. My only thoughts [then] were of making a living for my three kids and wife. And that's all I concentrated on. Never even thought about the war for those many years."

Miyamura said he was, to his surprise, swept up by memories of "being over there, fighting, wondering what could have happened if I didn't go . . . being confined, being a POW." The whole time he was working, he rarely discussed his experiences with his family—his children hardly knew a thing about his service in Korea. What they know now they've learned from attending his speeches, Miyamura says, that he now frequently gives at schools, events, and Japanese-American community centers.

The reason Miyamura decided to start speaking about his experiences, even though it forces him to relive them, is because he feels he owes a debt to the Japanese-American fighters who came before him. During his brief time with the 442nd, he first learned that the rest of the country was not as harmonious as Gallup. So he took it upon himself to attend every speaking engagement and event that would have him. "If I had my way, I wouldn't be speaking or going to any of these affairs that required speaking. But I feel also I have to let the American public know that the

Japanese Americans are serving and have served. And that we are as loyal Americans as anyone else. I feel I'm obligated to do that. Because I wear this medal."

He was thus relieved in more ways than one when the army reviewed the Second World War's Japanese-American recipients of the Distinguished Service Cross and presented 22 upgraded medals in 2000. He saw men like George "Joe" Sakato, the World War II hero with whom he had trained, receive the Medal of Honor, and he was no longer so alone. There are others who can fill his slot at the speaker's podium, like Medal of Honor recipient Senator Daniel Inouye from Hawaii. "I just regret that I'm not a better spokesperson for my people," Miyamura admits. "I don't know . . . I just can't express myself well enough.

"I feel like a different person whenever I put that medal on. I feel that so much is expected of me or anyone who wears it. You can't act yourself. You have to be more careful of what you say or do," says Hiroshi Miyamura. "I would rather just not be known. But when you do have to wear [the Medal of Honor], you have to act accordingly. You can't be ashamed of it, you *have* to be proud of it, which I am. But it's just not me. I'd just as soon be in the background."

CHAPTER NINE

William Charette

"Participating in a fierce encounter with a cleverly concealed and well-entrenched enemy force occupying positions on a vital and bitterly contested outpost far in advance of the main line of resistance, [Hospital Corpsman Third Class] Charette repeatedly and unhesitatingly moved about through a murderous barrage of hostile small-arms and mortar fire to render assistance to his wounded comrades."

— MEDAL OF HONOR CITATION

THE NAVY HOSPITAL CORPSMAN who serves with marines is an unusual hybrid in the U.S. armed forces. Since the marines have no medics of their own, they rely entirely on the navy to patch their many wounds. The navy obliges by sending members of their medical corps to marine training and outfitting them for ground warfare. These corpsmen often wear marine uniforms, carry marine-issued weapons, and go into the thick of battle as a marine would. Corpsman John Bradley helped the marines raise the flag at Iwo Jima. Corpsman Francis J. Pierce earned the Medal of Honor at Iwo Jima for saving the lives of wounded marines while risking his own. And of the seven U.S. Navy personnel who earned the Medal of Honor during the Korean War, five were hospital corpsmen. Of those five—Edward Benford, Richard Dewert, Francis Hammond, John Kilmer, William Charette—only Charette survived the action that earned him the medal.

Even before he got to Korea, William Charette had seen plenty of the psychological and physical scars that the war left on America's young men. Medical corpsmen finish their training in navy hospitals, and Charette served in both a psych ward and a "clean" (no infection) orthopedic ward in Charleston, South Carolina. "We had a lot of casualties out of Korea. Marines. The others were motorcycle accidents by sailors [stationed in Charleston]."

The war wounds and motorcycle accidents were one thing; the psych ward held its own horrors. "I saw some people who were catatonic, and one who was paralyzed from the waist down, but it was all in his mind. And there's not much you can do. And yes, I did watch electric shock therapy." The war had filled the hospital to overflowing: Usually there were 50 patients in the locked ward built for 25. Some had returned from Korea, some were marines who had "cracked up" during basic training at Parris Island, South Carolina. "When you mixed them all together, it created problems. Particularly with our combat fatigue patients." Combat fatigue, of course, used to be the catch-all diagnosis for what we now call post-traumatic stress disorder.

Neither phrase really explains what those who are suffering experience. "The doctors would teach us," Charette recalled, "there was usually something that occurred that the marine felt guilty about." The patient didn't even have to be a combatant. One patient had been trying to get his ambulance loaded with wounded to the hospital, took a corner too fast, and threw stretchers full of wounded men across the road. One of them died. He'd become overburdened with guilt, but had no idea why. "He didn't tie it to the accident, not at all," Charette remembered.

Seeing the aftereffects of war on the human mind and body didn't put Charette off the notion of serving in Korea. "As a matter of fact, I wanted to get out of Charleston. I volunteered to go, or, I volunteered to go [serve with] the Marine Corps, but that was the same thing." Up to that point, corpsmen were putting in 18-month tours, when the normal tour for a marine was a year, and they were going out on patrols every other night, when most marines were going out every third night. The rules changed to make things more equitable, but this resulted in a dearth of corpsmen, and that's how Charette knew that volunteering to serve with the marines meant serving with them in the ongoing Korean War.

The decision to join up in the first place had been made less than a year before, in the early hours of January 1, 1951. "New Year's Eve. We'd been out partying, and the decision was made: 'Well, let's go into the navy.'" There were five local boys from the small lakeside town of Ludington, Michigan, involved in the pact. They'd all worked on the auto ferries that ran across Lake Michigan, so they figured they knew a thing or two about ships. "And we figured if we waited on the draft there's not much we can do." So they went down to the post office for a pre-entrance and then to Chicago for their physicals. Only one didn't pass. The rest began training on the Great Lakes.

But the decision wasn't just a product of the party and the camaraderie. The Second World War hadn't been over all that long. The memories and the patriotism of that massive mobilization were still very much present, and service was almost second nature for Charette and the young men who marched down with him to sign up.

At the time of the attack on Pearl Harbor, Charette, age ten, and his sister, who was older, were under the care of their uncle Albert—he'd taken them in after their parents died, months apart, when Charette was five. Both children went to parochial school, while Albert worked at a bank. As a family, they achieved peace and normalcy despite the tragedies—a mother lost to cancer and a father lost to heart disease—

that brought them together. When the war came, Albert shipped to England with the Eighth Air Force in 1943. The fact that he knew how to type put him behind a desk instead of up in the air. Charette's sister's classmates signed up right after high-school graduation, and he watched the small town reel each time condolences arrived from the War Department. Meanwhile, his sister studied to become a nurse, preparing to serve overseas as soon as she was able. It seemed everyone around him was pitching in, but there was nothing Charette could do to help but work on his great-uncle's farm, where he'd been sent while his uncle was in England.

He remembers one great character-building lesson from that time: "[My great-uncle] decided my job was to clean out the horse barn. So I went over there and I'm trying to shovel the horse manure out the back door of the barn, and I'm gagging and I think I'm going to throw up. So I go back and tell him I can't do this. I'm going to throw up. He looked at me very calmly and said, well, just keep trying. You'll get used to it. He was so right. I got *very* used to it."

The war ended, Albert came home, and Charette came back off the farm in 1946. During the summers, he started working on the ships run by the C&O on Lake Michigan—odd jobs, making the beds, cleaning the crew's quarters. When he got older, he worked as a coal passer, which isn't quite as hard as it sounds. He used a conveyor belt, not a shovel, and the money was great. In fact, he earned more than his sister, who worked as a nurse. "I was thinking, 'This is terrible, here's someone who went to school for three years, and I'm making more money than she is.'" Even more unfair was the fact that she was the studious one. "I squeezed through. In Latin I got a D minus because the nun liked me." Add to this the freedom gained from working on the boats, and he says he became someone who was "not the best of people."

"I don't know. I just liked to drink beer. And when you consider—I was sixteen, seventeen, when I worked on the boats—we could go into Milwaukee and Sheboygan and they'd never question when we'd go into the bars and so forth." In the back of his mind was the belief that he would go to college, but as of graduation in 1950, he had no plan. "But along came the Korean War."

The terror and heroism at the Chosin Reservoir in late November and December 1950 had made it to Ludington thanks, Charette remembered, to *Life* magazine. The 1951 New Year's resolution that landed Charette in the navy was, in part, a response to this nearly cataclysmic event. In a matter of months, Charette was helping treat marines who had been wounded in Korea.

After his time at the hospital—after he decided to serve with the marines—Charette spent two months at Camp Pendleton, California, learning to fire the M-1 rifle, the carbine, and the .45, practicing amphibious landings, and assaulting pillboxes. Charette shipped to Korea and was inserted into a trench warfare scenario eerily similar to that witnessed by Woodfill in 1918. It was the end of January 1953, and after years of pushing forward and falling back, the Chinese and UN armies were locked in stalemate, and the deadlocked talks had been in recess since October 1952. There were no major offensives, just raids and probing actions.

Charette joined Fox Company, Second Battalion, Seventh Marines, a rifle company, near Panmunjon, the site of the peace talks on the western side of the peninsula, near the 38th parallel. At the time, he didn't know he was joining the marine regiment that had fought its way out of the Chosin Reservoir. Most of the men who'd been there had rotated out. But the Seventh was now holding the line along the preferred invasion route to Seoul, and Charette's company was in reserve in the shadows of three hills known collectively as Nevada, and individually as Reno, Carson, and Vegas. All was quiet at first, with Fox Company performing patrols, laying barbed wire, and digging trenches, but Charette heard that the Chinese had maybe 100,000 men facing their reinforced division of 20,000. "Of course they outnumbered us, but they didn't have the air, nor did they have the firepower." Charette worked with a corpsman who taught him the ropes. Then, in late March 1953, the attack came.

We were way back in reserves, and we were practicing a midnight patrol when all this started. You could hear the thunder off in the distance. And one of the guys said, "Oh my God, that's over there around Vegas and Reno, that's Chinese coming in." And he was quite right.

What they were hearing was the sound of thousands of Chinese troops in a coordinated offensive. It wasn't strictly a surprise attack, but it wasn't completely expected. The peace talks were stalled, but to the Chinese, these hills had no strategic value. They weren't, however, operating on a purely military level. They knew that the American home front had tired of the war. They assumed that by flexing their muscles and filling UN body bags they would gain an advantage when the peace talks resumed. The marines did their best to keep this from happening, but on these three hills, the tidal waves of enemy troops broke their resistance. Charette and his company were informed in the morning that the hills had fallen, and that his company would take part in the counteroffensive by the battalions to take them back. By noon, they were joined with three battalions to make an assault on Vegas. Charette went out with Fox Company's second platoon.

The marines are legendary for their determination never to leave one of their own behind, dead or alive. So the American casualties that Charette saw on the way up the hill—men still hanging from the barbed wire entanglements where they had died—spoke volumes about the intensity of the enemy attack. The first battlefield casualty that Charette ever treated was a man left from the night before. From there, the situation descended into chaos and Charette wouldn't see a moment's rest.

The next thing you know I was called to another area and [another] platoon . . . I don't know what happened to their corpsman, but I was in amongst them and it was decided they were going to be the frontal assault unit . . . When they told us to start going forward I thought, "I'll wait until my platoon catches up." But the sergeant stood up. He had a machine gun and his words were very encouraging: "Okay men, move on out, because if they don't kill you I will." So with those words of encouragement I went forward with his platoon.

The men on the point got farther up than they'd expected, took a casualty, and called for a corpsman. Charette moved up, treating the wounded man at the very edge of the conflict. "Then, at that point they started rolling grenades on us, because they had the high point. I started with one [wounded] guy and ended up with five of them." From there, Charette lost track of time and the numbers of wounded he treated. However, he remembers two things well: At one point he looked up and it was dusk. At another point he asked himself, "How the hell did I get into this?"

Night favored the other side. "They didn't have the firepower we had, and once they opened up with any artillery or mortars or so forth, we'd zero in on it . . . But at night, if you can't see more than twenty-five feet, that's all [your weapons] are good for." The enemy was also practiced in the dangerous maneuver of sending in attacking waves just under an artillery barrage, which gave the Americans a choice terrible to contemplate: Stand up and take the shrapnel, or hunker down and be overrun: "You've got your head down, and they're on top of you."

Charette kept up his grim work through the night, and according to his citation, "repeatedly and unhesitatingly moved about through a murderous barrage of hostile small-arms and mortar fire to render assistance to his wounded comrades." Then, when a grenade landed a few feet from a man he was treating, Charette covered the stricken body of his patient with his own and "absorbed the entire concussion of the deadly missile."

It's difficult to think of a higher example of self-sacrifice than that exhibited by those who protect others from explosions with their own bodies, but the roll of the Medal of Honor is filled with pages of such stories. The grenade is an ugly weapon that creates ugly wounds. It appears without warning, but unlike bullets, its victims usually have time to recognize its arrival. They have time to react.

Those few who actually survive the act of throwing themselves on grenades or in their path invariably say that they never thought about what they were doing, that it came almost naturally. They are, in this respect, no different from many of those who go through more sustained actions—the rational mind often shuts down and something else takes over.

"I could have been him and he could have been me," was Charette's explanation. He had somewhere in his training or in his brief time in Korea ceased to make distinctions between himself and other soldiers. Their fates were shared, their wounds were his own. And even further, Charette *knew*, with certainty, that the man he protected would do the same for him were their positions reversed. And that's what made the following story so funny to him.

A corpsman Charette knows, who earned the Medal of Honor in Vietnam, jumped on a live grenade that landed in his foxhole. The instant death that he assumed was coming didn't—he'd thrown himself on a dud. Charette was with him when he was relating this story to a small cadre of corpsmen, and the Vietnam vet, playing up on the perpetual navy-marine rivalry (which, incidentally, corpsmen are quite often excused from), joked about what he could have done instead: "Given a second thought, I probably could have thrown a marine on it."

When the marines sent in a party under cover of darkness to evacuate the wounded from Vegas, Charette helped them. As they worked their way downhill, however, they found a portion of their trench had been exposed by an explosion. Charette, without hesitation, lifted a man from the trench, carried him across the line of fire to safety, and then returned. He stood with his legs on either side of the trench, oblivious of the intense fire, and picked up a second man for the same treacherous trip. He continued like this until all five men in his care were in the rear, then he returned to the ongoing battle. His medical kit shattered by a grenade blast, he tore pieces of his uniform for bandages and tourniquets. He seemed to be everywhere, serving men from three different platoons throughout the night.

As the battle drifted into a second day, the situation on Vegas produced a second Medal of Honor recipient. Machine gun fire had Marine Sergeant Daniel Matthews' squad pinned, keeping a corpsman from ascending the hill to treat a deadly wound. Matthews was fatally wounded while drawing the machine gun's fire, but continued what his citation called a one-man assault until he dropped. By that time, the wounded man had been evacuated, and two enemy gunners had died at Matthews's hands.

They pulled Charette and the three battalions engaged in the attack off the hill in the morning using smoke. He and most of the others had been up all night. "When we got to the rear," he recalled, "there must have been five acres of dead people. And I think I read somewhere that you feel guilty to be alive when you are among the dead. It struck me that that is very true." No matter how hard Charette worked the hillside of Vegas, there were still five acres of dead. "That's the odd part of it. I didn't think I could do more, but I felt guilty."

The attack on Vegas was not successful. The next attempt, which Charette missed, was. "The next day I talked to a corpsman who came in after us, and he said they walked right up there. The Chinese had simply left. They couldn't afford to hold it." They had never really intended to. "It's a terrible thing to see people killed over a damn piece of real estate," Charette remarked, "that you're going to give back, or one way or another it's not going to do anything." This battle hadn't been for territory, only for leverage. Only for the purpose of inflicting casualties. In this it was successful.

During the battle, Charette had made a name for himself: "I'd been seen by so many people that a lot of things came out about how good I was and so forth." He felt, even then, that his actions were blown out of proportion by exaggerated memories. Two days after the battle for Vegas, he began to regret that he'd made such an impression. The hard-bitten sergeant who had motivated his men with a machine gun "volunteered" Charette for a dangerous combat patrol. "I thought, 'This is unreal. I don't even know these people.' But I went." They both survived, Charette and the sergeant, and the sergeant came away with a promotion. It didn't stick. "While he was operating back in reserves he commandeered the captain's jeep and a .45 and got busted back to staff sergeant." Charette said with a laugh, "So yeah, he was a marine."

In April, Charette rotated to battalion aid, which put him a little farther away from the battles still erupting on the hills around Panmunjon. But although he was removed from combat, he was still connected to it via the wounded. "You were always aware of what was going on on the front lines by the casualties you'd get." Some he said he'd never forget, like the large number of South Korean soldiers who lost their right hands in an unusually short period of time. "The Korean marines got the new type of grenade . . . The new ones were quite smooth, easier to throw, little lighter weight. Problem was, they'd put a shorter fuse on them . . . That was a screw-up. They never should have gotten those grenades."

Another soldier came in for treatment of an unusual wound that a number of doctors wanted to put in the textbooks. He'd been way behind the lines, and a bullet went through the back part of his upper arm and got stuck between his ribs. "You could see it. All the doctors got their cameras and were taking pictures of it. It was nothing life-threatening, just an oddity."

The next phase of his rotation was in June 1953 to a med company.

Battalion aid patched people up as they came in. The med company was a mobile hospital, the navy equivalent of an army MASH unit. Charette was still stationed near Panmunjon, where the deadlocked talks had reached a breakthrough. With the end of the war in sight, both sides started jockeying for position, trying to give their negotiators any advantage. Then, suddenly, at the end of July, the war ended.

The wounded soldiers now came to the hospital in a trickle rather than in waves, and the American doctors mostly treated Korean civilians. One man made a deep impression on Charette even before he entered the med company's perimeter. "You could tell he was one of the elders of the village, and how he survived through the Japanese and the North Koreans, I don't know. But he came up—you could tell he was in a great deal of pain but he stood [with] his ceremonial robes and so forth, and looked very distinguished. I thought 'My God, all the stuff they went through.' How this man could still carry that bearing was beyond me . . . To this day I can remember him coming up the hill to our camp."

As life in Korea slowly returned to something resembling normal, Charette found time to travel on leave to Seoul, Inchon, and through the countryside. The UN trucks were always on the move, so hitching a ride was as simple as waving one down. By this time, both sides were supposed to have disarmed. Charette disarmed himself in a manner outside the regulations, but it was at least one that gave him a chance to celebrate the peace. "I had an M-2 carbine . . . and these Canadians picked me up. I traded them that carbine for five quarts of liquor."

Back at the med company in late September, Charette learned he was up for the Medal of Honor. "It was pretty quiet, and then I found out I was to receive the medal . . . This friend of mine who was on the hill with me, another corpsman, I told him, 'I don't want this thing, this is ridiculous.'" Charette went to his CO, a navy doctor, and told him just that. "I don't know if he pursued it, because next thing you know, they told me 'Okay, we're going to get you home for Christmas.'" It was early December, and Charette had almost completed his year-long tour. A trip home started sounding pretty good, and he forgot about continuing a protest against receiving the Medal of Honor.

He spent Christmas with his family back in Ludington, and soon he accepted the fact that he was going to receive the nation's highest military honor. His family's reaction had something to do with that. His sister's husband had landed at Normandy and had gone all the way through to Germany, earning a Bronze Star near the very end of the war in Europe. His uncle had, as mentioned, served in England.

President Eisenhower presented the Medal of Honor to William Charette on January 12, 1954. Also receiving medals that day were First Lieutenant Edward Schowalter and Private First Class Ernest West, who appeared in a White House photo with Charette and Eisenhower.

Back in Ludington, Michigan, Charette got his parade. "This was the biggest thing that ever happened in my county." But all he could think during the festivities was "Why?" The citizens had gathered up $3,000— in those days enough to buy a pretty decent car—for the reluctant hero. "I put it aside and eventually put in a down payment on a house."

The nightmares bothered him for "a year or two." The nightmares and the guilt. He knew, from seeing the cases of battle fatigue back at the hospital in Charleston, that he'd gotten off easy as far as the aftereffects. A man who had gone through marine training with Charette wasn't as lucky. He'd also fought on Vegas, but was trapped behind enemy lines and was entirely alone. Trying to get back, he killed a number of the enemy at very close range. "Ended up killing one with an entrenching tool, and he gouged out one guy's eyes. This was years and years ago, until recently he never told anyone this, but he used to have nightmares of eyes."

While Charette was bothered about the futility of a war that degenerated into a fight for a few hills rather than a committed struggle against Communism, he, like most Korean War vets, look to the success of South Korea as a reward and justification: "I once said you can tell they're doing good because you can point to their signs: 'American go home.' In other words they're pretty free to do what they wanted to do politically. I have a cousin who was killed over there. And he was my aunt's only son. So when you think about that for a bit, you think well, was it worth it? And after many years I've come to the conclusion: yes it was."

He still had a few months left to serve, but because of the medal, he got to choose his next assignment. He decided to go back to Great Lakes, where his navy career had started. This homecoming turned out to be the beginning of his married life. His future wife, Louise, was in the Women Accepted for Volunteer Emergency Service (WAVES) reserve with the hospital corps, and it didn't take long for she and Charette to figure out that their meeting was going to have a greater meaning. They married in November 1954. When Charette was interviewed for this book, he said they were coming up on their 47th anniversary.

In A-school, the next step past basic training, Charette supervised new corpsmen. But he wasn't planning on staying—he was just biding his time. The remainder of his term with the navy was like a standard nine-to-five job, and he was looking forward to getting out. In January 1955 he left the navy, but didn't travel far. He took a civil service job at Great Lakes in an electronic supply postal section, "getting the mail and shipping it out. No big deal." Mostly, he was waiting to start college on the GI Bill, but one of his coworkers was an ex-marine. "He kept telling me, 'You're foolish. You ought to go back into the service, do twenty, and get out. You'd still be young.' I got to thinking about it, and the wife got pregnant, and I thought, 'Boy this is going to be a long row to hoe.'"

Charette went back into the navy in April 1955, still not exactly sure how he wanted to serve. He was in corpsman B-school, the additional training required before becoming a corpsman on a ship, when he learned about serving as medical personnel on submarines from an instructor who'd done just that. He signed up for sub school and "never looked back." It was, he said, as if he'd "found a home."

It's a different sort of person who can find a home in the cramped quarters of a submarine, and Charette got his start in January 1957, serving with the best of them. The captain and most of the crew of the USS *Quillback* were World War II vets who knew how to discipline moderately: "[The captain's] attitude was, 'If this boat's ready to go to sea, I don't care what you do on liberty.'" With an attitude like that, he got a group of men who were committed, independent, and loyal. Plus, they loved their boat. The engineering officer had been around since before the Second World War and knew his diesel engine "frontwards, backwards, and sideways." The chief of the boat was one of those guys who knew his ship and crew so well an officer would ask him his opinion rather than give a direct order, "because once he told that chief what he wanted done, forget it, the chief would do exactly that, no more, no less . . . That's why you get the idea that chiefs run the navy, and aboard ships like that, yes they do."

By 1960 it had become clear that the diesel boats that had served so well were on their way out. Charette attended nuclear power school in New London, Connecticut, where he went "from two and two is four to calculus in eight weeks." After six months of learning about reactors, he went on to study nuclear health medicine for another six months. At the same time, in 1960, the USS *Triton* was making history with its 84-day, around-the-world cruise, totally submerged. When Charette was done, he joined the crew of the *Triton*, which became the flagship of the Atlantic submarine force.

The *Triton* was the first and only U.S. submarine to carry twin reactors and twin screws. This was early in the history of nuclear-powered subs, and the Navy had originally conceived the boat as a "radar picket." It would work far ahead of the fleet, gathering information about enemy aircraft before submerging to avoid attack. It was, and to a large extent remained, an experimental craft, a bridge between the old subs and tactics and the new age of the submarine as strategic missile platform. Shortly after its cruise, however, it was designated an attack submarine, the original vision obscured by the reality that it and all submarines are sitting ducks when not fully submerged.

When Charette joined the *Triton* in April 1961, he received a promotion to chief, with two first-class corpsmen under him, and one navy doctor over him. He served under the legendary Captain Edward L. Beach, author of *Run Silent, Run Deep*, until he was replaced by Captain George Morin. With each new commander, Charette found, the Medal of Honor in his record didn't automatically earn him points. "If you're a commanding officer and you have a Medal of Honor recipient who comes to work with you . . . Of course they kind of view you a little different. They think, 'What am I going to do if he's a real foul ball?'" From an officer's perspective, that medal can be a little intimidating. How do you discipline a Medal of Honor recipient? "But after they found out I'm not different, and that I'm a good corpsman, and fairly dedicated, I should say, I never had any problems. None."

In October, the *Triton* found a new use as a spy against the Soviets. "We went way up into the Russian area, when they detonated the 50-megaton bomb—that's the largest that's ever been exploded—and we would take water samples and air samples. They were shooting missiles, and we watched them fire the missiles. Since we were fast enough, we could run downrange and watch them retrieve them. I think they knew we were there, but I don't think they wanted to do too much about it in those days." Charette had gone from serving in a shooting war in Korea to serving in a war of intelligence-gathering and deterrence. The Cold War had arrived, with the nuclear warhead at its center.

The *Triton* went into dry dock in 1962 for three years, just before the Cuban Missile Crisis. Charette was on leave in Florida when the tension was highest, but since his boat was in dry dock, he didn't get called up. The *Triton* had been state-of-the art, but now the Fleet Ballistic Missile (FBM) subs were taking the lead. Charette went to FBM school in

Charleston from November 1962 to September 1964, moving to the front lines of the Cold War with the Fleet Ballistic Missile submarine USS *Daniel Webster* in October 1964.

Fleet Ballistic Missile subs are essentially platforms for a nuclear missile launch, while attack subs like the *Triton* are designed for combat against ships and other subs. Where the *Triton* had made a few long patrols lasting more than 80 days, serving aboard the *Daniel Webster* meant that these long patrols in the North Atlantic would be routine. Each of these boats (the *Daniel Webster* was the last of nine Lafayette-class subs commissioned) had two crews, a gold and a blue, maximizing its time at sea. Whenever one crew would come into port the other crew would replace them, the sub would go back out, and they'd get 30 days off, followed by 30 days of classes, training, and general "upkeep," followed by another 65 to 70 days at sea. "But this meant that you'd be ashore with your family usually six months out of the year. That was the good part."

The bad part? Practicing medicine on a ship that was surrounded by water and under strict instructions to stay down there for over two months. Illnesses that counted as routine on shore could be life-threatening here. There was always a doctor on board, but he was typically an intern and a little green: "The doctor would show up in cutoffs and sneakers because he was navy reserve who'd just finished his internship," which inevitably led to the executive officer muttering to Charette, "Take these guys down and get them into uniform."

Fortunately, Charette was spared most of the medical emergencies that can spell disaster at sea. There was, however, one crew member who was struck with appendicitis. The navy doctor was in a near panic, "saying, 'where's our surgical gear, what do we have?'" They had the equipment, but what probably saved the patient's life was an article in the medical journal *The Lancet*. "What they'd done [experimentally] was use a lot of antibiotics—broad spectrum antibiotics—and wall it off. Even if the appendix ruptured, you could wall it off. And then you could do the surgery later at a regular hospital. Thank God I had that, because the worst place to do surgery is at sea, and with an intern who'd watched only two or three appendectomies."

The only things that can make being underwater for two months at a time bearable are a routine and a full schedule. Since Charette wasn't always needed unless someone was sick, he ended up as a diving officer, responsible for maintaining the depth set by the commanding officer. He got the responsibility because he often had more hands-on experience than the junior officers who rotated out frequently. During one patrol, Charette had been reading the Geneva Convention, and said, in passing, that medical corpsmen shouldn't be "enabling a man of war." The treaty insisted that they stick to medical duties. "So of course this lieutenant went and told the captain what I was talking about, and all the captain had to say was 'You tell Charette as soon as we go to war, I'll take him off dive.'" It was this kind of humor that took some of the tension off the fact that these men were, day after day, preparing for the end of the world. Amazingly, during all his years underwater, Charette says he only saw one man crack under the pressure.

In March 1968, Charette left the *Daniel Webster* and transferred to the naval hospital in Orlando, Florida. "You only have to do so much sea duty. I had a great deal of sea duty in back of me, and I never did get a complete tour of shore duty, so they put me ashore." He rotated back to sea duty with the USS *Simon Bolivar* in December 1971. While he was "riding" this FBM, he considered serving with the marines again, which would have put him in Vietnam. He "always felt that the people who served there were very honorable," and he would have joined them if the war hadn't ended before his term with the *Simon Bolivar* was up. He would have gone even though he questioned why the United States was fighting there. "I've always felt we could have talked to Ho Chi Minh" and reached an agreement. "Instead, we went to war for seven years."

When he finished his time on the *Simon Bolivar,* he returned to the hospital in Orlando in August 1975, where he ended his navy career on dry land in 1977. Since then, retirement has been fairly busy. After he realized that he'd spent nearly four years of his life completely submerged, Charette pursued second careers—carpentry, horticulture—that kept him outside. His wife opened up a crafts shop, and he worked for her for a while.

Charette's local paper recently ran a series honoring America's veterans. "They had a big thing about World War One, World War Two, and then they skipped right over to Vietnam . . . I don't understand that, because 54,000 Americans lost their lives in Korea . . . And you're talking about not quite three years . . . So your odds of getting killed in Korea are a hell of a lot greater [than in Vietnam] . . . And there are still eight thousand missing from the Korean War." That's why Charette's car still displays the bumper sticker "Korea: The Forgotten War."

Aside from attending the occasional get-together of fellow recipients, Charette's life doesn't have much to do with the medal he thinks he didn't deserve. But whether he deserved it or not, he recognizes one benefit it has brought: Without the medal, he wouldn't have had the choice of returning to Great Lakes after Korea. "So without the medal I wouldn't have met my wife, and that's probably one of the greatest things that ever happened to me."

Still, there has been one problem with his citation that has always bothered him. He says it has a serious factual error that has never been fixed. "It says I removed my bulletproof vest and put it on somebody . . . I did not take off a bulletproof vest. I had a jacket, and I was treating the guy for shock, and what I did was I put my jacket on him. This was the end of March and it was still very cold at night. And somehow that got misinterpreted and whatever." He's tried to get the citation corrected, but to no avail.

"My wife hates this, but it's a fact. I was originally written up for the Navy Cross . . . I was thinking it would get pushed down, maybe to a Silver Star. But instead of getting pushed down, it got pushed up. And I've often wondered why. You've got four dead corpsmen," he continued, "and if I don't get the medal, there'd be no live corpsmen out of the Korean War . . . I don't know. It's just a thought."

To Charette, it was never a matter of whether he was brave or not, heroic or not. It always ended up being a matter of degree. "Each man has a breaking point," he remarked. In the hospital, on the submarine, in Korea, he had seen men past their breaking points. He's just someone whose breaking point has never been reached.

From the Forgotten War to the
Living-Room War

At the time that William Charette risked his life to rescue his wounded comrades, U.S. troops had been bogged down in Korea for nearly three years, and the mood back home was one of weary impatience. Many Americans were counting on the new president, Dwight Eisenhower, to bring an end to the war, even if the terms of the truce were not all that satisfactory. And that is precisely what Ike did. He chose to settle for a tie in Korea rather than push for the decisive victory that had once been our objective. And in the years that followed—as Charette and the other veterans who served there would discover to their regret—the Korean War soon faded off our radar screens and all but disappeared down a memory hole.

I had occasion to look back on that war in 1997 when I was the correspondent on a series of historical documentaries called *The Twentieth Century* that CBS News produced for cable television. The programs were broadcast on the A&E Channel, and then later on its sister operation, the History Channel. The one we put together on Korea was basically an overview of the war structured around interviews with some of the men who had fought there. We called that program *The Forgotten War,* and my on-camera open began with these words:

"One way to memorialize a war is by the songs it inspires. 'It's a Long Way to Tipperary' from World War I. 'Praise the Lord and Pass the Ammunition' from World War II. 'Where Have All the Flowers Gone?' from Vietnam. There are no songs about the Korean War."

There are a number of reasons why the Korean War has been the victim of historical neglect. Coming so soon after World War II, it was bound to be eclipsed in the long shadow cast by that colossal conflict. And from the other direction—the future—it was destined to be overshadowed by Vietnam, for even though Korea was an unpopular war, it did not arouse the passions and protests that tore the country apart during our tragic misadventure in Vietnam. Finally, there's the fact that we neither won nor lost the Korean War. As I said in that *Twentieth Century* broadcast, "Nobody cheers for a tie."

By the time the war in Korea ended, our involvement in Vietnam was already looming on the horizon. Following the collapse of French forces at Dien Bien Phu in 1954, we took over the burden of resisting Communist aggression in Southeast Asia. When the Eisenhower administration made the decision to support the fragile pro-Western government in South Vietnam, it backed up the pledge with millions of dollars in aid and a few hundred military advisers. John F. Kennedy sharply escalated the commitment. During his presidency, the number of U.S. troops in Vietnam swelled to nearly 17,000.

Then in 1965 came the huge buildup in U.S. combat forces as President Lyndon Johnson made the fateful decision to transform the conflict into an American war. From that point on, there was no turning back. Over the next two years, the escalations proceeded at such a terrible pace that by the end of 1967 there were more than 500,000 Americans in Vietnam. And with the corresponding rise in casualties came an increase in the antiwar demonstrations back home. For by then, Vietnam had become a national obsession, the most divisive ordeal to afflict America since the Civil War.

—MW

CHAPTER TEN

Dwight Johnson

VIETNAM WAR

"Johnson's tank, upon reaching the point of contact, threw a track and became immobilized. Realizing that he could do no more as a [tank] driver, he climbed out of the vehicle, armed only with a .45 caliber pistol."

— MEDAL OF HONOR CITATION

DWIGHT JOHNSON HAD GROWN UP, to use his own words, as a "good boy." Explorer Scout. Altar boy. Good grades, active in choir and drama. Extremely bright, with an army GT rating equivalent to an IQ of 120. The E. J. Jefferies Homes, in the heart of Detroit's Corktown district, wasn't the easiest place to grow up, so "Skip," as everyone called him, learned how to run. "Don't you fight, and don't let them catch you" was his mother's refrain for him to remember whenever he had a confrontation. The only time he fought was on one occasion when older boys set upon his younger brother, and the anger came pouring out. The neighbors had to pull a kicking and screaming Skip away from the fight.

His mother, Joyce Alves, was a single mother of two, separated by an extradition order from her Jamaican-born husband, who was Skip's step-father and the only father he'd ever known. She worked as a nurse at an Ann Arbor VA hospital, a strong, nurturing figure to her patients and to her boys. Dwight Johnson was drafted in July 1966, just months after his graduation from high school. Six days after his first and last battle in Vietnam, he was back at his mother's home, in the last week of January 1968.

He'd missed the Tet Offensive, the January 30 across-the-board attack on American installations, by a hair's breadth, and his buddies back in Detroit thought it was good sport to tease him about how he'd gotten off easy. He never contradicted them. In fact, he agreed with them, insisting that nothing had happened during the war. He tried to appear unaffected and sociable. Those who didn't know him well couldn't tell that anything was wrong. He seemed to be filling up his days with as much activity as possible. No one knew he was having nightmares. One friend said, however, that he had color slides of dead Vietcong in his room.

In the fall, Johnson started trying to get a job, and his cousin Thomas Tillman got to see a side of him he didn't know existed. Johnson was a friendly, gregarious, outgoing guy, a practical joker. But when he tried for a job, Tillman said, "He'd just sit and mumble a few words when they'd ask him questions. It was like he felt inferior." He only tried for the jobs that had minimal qualifications, even though he'd qualified as a tank driver in the army. And even then, he got nowhere. "For two months we went around to place after place and got doors slammed in our face . . . People gave him a lousy break. Nothing happened decent to him."

Johnson assumed that the army was done with him until two military police came one day to his door in October 1968. They had a few questions but didn't stay long. They were especially interested in finding out if Johnson had been arrested since his discharge. They left, and the phone rang moments later. The man on the other end was calling from the Pentagon. Dwight Johnson was to receive the Medal of Honor, directly from President Johnson, on November 19, 1968.

This was huge news in Michigan, which had produced no Medal of Honor recipients since Korea. To reporters, Johnson gave no hint of the struggles he'd been through since he got back. According to the local papers, he had a job as a lineman for Michigan Bell Telephone Company. In actuality, he'd only just started the interview process. To another reporter, he remarked that he wanted to get into computer programming through the GI Bill, something that he had never mentioned before.

"I don't know how many I killed," he said in response to a reporter's question. "I wasn't thinking. I wasn't counting. I was just shooting." After the battle, he said, "They put me in a helicopter and flew me back to the base hospital where I was in shock for about ten hours."

President Johnson had used previous Medal of Honor ceremonies to vilify the war protesters. This time, however, with the peace talks in Paris between the United States and North Vietnam moving forward, and Johnson's administration about to leave the White House, he chose to focus on the distant possibilities of peace and national unity as he presented five medals to five Vietnam veterans. "In this company we hear again, in our minds, the sound of distant battles. This room echoes once more to those words that describe the heights of bravery in war—above and beyond the call of duty . . . These five soldiers, in their separate moments of supreme testing, summoned a degree of courage that stirs wonder and respect and an overwhelming pride in all of us."

Dwight Johnson stood at attention as his citation was read, staring straight at President Johnson. As the president draped the medal around his neck, he whispered, "Thank you." Dwight Johnson said his muscles "jumped like frogs." Then, when he saw his mother in the reception line, he broke down in tears. "Honey," she asked him, "what are you crying about? You've made it back." During the ceremony, the *Detroit Free Press* reporter watched Dwight Johnson's younger brother: "Twelve-year-old

David Alves of Detroit had to stand so he could see. And he wanted to tell everybody: 'That's my big brother.'"

Receiving the medal that day with Dwight Johnson was Sammy Davis, who manned a howitzer single-handed, fired three rounds across a river into an enemy position despite being wounded several times, and swam across the river on an air mattress to rescue three soldiers trapped on the opposite bank. Once there, according to his citation, "he stood upright and fired into the dense vegetation to prevent the Vietcong from advancing." James Allen Taylor became a Medal of Honor recipient when he rescued five men from a burning armored vehicle just before it exploded, running through intense machine gun and mortar fire. Taylor then killed a Vietcong machine gun crew and made his way to the evacuation site, where the enemy destroyed another vehicle. Again, Taylor pulled the wounded from the flames. Gary Wetzel, a helicopter gunner trapped on the ground, carried out a series of rescues and successfully repelled enemy troops after he'd lost an arm to a rocket blast. Even without his arm, he thought he could help his crew chief save his commander. He lost consciousness on his way, but woke up and made it to the side of the wounded officer. As he and his crew chief dragged the commander to a nearby dike, he passed out again from loss of blood.

Also being presented with a Medal of Honor that day that was a man remarkable not only for his action, but because he was one of a handful of chaplains who have received the Medal of Honor. Charlie "Angelo" Liteky was with a search-and-destroy mission when his company was ambushed and pinned down. It was his first time in combat. Seeing two wounded men, he interposed himself between them and the machine gun fire that had taken them down, and evacuated them during a respite in the fighting. Throughout the night, he made trips between the evacuation point and the wounded and dying. He stood upright to direct helicopters and he crawled to the casualties. He made it to one grievously wounded soldier with bullets whizzing directly above his head and pulled him onto his chest. He then inched his way back to the evacuation point using only his fingers and heels for 30 yards. By the time he was done, he'd saved the lives of 20 men. "When Captain Liteky went out there the first time, we knew we'd never see him again," one soldier told television reporters. "And by the end of that day we just knew he could walk on water." In 1986, Liteky left his medal at the Vietnam Veterans War Memorial in Washington, D.C., along with a letter to President Reagan protesting Reagan's Central American policies.

After the White House ceremony, Johnson once again was certain that the army was done with him. But the army was suddenly determined to see this African-American hero in uniform as a recruiter. To Johnson, the offers made by the army seemed too good to be true, definitely better than anything he'd seen during his months-long fruitless job hunt. Within a month, he'd signed up for a three-year contract as a recruiter. "Personally," one army employee who worked with Johnson told a reporter, "I think a lot of promises were made to the guy that couldn't be kept. You got to remember that getting this guy back into the army was a feather in the cap of a lot of people."

The pace of Dwight Johnson's life quickened, and he readily adjusted. In January 1969 he married Katrina May, the woman he'd been seriously dating since his return. The Pontchartrain Hotel in Detroit donated a bridal suite to the couple, and then they were off to Nixon's inaugural. In February, he was feted at a dinner in Detroit cosponsored by the Ford Motor Company and attended by Governor Milliken, Mayor Cavanagh, and General William C. Westmoreland, army chief of staff, who remarked, "The unsurpassed heroism of this Medal of Honor winner has reserved for him a special permanent place in the annals of history." Johnson met the ball players at Tiger Stadium, and saw Washington Boulevard renamed (briefly) Dwight Johnson Boulevard. Even at the time, Johnson's father-in-law, Leroy May, who by all accounts loved Dwight like a son, thought this whirlwind of activity wouldn't lead to happiness. His daughter and son-in-law were, he felt, like a couple of kids, getting "too much too soon."

Dwight Johnson quickly learned what it meant to have connections. He told a hometown reporter that what he wanted more than anything was to see the return of his stepfather, Brenton Alves, separated from Joyce, Dwight, and Brenton's son David, for 12 years.

Brenton had first come to the United States in 1949 as an agricultural worker from his native Jamaica, but had skipped out on his contract to come to Detroit. He returned to Jamaica, but before long he was back in the United States on another agricultural contract. Again he skipped out. Soon after, he married Joyce. Four years later, despite the marriage, despite the fact that he had a son, he was arrested and deported.

Johnson's wish was quoted in the *Detroit News*: "Nothing would make me happier than getting them back together. Maybe now that I've done something for my country, my stepfather can return." That was all he needed to say. After a 12-year bureaucratic impasse, a Michigan senator stepped forward. The law permitted the U.S. attorney general to waive an exclusion from the immigration quota if the admission was not contrary to national welfare, safety, or security, and Mr. Alves was a threat to none of these. Two days after the *Detroit News* quoted Johnson, they had occasion to quote a very satisfied Joyce Alves: "I was on top of the world with my son receiving the medal and I'm even happier now." Her quotation and a few words of thanks from Johnson to "all these nice people," appeared beneath the headline: A HERO GETS HIS WISH—HIS DAD WILL RETURN. Johnson called receiving the medal the "proudest moment of his life," but this was by far "the happiest."

Johnson's life had become the parade that was pointedly denied to other Vietnam vets, but he felt the army was using him. He believed that it was only the combination of his skin color and the Medal of Honor that created the constant demand for appearances. He could reach out to the young black men of Detroit in a way no white recruiter could. But what would happen to those young men when they shipped to Vietnam? He was deeply conflicted about his work, especially after one of his appearances was picketed by black militants who called him an "electronic nigger," a robot who did what he was told. He felt that when he appeared at the Lion's Club, the Rotary Club, or the Chamber of Commerce, he was only there because of the Medal of Honor. No black man from the projects got there through hard work, not in his experience.

He and Katrina bought a house in a better section of Detroit that had mortgage payments almost twice what they previously paid in rent. They couldn't quite afford it on Johnson's army salary, but it felt like something they should have. Johnson had become very good at appearing to be happy and successful. He laughed, and he was relentless with his practical jokes. When his son Dwight Christopher Johnson was born in 1969, Dwight couldn't resist needling his mom. Katrina had been to the hospital several times already—false alarms. Everyone in the family was a little on edge, waiting for the big event. One morning Dwight came over to his mother's house, as he often did. Brenton was at work, and Joyce made her son breakfast. He finished, talking as he always did about the little details of his life. Then, once he was done, he turned and said, "Oh, by the way, Katrina had the baby."

The practical joker also couldn't resist sending his wife back and forth, from the crib to the bed, by making the sounds of a baby crying. She wondered for a long time why she would hear the baby cry, only to find him sound asleep when she got there.

Dwight made friends with the neighborhood kids, who revered him whenever he came down to the playground to play basketball. And one neighbor remembered how he would wrestle for hours with her children in their backyard. His schedule at the recruiting office allowed him plenty of free time—his work mostly consisted of making public appearances.

Meanwhile, bills were piling up at an alarming rate. The lifestyle his celebrity seemed to demand didn't fit with his army salary. In fact, the two were miles apart. Johnson bounced a check for $41 at a grocery store, but a prominent black lawyer made up the difference. Johnson was habitually picking up all the tabs, and filling up his credit cards, but barely scraping by. As he fell deeper into debt, his feeling that the army was exploiting him grew. At the same time, he was still carrying around a terrific psychological burden from the war, and no one knew. "He never talked about it. It was like pulling teeth to get him to talk about it," remembered his father-in-law. His wife knew, but not because he was opening up to her. She learned quickly that whenever she had to awaken her husband, it was better to do it from the other side of the room. He could be dangerous when startled.

The cracks in the life that had been thrust upon him started to show after he had been a recruiter for about a year and a half, in summer 1970. He was by then missing meetings and recruiting appearances so frequently that the army assigned someone as an escort just to make sure he showed up. Neighbors called the police on him when he threatened to come over there and shoot them all because of a barking dog. He was tightly wound and complained of pains in his stomach. He finally went to see a doctor about his stomach pains and was diagnosed with bleeding ulcers and referred for psychiatric examination. In September 1970 Dwight Johnson was sent to the Valley Forge Army Hospital in Pennsylvania for further examination and treatment. Finally, he started talking to a psychiatrist about his time in Vietnam and the day he earned the Medal of Honor.

Johnson went through basic training at Fort Knox, Kentucky. One of his friends remembered a day in training when a "wise guy" asked him what NAACP stood for. Dwight told him, but the white soldier told him he was wrong—it stood for "Niggers Acting As Colored People." Witnesses to this provocation tensed up and waited for a fight, but Johnson laughed it off.

Johnson formed lasting friendships in basic training. He got drunk for the first time in his life in Fort Knox—and then got arrested for the first and only time for his drunken behavior. He was soon sent to Vietnam, where the tank duty to which he had been assigned brought him close to the four men in his crew. It was his first time away from home and he was getting along.

On January 14, 1968, eight days before he was due to ship home, Specialist Fifth Class Johnson was assigned to a new tank. He was given no reason for the change. The following day, he was driving his newly assigned tank in a column near Dak To, not far from Cambodia. In this column was his old tank, manned by the soldiers with whom Dwight had spent the last year, and two other tanks. They were heading toward an ongoing battle when a series of rockets flew from the trees and a battalion-sized enemy force appeared from nowhere. Two tanks, including the one Johnson would have been in, took direct hits, while Johnson's tank threw a track. Johnson looked to the side to see his former tank ablaze.

"No one who was there could ever forget the sight of this guy taking on a whole battalion of North Vietnamese soldiers," said one witness. With only a .45 caliber pistol, Johnson leaped from the safety of his own vehicle and ran through 60 feet of crossfire to reach the burning tank. He pulled a barely recognizable but still breathing crew member from the turret and carried him to the ground. At that moment, the ammunition exploded, turning the tank inside out. "When the tank blew up, Dwight saw the bodies all burned and black, well, he just sort of cracked up," the witness told a reporter years later.

He dove into the attack with only his .45. He kept running into the thick of the fight and firing until his clip was spent. He then turned around, returned to his tank, got a submachine gun, and continued the one-man battle. When he ran out of ammunition, he turned his rifle into a club and killed a Vietcong soldier with the stock.

For 30 minutes he continued, firing from the .50 caliber gun atop his tank, reloading and using his pistol at close range, and assisting in firing the main gun of his tank. At any time, a bullet or rocket could have killed him, but one incident during this sustained action would perpetually remind him of how close he'd come. Running through the jungle, he came face-to-face with a Vietcong soldier with his rifle raised to Johnson's chest.

Johnson watched him pull the trigger, and heard the click of a misfire. He quickly killed his would-be killer, and continued to fight.

Dwight killed between five and twenty men that day. No one knows for sure how many. He wouldn't stop fighting. He tried to kill the prisoners. He was held down and given shots of morphine. They took him away from the battlefield to a hospital in a straitjacket.

Six days later, he was back in Detroit.

William Charette and countless others have spoken about survivor guilt. Johnson had the guilt of surviving coupled with the knowledge that he would have died along with his friends in his original tank, but for the army's reassignment. He also had the experience of what officials in Vietnam called a "personal kill." Hardly any soldier, no matter how hardened, can walk away from a face-to-face killing like this without being affected. On top of that, he had the memory of the enemy's rifle pointed at his chest and the sound of the click. Everyone at the scene of the battle could see that he was highly disturbed by what he'd just experienced. At home, however, no one knew what he'd just been through and no one could even approach understanding what had happened to him. According to Dwight Johnson's father-in-law, "He always said he thought he should have died over there. He said he couldn't understand why he didn't."

In summer of 1970, more than two years after that day near Dak To, Dwight Johnson agreed to inpatient psychiatric treatment at the Valley Forge Army Hospital in Pennsylvania. Valley Forge was a joint orthopedic and psychiatric facility, with acres of wounded spread throughout seven miles of labyrinthine hallways. Because of his record and high visibility, Johnson was placed in the hands of the division's chief psychiatrist. The diagnosis: depression. The cause: post-Vietnam adjustment problem.

He was told that treatment would take some time, but he was given 30 days' leave from the hospital on October 16, 1970. He didn't come back until January 21, 1971. He'd spent his time AWOL, hanging out with his friends, shooting baskets with the neighborhood kids, and getting very good at dodging calls from the army and his creditors. When he returned to the hospital, he had a hearing for his absence. Not only were the charges dismissed, but he was given all his back pay. The reason given for this leniency was his exceptional war record.

On his first night back at Valley Forge, Johnson's superiors pulled him out of his hospital gown, put him in a dress uniform, and drove him out to speak at a nearby event. When he got back to the hospital that night, he warned the master of his ward that if they ever tried that again, he would go AWOL permanently.

Johnson's treatment began in earnest. "Since coming home from Vietnam," the chief psychiatrist recorded, "the subject has had bad dreams. He didn't confide in his mother or wife, but entertained a lot of moral judgement as to what happened at Dak To. Why had he been ordered to switch tanks the night before? Why was he spared and not the others? He experienced guilt about his survival. He wondered if he was sane. It made him sad and depressed."

The chief psychiatrist also wrote, "In first interviews he does not volunteer information. He related he grew up in a Detroit ghetto and never knew his natural father. He sort of laughed when he said he was a 'good boy' and did what was expected of him . . . In general, there is evidence the subject learned to live up to the expectations of others while there was a build-up of anger he continually suppressed." He may have suppressed that anger, but he was aware of it. That's why he was afraid. The chief psychiatrist wrote of one of their sessions:

The subject remembered coming face to face with a Vietnamese with a gun. He can remember the soldier squeezing the trigger. The gun jammed. The subject has since engaged in some magical thinking about this episode. He also suffers guilt over surviving it, and later winning a high honor for the one time in his life when he lost complete control of himself. He asked: "What would happen if I lost control of myself in Detroit and behaved like I did in Vietnam?"

On March 28, 1971, Johnson left the hospital with a three-day pass that allowed him to travel to Philadelphia. Within a few days, he was in Detroit, AWOL again. The army decided not to prosecute him or force him back into treatment. "How can you take punitive action against a Medal of Honor holder?" one army official asked. When his car was repossessed, he cashed his back pay and bought a used car. He took out a loan from the credit union. He changed his phone number. He stayed at home and slept or watched TV.

There were a number of disquieting events on the news that month. Lieutenant William Calley was convicted of the murder of 22 Vietnamese civilians the day after Johnson left the hospital. On April 23, approximately 800 protesters with the Vietnam Veterans Against the War "returned" their medals to the U.S. Capitol in an emotional display that was reported around the world. In the week following, Sergeant Rogers Mobley, an air force recruiter, was stabbed to death in public by a young man who screamed, "He's sending people to Vietnam! He's got to die!"

On April 28, Johnson took his car into the shop and took his wife to the hospital. His car needed new brakes, and his wife had to have an infected cyst removed. He had no money to pay for either, but promised the hospital that he would be back with the $25 deposit. The car he simply left in the shop for the time being. With his wife in the hospital, he was alone in their home—which was about to be foreclosed after nine months of nonpayment. He tried to get some friends to go out for beers, but finally ended up making a long distance call to an army buddy. He'd started a story he wanted published. "It starts out like this," he said, "Sergeant Dwight Johnson is dead and his home has been wiped out."

On April 29, 1971, Dwight Johnson visited his wife in the hospital.

She wanted her curlers and her bathrobe. She was in good health and spirits. He was, she said, "the same old Dwight, just kidding and teasing." He promised Katrina and the hospital that he would return shortly. The hospital was asking about the unpaid deposit. He left at 5:30 P.M.

At about 9:00 P.M., Dwight called a friend to ask a favor. He offered to pay $15 for a ride. He needed to see someone who was going to help him out with some money. The friend's stepfather had a car, and they turned the favor into a family outing, with his friend's mother joining them for the ride. They picked up Johnson at about 11:00 P.M.

About a mile from Johnson's home, they pulled onto a dark street, and he told them to wait.

Johnson walked down the block to the Sip 'n' Chat bar and sat down. He ordered a shot of Johnnie Walker and a Pabst. He drank slowly, paid, and left.

Johnson then walked across the street to the Open Pantry Market, what they call a "party store" in Detroit. He asked for a pack of cigarettes. He offered a bill to pay.

When the storeowner opened the register, Johnson pulled a .22 caliber pistol and told him to step aside.

The owner lunged for the gun when Johnson reached for the money. The pistol went off, twice. One bullet grazed the owner; the other entered his left arm. The owner reached under the counter and produced his own gun. He started firing.

"I hit him with two bullets, but he just stood there, with the gun in his hand, and said, 'I'm going to kill you.' I kept pulling the trigger until my gun was empty," the storeowner told police.

Dwight Johnson was taken to the hospital with three bullet wounds in his chest and one to his face. He died on an operating table at 4:00 A.M.

The police who went through his wallet for ID found a card that read "Congressional Medal of Honor Society, United States of America" and "This certifies that Dwight H. Johnson is a member of this society."

* * *

"We cannot probe a man's mind deeply enough," said Pastor Carl Hort of the Faith Memorial Lutheran Church at Dwight "Skip" Johnson's funeral. "We can never judge another person. This man did not know what he was doing." A number of people felt that way. Some 400 attended his funeral in Detroit. Most were black; the few white faces that appeared were army buddies who had learned of the tragedy from the evening news. Some mourners were complete strangers. Everyone, the reporters, the friends, the public, tried to make sense of what had just happened. "They say he shot somebody last night," father-in-law Leroy May told a reporter on April 30. "Well, that's what they taught him to do. That's what he did over there." A Pentagon spokesperson called him "the hero type," and added "It's too bad this had to happen." His commanding officer said he had "nothing but the highest regard for him."

The army gave Johnson full military honors at his funeral in Arlington National Cemetery on May 6, 1971. Across the Potomac, the Vietnam Veterans Against the War were still engaging the government, but Arlington that day was peaceful. Johnson's mother was there, and when she got back to Detroit, she received a call from a reporter from the *New York Times*.

On May 26, an in-depth article written by Jon Nordheimer appeared in the *Times*. A reader responded to the article with a letter to the editor that offered poverty as a possible answer: "Sergeant Johnson couldn't have bought a can of soup with his Medal of Honor at that grocery store." Another letter writer, a psychiatrist at Mt. Sinai School of Medicine, thought Johnson might have been saved if he'd taken part in the medal-throwing event at the Capitol, or in the "rap groups" of vets that were springing up around the country. Playwright Richard Wesley was inspired to write *Strike Heaven on the Face*, based on the article, while Playwright Tom Cole responded with *The Medal of Honor Rag*, which had a short run on Broadway and a well-received production on PBS. Poet Michael S. Harper wrote the *Debridement* series, published in 1973, "out of deep anguish about this whole business."

Years later, the Veterans Administration ruled that Johnson was not able to "make a rational decision," opening the way to an increased pension for his wife. They'd heard testimony from a representative of the Detroit Disabled American Veterans, who'd been fighting for Katrina for two and a half years. He said Johnson had been used "to motivate other blacks, not honoring [him] for what he did, saving lives by killing the enemy, but using him." Other testimony, from a Detroit psychiatrist, claimed that "Johnson's criminal behavior was an effort to get himself killed."

That's what Johnson's mother thought, and it was with a quote from her that Nordheimer chose to end his article. "Sometimes I wonder," she said, "if Skip tired of this life and needed someone else to pull the trigger."

CHAPTER ELEVEN

Thomas Kelley

VIETNAM WAR

"Lt. Comdr. [then Lt.] Kelley disregarded his severe injuries and attempted to continue directing the other boats."

— MEDAL OF HONOR CITATION

"IT WAS A SUNDAY, JUNE 15, and we had been down two days before in the same geographic area . . . It was kind of a tough area because supposedly there were a lot of Vietcong units in that area." Thomas Kelley was, on that day in 1969, in command of a small flotilla of navy boats that belonged to Task Force 117, the Mobile Riverine Force. Their assignment, as it was on most days, was to transport soldiers of the army's 9th Infantry from one patrol area to another. They were on a canal near Ben Tre in the Mekong River Delta. "We went down there two days before . . . and at one point, we came under attack and one of the rounds fired at us hit one of the boats, and through a fluke went into where the troops were . . . and we took some heavy casualties. We lost about six soldiers, many wounded. Six killed, several wounded. That was a very bad day. So when we found out we were going back to the same area two days later, we had a feeling it might be rough again."

What happened on that day, Kelley says, has to be given the proper perspective. "I don't dwell on it at all. If somebody brings it up, I would be happy to refer them to my citation, I would rather just have them read my citation than describe it. I don't feel comfortable telling people that story over and over again." It happened, he says, over 30 years ago. It lasted only 30 minutes. It was an "infinitesimal" part of his life.

Kelley's life started on May 13, 1939, in South Boston. He was born in Dorchester and raised in West Roxbury. He shouldn't have remembered the attack on Pearl Harbor, but maybe he does. "I'm not sure if it's possible, but I can almost remember being in the living room with people sitting around the radio listening to either the story of Pearl Harbor or the president's speech the next day. And I do have a memory of that." Before long, "every other house" on his short street had someone overseas.

Every house, it seemed, already contained someone in service at home. "It was a typical lower-middle-class neighborhood. The people who lived there were things like cops and firefighters and teachers and public servants. People who worked for the city and the state." Thomas's father was an English teacher at a Boston public school, but during the war he was also an air raid warden. Thomas's mother stayed home. When Thomas started thinking about what he wanted to be when he grew up, he first decided he wanted to be a priest. Then, he thought, maybe a cop. Then later, a professional hockey player.

The city didn't provide organized sports, but it did flood the playground in the wintertime so kids like Thomas could play hockey and skate. During the summer they used the street for team sports. In general they "kept busy all the time without much adult supervision." When he was seven, Thomas's uncle took him away from the fun and games for an afternoon to take a tour of the USS *Missouri*. The ship where the Japanese surrender had been signed was on a cruise around the country. "I remember seeing the sailors, and at that point I really wanted to become a sailor because it looked like a pretty good life. I was overwhelmed by the *Missouri*, the hugeness of it." That early desire to become a sailor, however, didn't stick. Thomas got his first job two years later.

His brother, three years his senior, had been working at the country club as a caddy and had been telling him "what a great life it was." And it wasn't bad at all. "But it made me think that golfers are a really strange breed of people. They wear funny clothes, they're cheap as hell, and they take it all too seriously." At any rate, that's what he thought then when he was working for them. Thirty years later he started playing golf himself. "And I found out I was right."

Then he had a paper route and a job at a family-owned fruit and vegetable stand. As Thomas entered high school, his brother "dragged him along" once again to a new job, working as a waiter for a catering outfit. Thomas had to buy his own tuxedo, but he found one that only put him back five dollars. Then, during the summers, their father would take the family to Maine where he had a job managing a resort hotel. Thomas worked his way up at the hotel, from dishwasher to room service waiter. "I was always working, but they were jobs in a fairly nice atmosphere."

He attended an all-boys Catholic school, where he played hockey and ran track, neither of them very well. When he was accepted to Holy Cross College in Worcester, he decided to study economics, "probably to make a million dollars. It didn't work out." He applied himself for the first two years, but "skated" for the next two. "There were other things going on, raising hell and things like that . . . But you couldn't get away with too much on campus, believe me." The Jesuit priests who taught there also instilled quite a bit of regimentation and "forced discipline," so by the time he got into the navy, Kelley says, going by the book was "a piece of cake."

In 1960, two weeks before graduation, Thomas Kelley was visited by two of his closest friends, who said they had just joined the navy. They told him it was a good program, a "good deal," so Kelley went down the next day and signed up for three years. "I tend to procrastinate—at least in those days I did—about what I'm going to do next in my life. It sounded like a good place to spend two or three years, have a little adventure, get a little responsibility, do some different things, and then see what I wanted to do with the rest of my life." Patriotism and the desire to serve may have been in the foundation of his decision, but they weren't the first thing on his mind.

After 120 days in officer candidate school, Kelley went aboard his first ship and found that "you have to put behind you everything that you learned in school and learn what the real navy's all about." The first thing he had to learn was how much he would depend on the men under his command. "That was kind of daunting . . . because I was twenty-one years old, trying to lead chief petty officers and senior petty officers who were twenty years in the navy, and might have been in their forties." In some cases, he would learn from them, in some cases "they'd put up with me and help as much as I wanted to be helped." In any case, he wasn't the first young officer they'd encountered, and wouldn't be the last.

Kelley's first assignment wasn't "the most glamorous." The USS *Pandemus*, a World War II landing ship, had been converted to a repair ship. Since it had only a few 40-millimeter guns, "which were not very effective" for defense, Kelley's job as weapons officer was manageable. He also served as operations officer, in charge of radar and communications. He served on the ship for three years, and was in the Caribbean during the Cuban Missile Crisis.

They were not part of the blockade but were certainly in a "high state of tension." Kelley remembers keeping his fingers crossed, but, as he remarks, "the advantage of being in the military or the navy during crises like that is you are so busy doing your job day to day that you don't really have time to worry . . ." Kelley had been aware of the Cold War before he went into service, perhaps a little more than most citizens, but he had no idea about how the standoff with the Soviet Union would affect him as a naval officer. He hadn't thought about what role he was going to play. The Missile Crisis brought this home.

When Kelley's three years were up, he decided to stay on for several reasons. "I'd gotten married . . . I couldn't be footloose and fancy-free." And also, he says, "A little patriotism had crept in there at that point." After the Second World War, and again after Korea, the men and women who served had returned to their lives. "[It was] like letting air out of a balloon, it just kind of deflated . . . I wanted to be part of the skeleton crew that stayed around to maintain things until the next time we were needed." Promoted to lieutenant in 1964, shortly after he'd made the decision to stay in the navy, Kelley started service on the destroyer USS *Davis*.

The ship's namesake, George Fleming Davis, had been commander of the destroyer USS *Walke* during the Second World War. On January 6, 1945, the *Walke* was in support of minesweeping operations that would clear the way for an invasion of Luzon, the main island in the Philippines, when four Japanese planes lined up against it for a suicide attack. Davis chose to coordinate the defense of his ship from the vulnerable wings of his bridge. His gunners shot down the first plane, then disabled the second, causing it to miss the bridge and crash into the sea. But the third plane struck the rear of the bridge. Davis was, according to his citation, "seriously wounded . . . drenched with gasoline and immediately enveloped in flames," but he refused to give up command. His men shot down the fourth plane and, under his direction, extinguished the fires. After he was certain that the *Walke* was safe, he relinquished control of the bridge and was carried below. He died several hours later. Secretary of the Navy James Forrestal presented the Medal of Honor to his widow in November 1945.

History, Kelley says, was another reason he decided to stay in the navy. He was drawn to the fact that "people had been doing this for a couple hundred years. It's a noble experience, and I wanted to be part of it." Kelley next served on the destroyer USS *Stickell*, also named after a Second World War hero, an aviator who posthumously received the Navy Cross. It was aboard this ship that Kelley got his first exposure to the war in Vietnam.

He never did go ashore. The *Stickell* was in support of the army and marines ashore with her big guns and provided rescue services for downed pilots. "It was a pretty high tempo of operations; we were generally operating with an aircraft carrier off the coast." But Kelley felt his training had prepared him, and what's more, he was doing exactly what he wanted to be doing:

> You could see the buildup coming, and it gave me kind of a rush. I said, "Hey, that's the place to be." I thought it was the right thing to do. We were told that if democracy failed in South Vietnam, it would fail throughout Asia, and so we were doing all we could to help make democracy work in South Vietnam. I found it very believable.

But as the pace quickened in Vietnam, Kelley was sent home to shore duty in Newport, Rhode Island. He worked with a development group, testing new tactics and equipment for the required two years. He had a family now—three girls born in 1963, 1964, and 1966—so he welcomed the chance to come home every night. But in 1968, once he had the option, he wanted to be in Vietnam.

"I didn't want to go over there and sit behind a desk." And he'd already been part of the fleet off the coast. So when he learned about what the navy was doing on the rivers of Vietnam, he knew that's where he would go. "It was a new form of warfare that sounded kind of exciting, and I knew they needed people. They'd been in existence for a year or so, and they'd seen plenty of action. So I decided that was the thing to do, go to the place where there's plenty of action."

The Mekong Delta was a twisting maze of canals, rivulets, and marshes that accounted for one-quarter of the land mass of South Vietnam. The impassible terrain—there was practically only one road through the delta—and its proximity to Saigon made it a vitally important stronghold and series of supply lines for the Vietcong. The first U.S. advisers realized this immediately and were disheartened to find that the South Vietnamese Navy still made extensive use of sail-powered junks to patrol the waterways. The U.S. Navy thus waded into river warfare for the first time since the Civil War, when its contribution forced the Mississippi from Confederate control.

The navy entered the muddy waters of the delta in December 1965 with Operation Game Warden, disrupting the supply lines and river operations of the Vietcong with lightly armored speedboats. But as American involvement deepened, the navy was called upon to put forces on the ground. They then came up with the Mobile Riverine Force (MRF).

The MRF was based around barracks ships that could navigate the deeper channels of the delta and provide support to the troops and boats alike. The army's 9th Infantry slept and ate on the ships while they awaited their next assignment; the navy personnel usually chose to sleep aboard their smaller boats, just in case they came under attack. The craft of the force were modified Second World War–era armored troop carriers. They were about 50 feet long and rectangular, with a bow ramp that could drop to the beach, allowing the soldiers waiting inside to disembark. Each craft was crewed by about 5 sailors, but could carry up to 25 soldiers.

Some of these troop carriers were further modified to serve as fire support craft. These boats had their bow ramps removed and were outfitted with a 40-millimeter gun and extra armor. After the welders were done with them, they looked a little like the ironclads of the Civil War, and so they were dubbed "monitors." Others had a flight deck fixed to the top, just large enough for a helicopter to land and load passengers. Still others were converted into hospital ships, the interior devoted to operating tables and cold storage of blood supplies. Every craft was highly improvised, but the navy managed to create an ambulatory force that was remarkably self-sufficient.

The Mobile Riverine Force started training as a joint army/navy force in January 1967 and undertook its first major operation in February. The force's first serious incursion into the Mekong Delta was in May. By September, they were engaging the Vietcong in great numbers, taking and receiving high casualties, and becoming an undeniable presence in the delta.

Because helicopters and armored troop carriers gave increased mobility to the U.S. forces in Vietnam, soldiers there were put more frequently into the line of fire than ever before. Foot soldiers in the South Pacific during World War II, for example, saw 40 days of fighting, on average, over four years. Their counterparts in Vietnam saw, on average, 240 days of combat in a single year. And in a place like the Mekong Delta, it could happen at any time. "You were always on edge because you didn't know when the first round would come in. You were always on edge."

Kelley arrived in August of 1968 and for his first six months was on the staff of a squadron, which was comprised of 50 boats. Then he was put in charge of a division of 25 boats. Their mission was simply to take the army wherever it wanted to go. "We were wedded, married to what the army wanted us to do. If the army was sending out a company-sized operation, then we'd have boats to carry a company."

They usually got their orders the night before an operation. The boat captains would gather and go over the route, cover what intelligence was available about enemy strength, and discuss the rules of engagement. In the morning, the boats would load up the army's infantrymen, and they'd shove off before dawn. The boats would drop off the soldiers, then later extract them from another location. They might do several insertions and extractions in a single day. All the while, these slow-moving boats were totally exposed on the river, whereas their enemy was completely concealed in the jungle that stopped only at the river's edge.

Six months after he arrived, January 1969, Kelley was sent on a long assignment to the Cambodian border with a small force of eight to ten boats. "It was kind of independent duty for about four weeks. We just kind of hung around up there, had a few firefights up there . . . There was some sort of mystique about [the Cambodian border]. I'm not sure how much more dangerous it was, but the farther you got away from the main forces, Saigon and where the U.S. forces were heavily concentrated, the farther away you got, the more risks there were."

The risks were more apparent to others involved in an ongoing operation in which Kelley had a brief part. Operation Giant Slingshot, started in December 1968, was an attempt to stop the flow of arms and personnel across the Cambodian border, and it became one of the toughest assignments of the "brown water navy." The South Vietnamese took over the operation in May 1970, after the navy had suffered 58 killed and 518 wounded. The navy's river force was, outside of SEAL operations, one of their most dangerous assignments in Vietnam, a fact that Kelley knew as he joined. He'd read about the high casualty rates in a magazine article back home.

On June 15, 1969, the bad feeling that Kelley had, about going back to an area where six men had been killed two days before, was somewhat lessened by the fact that they received air support. "[A helicopter] was on call and was actually in the air. So we felt fairly well protected. I felt fairly well protected. When [the Vietcong] knew helicopters were there, they kind of kept their heads down and didn't bother you too much. That was what I experienced." They made three or four insertions and extractions early on, and it looked like the day would pass uneventfully. "As mid-afternoon came along, they told us we had to go one more place, pick up the troops, and take them one more place. And we wouldn't have helicopter support for this one. It was deeper and deeper [into the jungle]. So it had kind of a feeling that this is what they had been waiting for all day."

As Kelley's group of six boats dropped their ramps and picked up the infantrymen, Kelley stayed midstream aboard one of the MRF's monitors. All seemed clear until one of the boats found that its hydraulics were out and it couldn't lift its ramp. They were lifting it back into place when the firing started from the opposite bank. "Rocket-propelled grenades, machine guns, rockets, mortars, God knows what. They saw the boats exposed on the beach there and probably thought they could make some points on these boats."

Kelley directed the monitor, his command vessel, to a position between the disabled craft and the incoming fire, and then had the monitor fire into the jungle. "During the course of that, a rocket-propelled grenade came in and detonated right next to my head and kind of knocked me for a loop. That's when my Medal of Honor action, if you will, took effect."

Kelley was holding a radio when he was hit, and it fell with him about 10 feet down to the deck. He heard someone on the radio yell, "He's dead, he's dead!" He couldn't get up, but he could continue to give orders through the radio, helping to direct the fire and keep the situation from disintegrating in the intense firefight. Another boat pulled alongside, and in the middle of all this, a corpsman leaped onto the monitor and to Kelley's side, tending to his severe head wounds while Kelley continued to bark orders into his headset. "I didn't tell him to do that," Kelley said. "He did that on his own." It was, he reflects, typical of corpsmen: "They're incredible."

"The adrenaline was going and I was trying to get the job done and get the boats out of there . . . I knew I was hurt badly because I was in a fair amount of pain, and I knew I wasn't functioning the way I normally did, but I was able to keep enough of my composure to keep from falling apart, I guess." The firefight lasted for about 20 to 30 minutes, until the disabled boat was under way. From there, Kelley's memory of the event gets spotty. He doesn't remember getting into the helicopter, but he remembers being flown to a field hospital. "I remember a doctor saying 'I don't think he's going to make it,' and that's the last thing I remember. So when I woke up, I wasn't sure if I had made it or not, to tell you the truth."

The doctor had reason to worry. "My head had been banged up and I'd lost an eye, and a good part of my skull had been blown away." He had been in a coma for two weeks and had made a tour of navy hospitals—a few in Vietnam, one in Japan, one in the Philippines, where he regained consciousness. He was then moved to Hawaii, where his family was waiting for him.

In Hawaii, Kelley made a rapid recovery. He contracted hepatitis from the blood transfusions, but after undergoing reconstructive surgery that replaced the pieces of skull he'd lost with plastic and getting a prosthetic eye that "looks almost like a real one," he was out and on his feet. "I felt fortunate. Once I got back on my feet and out of the hospital, I felt pretty good. I got my strength back and I was able to resume my life. I was very fortunate."

Before long, he was back at work. He worked with the Pacific Fleet commander, but after two months, he had to undergo a medical review to determine if he could still serve, a routine procedure. "And they said I had to get out, because I was not physically fit to continue in the navy."

Kelley took exception with that. "I'm sure it was a matter of pride, [but I also] really liked the navy . . . and there was no reason to get out." He appealed, with the result that he could stay in, but on a restricted status. He could work behind a desk, or in the supply corps, but he couldn't go back to sea, and he could never go back into combat. "I appealed that also." At that point, the commander of the navy in Vietnam, who Kelley had been working for, interceded. "So I was allowed to stay. I was finally cleared for full duty about a year later." In theory, he could have gone back to Vietnam.

But the navy decided he'd seen enough of Southeast Asia and put him in graduate school in Monterey, California, where he studied management. It was in the spring of 1970 that he learned he had been recommended for the Medal of Honor. "I honestly didn't think I'd receive it, because I didn't know anybody who had the Medal of Honor and I didn't feel that what I had done really warranted that particular award, but I didn't argue about it. And I was quite surprised when I finally found out it had been approved."

The ceremony took place at the White House in May of 1970 under a cloak of secrecy: "They told me I had to be in Washington at such and such a day for something, they didn't tell me what. I wasn't officially told about the Medal of Honor until I got to Washington, but I, being a pretty smart guy, put two and two together. [They told me] you can't even tell your friends about this." They weren't trying to surprise the recipients—they were trying to fool the war protesters. There had been a marked increase in the size and number of demonstrations since Kelley had left in 1968, and the White House feared that protesters might try to keep the recipients from getting in. "While I was in Vietnam, I'm sure I knew it was going on, but I was too busy to worry too much about it. I never felt that the country didn't love me or anything like I'm sure some people feel. I was fortunate not to have that feeling."

Nor did Kelley hate the protesters. He still firmly believed in the war, but as he learned more about the antiwar movement, he decided it was more complex than he'd originally thought. It wasn't just a group of vocal cowards avoiding the draft. "One of the people who really influenced me was Muhammad Ali, when he went to jail rather than join the army. That was a pretty noble thing to do. I had a fair amount of respect for people who were willing to go to jail for their principles." Not winning Kelley's full admiration were those who fled the country or committed fraud, but he was affected by those who "paid the price for their beliefs," even if he didn't agree with them.

The White House ceremony was appropriately impressive, with a dozen men receiving the Medal of Honor from President Nixon. "He asked me where I was from, shook my hand and all that, and I said, 'Boston,' and he said, 'Oh, do you eat baked beans every night?' And I said, 'No, only on Saturday night.' And he walked on to the next person. That was my conversation with Richard Nixon."

Down the line was Navy SEAL Bob Kerrey, who that day received the

Medal of Honor for his action near Nha Trang Bay. In 2001, Kerrey, then a former U.S. senator for his home state of Nebraska, was accused by a former comrade of ordering the execution of civilians the night he earned his medal. Kerrey, in speeches and interviews, denied ordering executions but said that during a confusing firefight some 13 to 20 noncombatants, including women and children, were killed. In a speech at the Virginia Military Institute in 2001, he said that he had been "haunted by it for thirty-two years."

After completing his management course at the navy's graduate school, Kelley served as executive officer, "the number two guy," on the frigate USS *Sample* from 1973 to 1975. From 1975 to 1977, he worked for the Bureau of Personnel located in the navy annex near the Pentagon in Arlington, Virginia. Then, in 1977, after 17 years in the navy, Kelley was given a ship. "Command of a ship is really the ultimate goal of every naval officer. It's very competitive, and there are far more people who want command than there are available ships." Kelley was given the USS *Lang*, a fast frigate based in San Diego, from 1977 to 1980. This ship was primarily used for antisubmarine warfare, and the typical cruise involved doing "just what ships do, we went out and looked for submarines." In 1979, with the hostage crisis and the Soviet invasion of Afghanistan, Kelley's ship was sent into the Indian Ocean. "Nothing came of it, but it was another example of having to be there in case something happened."

Kelley had been through a number of promotions along the way—lieutenant commander in 1970, commander in 1976, captain in 1982. His service kept him globe-hopping, from a brief return to Rhode Island to a two-year stint in Yokohama, Japan. In 1985, he went to Korea to serve as chief of staff for U.S. Naval Forces in Korea. His earliest memory had been of Pearl Harbor. His naval career had taken him from the Cuban Missile Crisis to the Mekong Delta to several fronts of the Cold War. Now he saw firsthand the ongoing tensions of the unresolved war in Korea. "It was an eye-opener, because I hadn't realized, or I hadn't stopped to think about the fact that the Korean War is only in an armistice period, [with] two countries still staring at each other across the DMZ."

The tensions were visible in many ways. Seoul still had frequent air raid drills. On the golf courses, Kelley noticed that at night they strung wire across the fairway so planes couldn't use them as landing strips. "Things like that which the average American would never think about."

He left Korea in 1987, as he was coming up on 30 years in the navy. His last assignment—working for the chief of naval personnel in Washington—might sound like a dull way to end an exciting career, but the fact that he was working with Congress, face to face with "civilian control of the military," gave Kelley something to consider as he finished his service. "It made me realize more and more how we in the military are the public servants and the ships that we sail and the airplanes that we fly in, they belong to the American people, we're just the caretakers. The young men and women who join [the armed forces], we leaders of the armed forces, are responsible for this great American treasure."

After retiring, taking a year off, and then working for the navy in a civilian capacity for three years, Kelley took four years completely off. "I just kind of hung around for about four years to be very honest." But during this time he did a great deal of reading, and over the last ten years he's read quite a bit more about the Vietnam War. "I'm very, very proud of my service and I know most people are who served over there, but I think it was a tragic, tragic waste of men, time, money, everything else. For really the wrong reasons."

He doesn't describe this new perspective as a radical transformation, even though it could count as one. "When I was actually serving in Vietnam and serving in the navy afterward, I didn't really look outside my own little universe. I didn't really question the motives and actions of our leaders. And as I started reading more about it . . . I said, 'Gee, this never should have happened.'" He is now of a mind with David Shoup when he wonders if we ever had a mission or plan to defeat the forces of the enemy. In the future, he hopes we can be a little more clear. "It involves real men, real women out there, not just ships and airplanes and divisions and things like that, these are kids. And do we want to send them into a tough situation, and if so, are we going to back them up and take care of them when they get home? And is it worth it? Is it really worth it? And if it's worth it, then do it. And if it's not worth it, cut your losses and get out."

Back in Vietnam, even if he had objected to the war personally, he couldn't have done so publicly. "It's incumbent on a well-informed public. A well-informed electorate. I see it even now. Since September 11, people who question some of our policies . . . are kind of looked down upon, or called less than patriotic . . . And that stifles public discussion, public disclosure. I think that's wrong. Full disclosure is absolutely necessary."

Back in the mid-seventies, when it first came out, Kelley saw *The Medal of Honor Rag*, the play inspired by the life of Dwight Johnson. "I didn't particularly care for it at the time . . . I thought it was quite a negative portrayal of soldiers. People who had served. Then I recently reread it, the script, and I can see that this individual, Johnson . . . wore his wounds on the inside." But he firmly believes that Johnson is an exceptional case.

Kelley counts himself as fortunate to not have the guilt or the nightmares, and to have been spared the hate that other veterans experienced when they got home. The reason, he believes, is that he stayed in the navy, a "protective society" with a strong support system. But even as he went into civilian life, much later, he found that "there's a myth, that [the Vietnam vet] came back and was a failure, and wasn't able to get on with his life . . . but if you look at the numbers . . . veterans came back, picked up the pieces, went back to school, went back to work, and reintegrated themselves into society with a minimum of fuss." And although there are, he says, exceptions to this rule, he really feels that "fellow veterans are trying to find these less fortunate people and help them reestablish themselves."

Kelley remarried in 1993, to a woman from Boston, so in 1997 he returned to his hometown. He'd been back very seldom since his mother passed away—in the same year he received the Medal of Honor. Kelley went to work at the Massachusetts Department of Veterans Services, then headed by Thomas Hudner, a former navy pilot and fellow Medal of Honor recipient for an action near the Chosin Reservoir. Hudner had tried, without success, to rescue a downed pilot who was trapped in his cockpit by landing his own plane, with wheels up and near advancing enemy troops. When Hudner retired from the department in 1999, Kelley, through gubernatorial appointment, succeeded him as commissioner of veterans services.

This is the job life prepared him for: "When you finish your military service, you tend to gravitate toward groups of veterans, and you find some of them are not doing as well as you would like to see them doing. The benefits might not be what they should be, and there's a general feeling that we could do better. So I decided to try to take that on as a personal endeavor. This job is just perfect for that."

No one would openly disagree with a measure to care for our veterans. No lawmaker could survive an election if he or she objected to keeping a promise to our veterans. And if an overwhelming majority wants something in a democracy, one would think they'd get it. In this case, that hasn't happened. Kelley repeatedly finds himself in the halls of the state and federal governments, pushing for basic benefits or asking government to keep a perceived promise. And he finds he's virtually alone: "The only people lobbying the legislature and Congress to take care of veterans are veterans themselves."

He knows we probably won't ever see the military or veterans get the kind of support they got during the Second World War, when every other house on Kelley's block sent someone overseas. These days, the military is, he feels, somewhat detached from the public. "There's no sense of owner-ship . . . Now, your average citizen probably doesn't even know somebody in the military." The politicians won't make the effort, because the condition of our veterans isn't a daily part of enough people's lives. So, Kelley believes, "Until the average citizen stands up and says veterans programs are important . . . then nothing's going to happen."

AFTERWORD

By Mike Wallace

My first exposure to Vietnam was in the summer of 1962. At the time, even with the escalations that had been ordered by the Kennedy administration, the U.S. military presence there was quite limited. Slightly more than 15,000 Americans were stationed in Vietnam, largely confined to the role of advisers and support personnel. Our troops had been sent there to train, instruct, and provide transport for the South Vietnamese Army in its struggle to defeat the Communist insurgents, the Vietcong. In short, it was still a very small war in 1962, and U.S. forces had not yet been committed to engage in the actual fighting.

The reports I broadcast during my weeklong stay in Vietnam reflected the prevailing optimism. Yes, it was going to be tough, but we would prevail. We had to, because the dominoes would fall all across Southeast Asia if we failed there, as the French had before us in the 1950s.

But little by little over the next five years, it became clear that the enemy over there was far more tenacious and resistant than we had anticipated. The consensus that we Americans had been right to commit our military to the Vietnam enterprise began to crack. And one of the fault lines was generational. Those of us who were old enough to have served in the Second World War were more inclined to place our trust in the judgment and veracity of our military leaders. After all, many of the senior commanders in Saigon and even at the Pentagon were our contemporaries, men who had been young officers at a time when many of us civilians had served as young officers. Having shared the experience of winning World War II, we naturally felt a certain kinship toward one another.

Skepticism came more easily to younger Americans, especially those who had never before served in the military, and for the most part it was the younger generation that first turned against the war in Vietnam. By the end of 1966, the consensus had shattered. I remained to some degree a hawk, a supporter of the intervention. But more than hawk or dove, I was first and foremost a reporter, and since Vietnam had become, by then, the major story of a turbulent decade, I wanted a piece of the action. So I persuaded my CBS News superiors to send me back to Vietnam in March 1967 to help cover a war that was dramatically different from the light skirmishes I had observed there five years earlier.

And this time the officer leading the propaganda parade was the man in charge of the U.S. combat mission—General William C. Westmoreland. With his erect bearing, his firmly set jaw, and his crisply starched fatigues, "Westy" was the very model of military assurance, and no one was more adept at talking a good game. During the early days of my return to Saigon, I was repeatedly told by the general and his top aides that even though the U.S. mission had gone through some rough patches, we had finally turned the corner and gained the upper hand. It was now only a matter of time before the enemy would have to give up the fight and the war would be over. (In hindsight, my main regret is that Westmoreland refrained from uttering in my presence the phrase that would later take on such notoriety, his confident boast that there was "light at the end of the tunnel.")

But the reporters I talked to provided a much different version of how the war was going. Some of them, for instance R. W. Apple of the *New York Times* and William Touhy of the *Los Angeles Times*, had been in Vietnam since the start of the big buildup in 1965, and they had discovered, in one combat exchange after another, that the enemy was much stronger and more resourceful than the U.S. Command cared to admit. In their conversations with me, these reporters went out of their way to emphasize that they had not come to Vietnam with antiwar chips on their shoulders. Moreover, during their first few weeks there, they, too, had been inclined to accept at face value the smug predictions of a quick and decisive victory. It was only after they had a chance to compare those assessments with the grim realities they encountered in the war zones that they began to scoff at Westmoreland's optimistic claims.

I spent two months in Vietnam, and the more deeply I dug into the story, the more I became aware of the decisive change taking place in my own point of view. The more I saw and heard, the closer I moved toward the position that we had blundered into a war we were not winning and had no business fighting. We were intruders in what was essentially a civil war, and thus our intervention in Vietnam had been a devastating mistake, a tragic waste of lives and resources, as well as a military and political fiasco of towering magnitude. By the time I returned to New York, I had made a complete conversion from hawk to dove.

The America I came back to that spring was more bitterly divided than ever over Vietnam, and as 1967 drew to a close it seemed apparent to me that one of the casualties of the war was going to be Lyndon Johnson. The war policies he had pursued over the past three years had all but destroyed his presidency, which is a conclusion LBJ himself must have reached when, in March 1968, he stunned the nation with his announcement that he would not seek reelection to "another term as your President."

I was among those Americans who believed that because of Vietnam, the Democrats deserved to lose the White House, regardless of who wound up running in Johnson's place. It seemed to me that a Republican administration, starting out with a clean slate, would be in a stronger position to negotiate a speedy and honorable withdrawal from Vietnam. As it happened, my assignment during the early months of 1968 was to cover Richard Nixon's quest for the presidency, and I latched on to the hope that if elected, he could get us out of Vietnam as quickly as the newly elected Eisenhower had gotten us out of Korea back in 1953. Needless to say, I and other American voters who shared that hope were in for a big disappointment.

Nixon had opportunities to bring about a swift resolution to the war, especially during the early months of his presidency when he still had no heavy personal stake in the commitment he had inherited. But he and his foreign policy team let those prospects for peace slip through their grasp. I thought of those squandered opportunities when I read about Thomas Kelley's act of heroism in Vietnam. There is no doubt that Commander Kelley deserved the Medal of Honor for what he did that day to save the lives of his navy comrades. Nevertheless, there is something obscene in the fact that at that late date—June of 1969—American troops were still being exposed to such peril in a war that we no longer had any hope of winning. And Americans continued to fight and die in that war until January 1973, four years after Nixon became president. Not until then did he finally manage to pull us out of the Vietnam quagmire. By then, of course, his own presidency was on the road to ruin, and in a sense that, too, was a casualty of the war in Vietnam.

No fewer than four presidents—Eisenhower, Kennedy, Johnson, and Nixon—share the blame, in varying degrees, for our tragic intercession in Vietnam. In fact, you can make that five, because the fall of Saigon occurred on Gerald Ford's watch, and so he had to take at least some of the heat for that final humiliation. And in one way or another, every president since Ford has had to bear the cross that comes with the heavy responsibility of being the nation's commander in chief.

Jimmy Carter was driven to such a state of desperation by the Iranian hostage crisis that in the spring of 1980, he ordered an ill-advised rescue mission that ended in ignominious failure. Eight members of the rescue team were killed when one of the misson's helicopters crashed in the Iranian desert. The reckless blunder also destroyed whatever faint hope there had been for an early resolution of the crisis. The hostages were kept in captivity until after the November election, which is the main reason why Carter was defeated that fall in his bid for reelection.

In October 1983 Ronald Reagan dispatched a contingent of marines and army rangers to Grenada because of concern that the small Caribbean island was falling under the control of a rebel group said to be in league with Cuban communists. The purpose of the invasion, said Reagan, was to "restore order and democracy" in Grenada. But critics charged that the *real* purpose of the exercise was to distract attention from a more damaging military episode that had taken place in Lebanon just two days earlier.

In a suicide mission that would later be seen as a grim harbinger of far more devastating terrorist acts, a Muslim fanatic drove a truck full of explosives into the U.S. Marine barracks at the Beirut airport, and the explosion it set off killed 241 American servicemen. Not since the Vietnam War had there been so many U.S. military casualties in one day.

George Bush *père* ordered an invasion of Panama in 1989 to overthrow and capture that country's ruler, General Manuel Antonio Noriega. And two years later, his approval ratings soared to record highs when U.S. forces emerged from the Persian Gulf War with an overwhelming victory and extremely low casualties. But in the waning weeks of his presidency, Bush authorized another military operation that proved to be much less triumphant. As part of a UN humanitarian mission, he sent 7,000 American troops to the East African nation of Somalia, which had been ravaged by severe famine and vicious inter-clan warfare. Their assignment was to safeguard the delivery and distribution of food supplies, and to impose restraint on the various warring factions.

The military commitment ordered by Bush was inherited by his successor, Bill Clinton, who soon had reason to regret that American soldiers were in Somalia on his watch. The food deliveries met with enough success in 1993 to save an estimated one million lives, but the peacekeeping phase of the operation did not go so well. The UN forces failed in their efforts to disarm the rival clans and maintain a cease-fire. The most belligerent of the warlords was General Mohammed Farrah Aidid, and in June, Somali guerrillas loyal to him ambushed and killed 24 Pakistanis who were part of the UN mission. In response, the UN called for the arrest and imprisonment of Aidid, and from then on the peacekeepers and Aidid's clan were in open conflict with each other.

On October 3, U.S. army rangers who were members of the UN team took part in an abortive raid on a hotel in the Somali capital, Mogadishu, where Aidid and his top aides were gathered. In the ensuing gun battle, 18 American soldiers were killed. Two of the victims were Master Sergeant Gary Gordon and Sergeant First Class Randall Shughart, who voluntarily jumped from their helicopter to help fellow commandos whose choppers had been shot down. One of the men they rescued was Warrant Officer Michael Durant, copilot of a Black Hawk helicopter. After pulling the severely wounded Durant from the wreckage and thus saving his life, Gordon and Shughart were shot and killed by Somali gunmen. (The story of their heroism is told, with graphic and gripping force, in the recent book and movie *Black Hawk Down*.)

For their acts of valor, Gordon and Shughart were posthumously awarded the Medal of Honor, the first combatants to receive the medal since the war in Vietnam. At a ceremony in the White House on May 23, 1994, President Clinton presented the medals to the widows of the two soldiers, Carmen Gordon and Stephanie Shughart. In his remarks to them, Clinton described their husbands as "real American heroes" whose "actions were clearly above and beyond the call of duty." And he went on to say that Gordon and Shughart had "died in the most courageous and selfless way any human being can act."

Two months before that White House ceremony, Clinton withdrew U.S. forces from Somalia, thereby ending American participation in what had started out as a UN humanitarian mission. In the years that followed, Clinton would send our troops into harm's way on other fronts—in Bosnia, for example, and later in Kosovo—but fortunately they were able to avoid the kind of bloody encounters that are needed to make warriors eligible for the Medal of Honor.

Can we look toward a future in which there will be no more Medal of Honor recipients? Unlikely. In the aftermath of the terrorist acts of September 11, 2001, we hardly need be reminded that the world remains a very dangerous place, and as the world's reigning superpower, we cannot shirk our responsibility to defend and advance the cause of freedom. So there are bound to be future battlefields on which Americans will fight and die and, in a few rare instances, act with such extraordinary bravery that they will receive the ultimate award—the Medal of Honor.

NOTES

THE STORY OF THE MEDAL OF HONOR

Both of the major reference works on Medal of Honor recipients—*United States of America's Congressional Medal of Honor Recipients and Their Official Citations* (2nd ed., edited by R. J. Proft, Columbia Heights, MN: Highland House II, 1998) and *Medal of Honor Recipients 1863–1994,* by George Lang, M. H., Raymond L. Collins, and Gerard F. White (two volumes, New York: Facts on File, 1995)—contain brief but useful histories of the Medal of Honor. Both of these works were consulted for names, dates, and citations that appear throughout this book.

A Shower of Stars: The Medal of Honor and the 27th Maine, by John J. Pullen (Mechanicsburg, PA: Stackpole, 1997), gives quite a bit of detail on the changes in Medal of Honor law, not just those that pertain to the 27th Maine. A broad history of the medal, given mostly through the stories of specific recipients, can be found in *Above and Beyond: A History of the Medal of Honor from the Civil War to Vietnam,* by the editors of the Boston Publishing Company in cooperation with the Congressional Medal of Honor Society (1985).

CHAPTER ONE: DR. MARY E. WALKER

Despite its diminutive title, *Dr. Mary Walker: The Little Lady in Pants,* by Charles Snyder (New York: Vantage, 1962), is actually a very appreciative biography that attempts to fully explain her life.

Paul Starr's Pulitzer Prize–winning *The Social Transformation of American Medicine* (New York: Basic Books, 1982) provided background on the medical controversies of Dr. Walker's time.

Among other works consulted were:
Emert, Phyllis Raybin. *Women in the Civil War: Warriors, Patriots, Nurses, and Spies, Perspectives on History Series.* Lowell, MA: Discovery Enterprises Ltd., 1995.

Leonard, Elizabeth D. *All the Daring of the Soldier: Women of the Civil War Armies.* 1st ed., New York: W.W. Norton & Co., 1999.

————. *Yankee Women: Gender Battles in the Civil War.* 1st ed., New York: W.W. Norton, 1994.

"Records Relating to the Correction of Military Records, Nnm 377-2, Mary Walker." In *Records of the Adjutant General's Office, 1780's–1917, Record Group 94.* National Archives, Washington, DC.

Spiegel, Allen D., and Andrea M. Spiegel. "Civil War Doctoress Mary: Only Woman to Win the Congressional Medal of Honor." *Minerva: Quarterly Report on Women in the Military* 12, no. 3 (1994): 24.

Thomas, Martha. "Amazing Mary." *Civil War Times Illustrated* 23, no. 1 (1984): 36–41.

United States. Congress. House. Committee on the Judiciary., Mary Edwards Walker, Edward Thomas Taylor, and Jane Addams. *Woman Suffrage . . . Hearings.* Washington, DC: Government Printing Office, 1912.

Walker, Mary Edwards. *Hit.* New York: The American News Company, 1871.

[Walker, Mary Edwards]. *Unmasked.* Jersey City, N.J.: The Walker publishing company, 1888.

CHAPTER TWO: LEOPOLD KARPELES

This chapter would never have come together without the help of Joyce Blackman, who generously gave her time and photocopies of family papers. Also of crucial assistance was the Connecticut Valley Historical Museum in Springfield, Massachusetts. The several pieces of original correspondence mentioned below came from these two sources.

Of special help was Warren Wilkinson's incredibly detailed *Mother, May You Never See the Sights I Have Seen: The Fifty-Seventh Massachusetts Veteran Volunteers in the Army of the Potomac, 1864–1865.* (New York: Harper & Row, 1990). Wilkinson writes as if he knew personally every man of the 57th Massachusetts, and every step they took on behalf of the Union.

Also consulted were:

Anderson, John. *The Fifty-Seventh Regiment of Massachusetts Volunteers in the War of the Rebellion, Army of the Potomac.* Boston: E. B. Stillings & co. printers, 1896.

————. Letter to Leopold Karpeles, 1 June 1888.

Blackman, Joyce. "A Civil War Hero and His Rhode Island Family." *Rhode Island Jewish Historical Notes* 12, no. 1 (1995): 93–113.

Douglas, C. L. *The Gentlemen in the White Hats: Dramatic Episodes in the History of the Texas Rangers.* Dallas: South-West Press, 1934.

Foote, Shelby. *The Civil War: A Narrative.* III vols. Vol. III: Red River to Appomattox. New York: Vintage, 1974.

Graham, Samuel Butler, and Ellen Newman. *Galveston Community Book, a Historical and Biographical Record of Galveston and Galveston County.* Galveston, TX, 1945.

Gumpertz, Sydney Gustave. *The Jewish Legion of Valor: the Story of Jewish Heroes in the Wars of the Republic and a General History of the Military Exploits of the Jews through Ages.* New York: S.G. Gumpertz, 1934.

Hayes, Charles W. *Galveston: History of the Island and the City.* Austin: Jenkins Garrett Press: distributed by the Jenkins Pub. Co., 1974.

Karpeles, Leopold. Letter to James Otis, 6 July 1890.

Keating, Bern. *An Illustrated History of the Texas Rangers.* Chicago: Rand McNally, 1975.

McComb, David G. *Galveston: A History.* 1st ed. Austin: University of Texas Press, 1986.

Miller, J. Michael. *The North Anna Campaign: "Even to Hell Itself," May 21–26, 1864.* 2nd ed. *The Virginia Civil War Battles and Leaders Series.* Lynchburg, VA: H.E. Howard, 1989.

Norkin, Bonnie. "Landmarks Reveal Springfield Jewish History." *The Jewish Advocate* 189, no. 47 (1999): 1.

Shostek, Robert. "Leopold Karpeles: Civil War Hero." *American Jewish Historical Quarterly* 52, no. 3 (1963): 220–33.

Spooner, Samuel. Letter to Leopold Karpeles, 17 May 1863.

Springfield City Directory and Business Advertiser. Springfield: Samuel Bowles and Company, 1865.

Springfield Scrapbook. "Jewish Hero from City Revealed as Having Won Civil War Honor Medal." 24 January 1964, 33.

Taussig, Theresa Karpeles. Letter to Richard Schostek, 27 July 1959.

Winegarten, Ruthe, Cathy Schechter, Jimmy Kessler, and Texas Jewish Historical Society. *Deep in the Heart: The Lives and Legends of Texas Jews: A Photographic History.* 1st ed. Austin: Eakin Press, 1990.

Wolf, Simon, and Louis Edward Levy. *The American Jew as Patriot, Soldier and Citizen.* Philadelphia, New York, etc.: The Levytype Company; Brentano's, 1895.

CHAPTER THREE:
EDOUARD VICTOR MICHEL IZAC

Cabell Waller Berge provided her many recollections of her father for this chapter, as well as a stack of recollections by others. The San Diego Public Library has provided an invaluable service by indexing the *San Diego Union,* and they were kind enough to send photocopies of all references to Edouard Izac in their index. There are too many articles gleaned from this source to list here.

One other very interesting source was in the records of the USS *President Lincoln* Club, a curious collection of letters and articles in the Library of Congress Manuscript Division.

Izac himself wrote a detailed account of his POW days called *Prisoner of the U-90* (Boston and New York: Houghton Mifflin, 1919). I also consulted his memo to the secretary of the navy, written up on his return to the United States, and finally, Izac's comments before Congress in the Congressional Record.

Izac's partner to the Rhine, Harold Willis, tells his side of the account in *Escape!* by Harold Cournenay Armstrong (New York: R. M. McBride & Company, 1935).

The following sources were also consulted:

Alexander, W. E. *History of Chickasaw and Howard Counties, Iowa.* Decorah, IA: Western Publishing Company, 1883.

Cameron, John Stanley, and Cyril Brown. *Ten Months in a German Raider: A Prisoner of War Aboard the Wolf.* New York: George H. Doran Company, 1918.

Compton-Hall, Richard. *Submarines and the War at Sea, 1914–18.* London: Macmillan, 1991.

Crews, Ed. "Medal of Honor: The U.S. Navy Officer Had Vital Information to Deliver." *Military History* 7, no. 3 (1990): 16, 68, 70, 72.

Current Biography. "Izac, Ed(Ouard) V(Ictor Michel)." 1945, 300–301.

De La Pedraja Tomán, René. *The Rise and Decline of U.S. Merchant Shipping in the Twentieth Century, Twayne's Evolution of American Business Series; [No. 8].* New York and Toronto: Twayne Publishers, 1992.

Foote, Percy Wright. Letter to Lt. Commander Wallace L. Lind, USN, 17 February 1920.

Gleaves, Albert. *A History of the Transport Service.* New York: George H. Doran Company, 1921.

Glewwe, Lois A., and Dakota County Historical Society. South St. Paul Area Chapter. *South St. Paul Centennial, 1887–1987: The History of South St. Paul, Minnesota.* South St. Paul, MN: The Chapter, 1987.

Grant, Robert M. *U-Boat Intelligence, 1914–1918.* Hamden, CT: Archon Books, 1969.

Gray, Edwyn. *The Killing Time: The U-Boat War, 1914–18.* New York: Scribner, 1972.

Harlan, Edgar Rubey, and American Historical Company New York. *A Narrative History of the People of Iowa, with Special Treatment of Their Chief Enterprises in Education, Religion, Valor, Industry, Business, etc.* Chicago: American Historical Society, 1931.

Howard County Historical Society. *The History of Howard County, Iowa.* Dallas: Curtis Media Corp., 1989.

Izac, Edouard V. Memo to Secretary of the Navy on Imprisonment in Germany and Escape Therefrom, 13 November 1918.

————. Letter to supporters of 1944 Congressional campaign, 29 April 1944.

————. "Former Member Recalls Wilson's Inauguration." *Roll Call,* 7 February 1957, 3.

————. *The Holy Land—Then and Now.* [1st] ed. New York: Vantage Press, 1965.

Joint Committee on Conditions in Concentration Camps in Germany. Atrocities and Other Conditions in Concentration Camps in Germany. Report to United States Congress. 15 May 1945.

McCarthy, Daniel J. *The Prisoner of War in Germany: The Care and Treatment of the Prisoner of War with a History of the Development of the Principle of Neutral Inspection and Control.* New York: Moffat Yard, 1918.

Mitchell, Henry. "Torpedoes for Breakfast and a Medal from FDR." *Washington Post,* 23 December 1977, D1.

Neureuther, Karl, Claus Bergen, and Eric Sutton. *U-Boat Stories: Narratives of German U-Boat Sailors.* New York: R. Long & R. R. Smith, 1931.

New Republic. "Mr. Wallace Inches Along." 1 February 1939, 368.

New York Times. "U.S. Will Dispatch Planes to Pacific." 21 February 1941, 4.

————. "Veterans Express Neutrality Doubts." 17 March 1937, 21.

Newsweek. "A Bill for the Japs." 3 May 1945, 27.

———. "Narrow Escapes." 23 November 1942, 42.

Palen, Margaret Krug. *German Settlers of Iowa: Their Descendants, and European Ancestors.* Bowie, MD: Heritage Books, 1994.

Schepers, C. J. "Cresco Native a Little-Known Hero of 'War to End All Wars.'" *Des Moines Register,* 11 November 1990.

———. "Edouard Victor Izac." Manuscript of a Proposed Article. In Collection of Cabell Waller Berge.

Sims, William Sowden. *The Victory at Sea, Classics of Naval Literature.* Annapolis, MD: Naval Institute Press, 1984.

Zamichow, Nora. "Edouard V. Izac: WWI Medal of Honor." *Los Angeles Times,* 27 January 1990, B1.

CHAPTER FOUR: SAMUEL WOODFILL

Three Cincinnati papers, the *Commercial-Tribune,* the *Enquirer,* and the *Post,* as well as the Kentucky *Post* and the Kentucky *Times-Star,* closely followed Woodfill from 1919. But I would never have been able to access those papers so completely without the efforts of the Public Library of Cincinnati and Hamilton County and the Kenton County Public Library, and their dedicated staff.

We're also very lucky to have Lowell Thomas's *Woodfill of the Regulars: A True Story of Adventure from the Arctic to the Argonne* (Doubleday, Doran & Co., 1929), and should be thankful that Thomas chose to present the stories in Woodfill's own words (it should be mentioned that the book is also a painful reminder of how casually and frequently racial epithets were used in those days). I also consulted Martin Blumenson's 1967 article, "The Outstanding Soldier of the A.E.F." in *American History Illustrated* (vol. 1, no. 10), and the following sources:

Cincinnati Commercial-Tribune. "Bettman's Aid to Woodfill Acknowledged." 23 October 1929, 12:5.

———. "Hero of Argonne Has New Job." 25 July 1929, 1:4.

Cincinnati Enquirer. "Arlington Burial Awaits Kentucky Hero." 9 October 1955, 6:4.

———. "Army Recalling Woodfill to Active Duty July 1." 10 June 1942, 10:4.

———. "Hero of World War I Is Back in Army; Samuel Woodfill Is Sworn in as Major." 16 June 1942, 16:6.

————. "Maj. Samuel Woodfill Is Dead." 14 August 1951, 12:6.

————. "Still Has That Eagle Eye." 21 July 1942, 9:2.

————. "Woodfill Joins Chief for Eternal Sleep in Heroes' Cemetery." 18 October 1955, 21:2.

Cincinnati Post. "Hero Serves Again." 3 June 1942, 19:4.

————. "Maj. Woodfill, Once a Forgotten Hero, Sleeps Forever with Happy Warriors." 18 October 1955, 37:1.

————. "Major Woodfill Laid to Rest near Pershing at Arlington." 17 October 1955, 4:5.

————. "Major Woodfill, Leading Hero of 1918, Dies in Vevay." 14 August 1951, 4:5.

————. "Mrs. S.W. Woodfill, Wife of World War Hero, Dies." 26 March 1942, 11:1.

————. "Woodfill, York Named Majors in Infantry." 7 May 1942, 1:5.

————. "World War Hero Back in Army (Photo)." 16 June 1942, 13:3.

Kentucky Post. "Big Bertha's Answer Present." 30 September 1929, 1.

————. "Capt. Woodfill Re-Enlists." 16 December 1919, 1.

————. "Hero's School: New Ft. Thomas Building to be Known as Woodfill." 21 July 1922, 1.

————. "Medal for Ft. Thomas Man." 5 February 1919, 1:1.

————. "Sees Hero Husband Fight Germans Thru Film Reproduction." 11 April 1919, 1.

————. "Super-War Hero Is Boomed for Congress." 16 April 1924, 1.

————. "Woodfill Is Chosen." 7 October 1929, 4.

————. "Woodfill Will Not Run." 4 June 1924, 1.

Kentucky Times-Star. "Hero Adopted Same Tactics in Pursuing Germans That He Used in Hunting Wild Animals." 9 August 1919, 16.

————. "Hero Re-Enlists as Army Sergeant." 16 December 1919, 27:2.

————. "Hero Spoke at Unveiling of Monument." 9 April 1923, 27.

————. "Medal of Honor Wearers to Go to Convention." 7 September 1921, 25:7.

————. "Super-Hero of the World War Receives Another Decoration." 8 September 1920, 25:3.

————. "Super-Hero to Be Filmed as Lover of Peace." 2 March 1928, 7.

————. "Woodfill Film in Covington." 25 April 1919, 27.

————. "World War Hero Seeks Recruits." 2 April 1923, 18.

———. "World War Hero Takes Part in School Review." 27 June 1923, 25.

———. "World War Super-Hero Will Retire." 6 December 1923, 1.

Literary Digest. "How Our Greatest Soldier and His Buddies Carried On." 15 March 1930, 56.

———. "The Outstanding Heroism of Woodfill, Rifleman." 26 November 1921, 40–46.

New York Times. "Ask Woodfill Promotion: Veterans Want Hero Honored before Armistice Day." 7 November 1921, 16:2.

———. "Burial of Unknown Heroes: Body Placed in State in Capitol Rotunda in Washington: Bodyguard Headed by Sgt. Woodfill." 10 November 1921, 1:7.

———. "Burial of Unknown Heroes: Editorial on Woodfill's Appointment." 7 November 1921, 14:3.

———. "Greet Sergeant Woodfill." 20 November 1921, 1:5 (sect. II).

———. "The Hero of Cunel (Editorial)." 7 November 1921, 14:3.

———. "Italy Decorates Woodfill." 6 December 1921, 3:4.

———. "Made Major." 18 May 1942, 11:6.

———. "Major Woodfill Back in Army." 3 July 1942, 4:4.

———. "Major Woodfill Called to Duty." 18 June 1942, 5:5.

———. "Members of Society of Fifth Division Ask That He Be Promoted to Former Rank of Captain." 7 November 1921, 16.

———. "Our Unknown Dead in Capitol Rotunda." 10 November 1921, 3:1.

———. "Outstanding War Hero Helps with the Dishes." 2 November 1921, 4:6.

———. "Sergeant Woodfill Sees the President." 5 November 1921, 6:2.

———. "Unsung Hero to Be Bearer of Unknown's Body." 1 November 1921, 1:2.

———. "Woodfill Takes a Job." 6 September 1922, 14:7.

———. "Woodfill, Rifleman." 6 November 1921, 4:1 (section VII).

Newsweek, "Major Heroes." 18 May 1942, 30.

Reis, Jim. "Pieces of the Past: Samuel Woodfill: Battlefield Hero." *Kentucky Post,* 5 December 1994, Editorial.

Stenger, Bentley. "World War Hero Has Dreams of Peace." *Kentucky Enquirer,* 5 July 1938, 1.

Time. "Old Soldiers." 18 May 1942, 63.

United States. Congress. Senate. Committee on Military Affairs. Authorizing the President of the United States to Appoint Sgt. Samuel Woodfill a Captain in the United States Army and Then Place Him on the Retired List: Report to Accompany S. 300. Report. 75th Congress. 1937.

———. Samuel Woodfill: Report (to Accompany S. 2608). Report. 76th Congress. 18 July 1939.

CHAPTER FIVE: DAVID M. SHOUP

Thanks to the oral history projects of the John F. Kennedy Presidential Library and the Oral History Research Office at Columbia University, we have the voice of David Shoup, reflecting candidly on the two presidents he knew, his early life on the farm, and his time in the marines. Quotations from the Reminiscences of David M. Shoup (1972), in the Oral History Collection of Columbia University, are used by permission, and appear on pages 10–15 of the transcript.

Howard Jablon, of Purdue University North Central, has done more research on this remarkable man than anyone, and published a number of his findings in a 1996 article in *The Journal of Military History*. Jablon also edited Shoup's China diaries for publication as *The Marines in China, 1927–1928: The China Expedition Which Turned Out to Be the China Exhibition: A Contemporaneous Journal* (Archon Books, 1987). I also consulted Robert Buzzanco's *Masters of War: Military Dissent and Politics in the Vietnam Era* (Cambridge University Press, 1996), and several of his shorter articles on the same subject. He also has an article directly dealing with Shoup, co-authored with Leigh Fought, in *The Human Tradition in the Vietnam Era* (Scholarly Resources, 2000).

There are two exceptional books on Tarawa. Robert Sherrod's *Tarawa: The Story of a Battle* (Duell Sloan and Pearce, 1944) is a terrifying firsthand account. *Utmost Savagery* (Naval Institute Press, 1995) by Colonel Joseph H. Alexander, USMC (ret.) is a detailed historical account of the battle.

The story of Shoup's visual demonstration during the Cuban Missile Crisis is from David Halberstam's *The Best and the Brightest*. Halberstam places the anecdote in the context of the Bay of Pigs. Jablon places it in the context of the Cuban Missile Crisis.

Also consulted were:
Alexander, Joseph H. "David Shoup: Rock of Tarawa." *Naval History* 9, no. 6 (1995): 19–24.
———. "The Turning Points of Tarawa." *MHQ: The Quarterly Journal of Military History* 8, no. 4 (1996): 42–51.

Associated Press. "Former Marine Commandant Dead at 78." 15 January 1983.

Baldwin, Hanson W. "The Bloody Epic That Was Tarawa." *The New York Times* magazine, 16 November 1958, 19–21, 68–73.

Barrow, Clay. "The Stick Wavers." *Naval History* 4, no. 3 (1990): 28–32.

Beschloss, Michael R., ed. *Taking Charge: The Johnson White House Tapes, 1963–1964.* New York: Simon & Schuster, 1997.

Brown, Jerold E. "No Cheap Victory: Tarawa." *Military Review* 73, no. 11 (1993): 69–72.

Brown, Richard G. "Tarawa: Lest We Forget." *Marine Corps Gazette* 64, no. 11 (1980): 46–50.

Buzzanco, Robert. "The American Military's Rationale Against the Vietnam War." *Political Science Quarterly* 101, no. 4 (1986): 559–76.

Buzzanco, Robert, and Leigh Fought. "David Shoup: Four-Star Troublemaker." In *Human Tradition in America; No. 5,* edited by David L. Anderson. Wilmington, DE: Scholarly Resources, 2000.

Commonweal. "A Fresh Wind." 16 February 1962, 528.

Deakin, James. "Big Brass Lambs." *Esquire,* December 1967, 144.

Earls, Bill. "Tarawa: A Monument to Marine Bravery." *The Buffalo News,* 22 November 1993, 3.

Edwards, Owen. "Send Me a Memo, or Better Yet, Don't." *Across the Board,* November 1992, 12.

Fox, Thomas. "Tarawa Landing: Proving Ground for Pacific Victory." *New England Journal of History* 47, no. 2 (1990): 2–18.

Hammel, Eric M., and John E. Lane. "1st Battalion, 8th Marines Lands at Tarawa." *Marine Corps Gazette* 67, no. 11 (1983): 84–91.

———. "Third Day on Red Beach." *Marine Corps Gazette* 54, no. 11 (1970): 22–26.

Hickman, Martin Berkeley. *The Military and American Society.* Beverly Hills: Glencoe Press, 1971.

Jablon, Howard. "General David M. Shoup, U.S.M.C.: Warrior and War Protester." *The Journal of Military History* 60, no. 3 (1996): 513–38.

Kernan, Michael. ". . . Heavy Fire . . . Unable to Land . . . Issue in Doubt." *Smithsonian,* August 1993, 118–32.

Knoll, Erwin. "Obituary." *The Progressive,* March 1983, 4.

Levins, Harry. "War Doesn't Always Go According to Plan." *St. Louis Post-Dispatch,* 23 May 1993, 25A.

Life magazine. "Now Listen to a Marine." 23 February 1962, 4.

———. "Shoup of the Marines: 'We Teach Men to Fight—Not Hate.'" 23 March 1962, 49–61.

Lillibridge, G.D. "'Not Forgetting May Be the Only Heroism of the Survivor.'" *American Heritage* 34, no. 6 (1983): 26–35.

Mansfield, Mike. "Extension of Remarks." *Congressional Record,* 20 December 1943, A5594.

Marling, Karal Ann, and John Wetenhall. *Iwo Jima: Monuments, Memories, and the American Hero.* Cambridge, MA: Harvard University Press, 1991.

Maverick, Maury. "Flag Amendment Curtails Spirit of Free Speech." *San Antonio Express News,* 8 August 1999, 3G.

May, Ernest R., and Philip Zelikow. *The Kennedy Tapes: Inside the White House During the Cuban Missile Crisis.* Cambridge, MA: Belknap Press of Harvard University Press, 1997.

McKiernan, Patrick L. "Tarawa: The Tide That Failed." *U.S. Naval Institute Proceedings* 88, no. 2 (1962): 38–50.

Nation. "Plain Talk." 17 April 1967, 484.

New York Times. "Gen. Shoup Calls Johnson View on War 'Poppycock.'" 3 July 1967, 12:3.

———. "Gen. Shoup Critical of Article by Kennedy on '62 Cuba Crisis." 26 October 1968, 10:3.

———. "Group Gives Plan for World Peace." 19 February 1968, 14:1.

———. "The New Militarism." 6 April 1969, IV, 10:2.

———. "Veterans Plan a War Protest in Capital." 17 March 1971, 21:3.

Newsweek. "Now Hear This, You People: Knock It Off!" 18 January 1960, 23.

———. "People, Not Blips." 14 January 1963, 23–24.

Sherrod, Robert. "Tarawa: The Second Day." *Marine Corps Gazette* 57, no. 11 (1973): 38–47.

Shoup, David. *ABC Scope: The Vietnam War, Part 85—An Uncommon Breed.* Interview by John Scali, 5 August 1967. In *Congressional Record, Senate. 11 September 1967.* Washington, DC: Government Printing Office.

———. "The New American Militarism." *Atlantic Monthly,* April 1969.

———. "Patriotism." *Nation's Business,* October 1962, 39, 49–50.

———. "Remarks by General David M. Shoup, U.S. Marine Corps (Retired) at the 10th Annual Junior College World Affairs Day, Pierce College, California." *Congressional Record, Senate.* 20 February 1967, 3976.

Smith, J. Y. "Gen. David Shoup Dies; Was Marine Commandant." *The Washington Post,* 15 January 1983, B6.

Time. "Marines' Marine." 24 August 1959, 17.

———. "Medals: Tarawa's Third." 30 October 1944, 72.

———. "Uncle Dave." 23 February 1962, 27.

Trumbull, Robert. "Golden Beaches Bear War Debris." *The New York Times,* 23 November 1968, 16.

U.S. News & World Report. "General Shoup: War Critic with a Peace Plan." 1 April 1968, 14.

———. "Hero of Tarawa to Get Command of Marines." 24 August 1959, 23.

———. "The Marines and Cuba: 145,000 of Them Were Ready." 14 January 1963, 13.

United States. Congress. Senate. Committee on Armed Services. *Nominations of J. Vincent Burke Jr. and Maj. Gen. David M. Shoup: H. R. 6269 and H. R. 8189.* September 3, 1959. Washington: Government Printing Office, 1959.

United States. Congress. Senate. Committee on Foreign Relations, and David M. Shoup. *Present Situation in Vietnam. Hearing, Ninetieth Congress, Second Session, with General David M. Shoup, Former Commandant, United States Marine Corps. March 20, 1968.* Washington: Government Printing Office, 1968.

Wheeler, Richard. *A Special Valor: The U.S. Marines and the Pacific War.* 1st ed. New York: Harper & Row, 1983.

CHAPTER SIX: MAYNARD H. SMITH

Above all, the interview with Maynard Smith Jr. made this chapter possible. Maynard's son's account renders his father more fully human, something so many newspaper accounts failed to do. Maynard Smith Sr.'s ex-wife, now Mary O'Brien, also gave her time for a very helpful interview.

The Caro Area District Library keeps a file on Smith, and gladly provided references. Likewise, Stanley Bozich, of Michigan's Own Military and Space Museum, was very gracious in lending his own research. Most of the remaining sources for this chapter were from the reports from the *Washington Star,* on microfilm at the Library of Congress, and from various accounts of the storied Eighth Air Force.

Anderson, Christopher J. *The Men of the Mighty Eighth: The U.S. 8th Air Force, 1942–1945, The G.I. Series; 24.* Mechanicsburg, PA: Stackpole Books, 2001.

Astor, Gerald. *The Mighty Eighth: The Air War in Europe as Told by the Men Who Fought It.* New York: Donald I. Fine Books, 1997.

Bamford, Hal SMSgt. "Hinges of Hades." *The Airman,* July 1959, 38–39.

Boal, Sam. "The Deal." *The New Yorker,* 18 September 1943, 30–39.

Detroit Free Press. "Stimson Awards Highest Medal to Michigan Hero." 16 July 1943.

Evening Star (Washington, DC). "Judge Studies Plea to Void Smith Charge." 26 August 1952, B-1.

——. "Medal-of-Honor Man Saves Young Mother from Suicide Plunge." 1 August 1952, A-2.

——. "Mrs. Whomble Sticks to Fake Rescue Story at Snuffy Smith Trial." 18 September 1952, A-14.

——. "One of Pair Accused of Suicide Try Hoax Surrenders to Police." 5 August 1952. A-1.

——. "Police Can't Locate 'Snuffy' Smith to Serve Suicide Hoax Warrant." 6 August 1952, A-2.

——. "Snuffy Smith Denied Motion to Dismiss False Report Case." 29 August 1952, A-22.

——. "Snuffy Smith, Bennett Convicted on Reports in Suicide Hoax Here." 23 September 1952, A-2.

——. "'Snuffy' Smith Denies He Had Met Woman before Rescue at YW." 19 September 1952, A-25.

——. "'Snuffy' Smith Given Suspended Sentence." 12 May 1948, A-18.

——. "U.S. Moves to Condemn Preparation under Drug Act." 8 August 1947, A-14.

——. "War Hero Wins Delay as Ex-Wife Presses Non-Support Claim." 3 August 1946, B-15.

Freeman, Roger Anthony. *The Mighty Eighth: A History of the Units, Men, and Machines of the US 8th Air Force.* 2000 ed. London and New York: Casssell, 2000.

——. *Mighty Eighth War Manual.* London; New York: Jane's, 1984.

Freeman, Roger Anthony, Alan Crouchman, and Vic Maslen. *The Mighty Eighth War Diary.* Rev. ed. London: Arms and Armour, 1990.

Hastings, Donald W., David G. Wright, Bernard C. Glueck, United States. Army Air Forces. Air Force 8th., and Josiah Macy Jr. Foundation. *Psychiatric Experiences of the Eighth Air Force: First Year of Combat (July 4, 1942–July 4, 1943).* New York: Prepared and distributed for the Air Surgeon Army Air Forces by the Josiah Macy Jr. Foundation, 1944.

Hess, William N., and Thomas G. Ivie. *Fighters of the Mighty Eighth, 1942–45.* Osceola, WI: Motorbooks International, 1990.

Hicks, George E. "First Mission." *Sergeants,* January–February 1990, 49.

Kosier, Edwin J. "It Was My First Trip Out." *Sergeants,* January–February 1979, 9–12.

Lewis, Bruce. *Aircrew: The Story of the Men Who Flew the Bombers.* London: Leo Cooper, 1991.

McCrary, John Reagan, and David Edward Scherman. *First of the Many: A Journal of Action with the Men of the Eighth Air Force.* London: Robson, 1981.

Miel, Rhoda. "Caro Roared When Hero Came Home." *The Saginaw News,* 15 July 1993, A-1.

Murphy, Edward F. *Heroes of World War II.* Novato, CA: Presidio, 1990.

Nalty, Bernard C., and Carl Berger. *The Men Who Bombed the Reich.* 1st ed., *Men and Battle.* New York: Elsevier-Dutton, 1978.

New York Times. "Flying Fortress Gunner Beats Off German, Puts Out Fire and Saves Lives of All Aboard." 17 May 1943, 4:3.

———. "The Peeler-Bomber." 17 July 1943, 12:2.

———. "Sergt. M. H. Smith Gets High Honor." 16 July 1943, 6:2.

Oates, Morgan. "A Bad, Bad Boy Returned in Glory." *Detroit Free Press,* 15 February 1959.

Peaslee, Budd J. *Heritage of Valor: the Eighth Air Force in World War II.* [1st] ed., *Airmen & Aircraft.* Philadelphia: Lippincott, 1964.

Rooney, Andy. *My War.* New York: Times Books, 1995.

Shine, Neal. "Snuffy Was a Certified War Hero, but He Wasn't Always on the Mark." *Detroit Free Press,* 2 September 1984.

Sparling, Jim. "That Smith Boy." *Tuscola County Advertiser,* 23 February 2000.

Tuscola County Advertiser. "Caro Man Goes on First Bomb Raid." 14 May 1943.

———. "Death Claims Medal of Honor Winner Smith." 23 May 1984.

———. "English Girl and S.Sgt Smith Wed." 11 August 1944 1944, 1.

———. "Finest War Medal Given Sgt. Smith." 16 July 1943.

———. "Highest Decoration for Valor May Be Won by Caro Sergeant." 21 May 1943.

———. "'Hokie' Smith Is Given Discharge." 1 June 1945.

———. "S.Sgt. Smith Is Awarded Air Medal Oak Leaf Cluster." 15 October 1943.

———. "Welcome Planned for S.Sgt. Smith." 9 March 1945.

United States. Army. Headquarters, European Theater of Operations. Eighth Air

Force Waist Gunner Decorated with Medal of Honor. Press release. 15 July 1943.

Wells, Mark K. *Courage and Air Warfare: The Allied Aircrew Experience in the Second World War, Cass Series—Studies in Air Power; 2.* Essex, England; Portland, OR: F. Cass, 1995.

Woolnough, John H., and Eighth Air Force Historical Society. *8th AF News: Journal of the Eighth Air Force Historical Society.* Vol. [Issue no. 1 (Jan. 1975)]. Miramar, FL: The Society, 1975.

CHAPTER SEVEN: VERNON BAKER

Much of the story of Vernon Baker came from Baker himself. He generously gave his time for an interview, and his autobiography, *Lasting Valor* (with Ken Olsen. Columbus, MS: Genesis Press, 1997), is a fascinating record of the time in which he grew up, and a powerful telling of his time in the war.

The anecdote about John Lawson and the slave owner came from a conversation with Lawson's family members, two who of whom were old enough to remember him. Additional information on African Americans in the Union Navy came from several sources, listed below. The recommendations for the Medal of Honor for black sailors mentioned in this chapter can be found in the *Official Records of the Union and Confederate Navies in the War of the Rebellion.*

Details on desegregation and African Americans in the military can be found in many sources, but a good, recent one-volume account is Gail Buckley's *American Patriots: The Story of Blacks in the Military from the Revolution to Desert Storm* (New York: Random House, 2001).

Also consulted were several newspaper articles on Baker, the most important of which are listed below:

Aptheker, Herbert. "The Negro in the Union Navy." *Journal of Negro History* 32, no. 2 (1947): 169–200.

Farr, James Barker. *Black Odyssey: The Seafaring Traditions of Afro-Americans, Culture, Ethnicity, and Nation, Vol. 1.* New York: P. Lang, 1989.

Fleming, Marcella. "A Medal That Honors Their Buddies." *Indianapolis Star,* 23, May 1999, A1.

Gibbs, C.R. "Blacks in the Union Navy." *Negro History Bulletin* 36, October (1973): 137–39.

Idaho Statesman. "Baker the Ideal Selection to Speak at King Tribute Dinner." 23 January 1998, 16A.

———. "To His Surprise, Baker Enjoys Sudden Fame." 22 January 1998, 1B.

Kasindorf, Martin. "Belated Honors? Search Is on for WWII Heroes Some Say Were Shortchanged." *USA Today,* 17 September 1997, 1A.

Katz, William Loren. "Six 'New' Medal of Honor Men." *Journal of Negro History* 53, no. 1 (1968): 77–81.

Kempthorne, Dirk. "African-American Medal of Honor Nominees." *Congressional Record,* 19 June 1996, S6508.

Long, Gloria J. "Vernon Baker and Others Awarded Medal of Honor Because of Shaw University." *Washington Afro-American,* 8 March 1997, B7.

Marshall, John. "Hero Triumphed in Battles Abroad, and Finally at Home." *Seattle Post-Intelligencer,* 16 February 1998, F1.

Simonich, Milan. "Medals of Honor Bucked a Dishonorable Trend." *Pittsburgh Post-Gazette,* 31 May 1999, E1.

Spokesman-Review, Spokane. "Baker Finally Receives Pay for Medal of Honor." 24 December 1997, B2.

CHAPTER EIGHT:
HIROSHI "HERSHEY" MIYAMURA

Mr. Miyamura gave three long and very frank interviews for this book. He left very few details out, but some were gleaned from the following:

Bartelt, Eric S. "Secret Hero Recounts His Unforgettable Korean War." *KorUS* magazine, July 2000.

Duggan, Paul. "In Final Salute, Applause for Korean War Vets." *Washington Post,* 30 July 1995, B5.

Hickey, Michael. *The Korean War: The West Confronts Communism.* Woodstock, NY: Overlook Press, 2000.

Murphy, Edward F. *Korean War Heroes.* Novato, CA: Presidio, 1992.

Reed, Ollie Jr. "Honorable Mettle." *Albuquerque Tribune,* 28 May 1999, A1.

Zoretich, Frank. "City Honors Forgotten Veterans." *Albuquerque Journal,* 26 June 1995, B8.

CHAPTER NINE: WILLIAM CHARETTE

Like Hiroshi Miyamura, Mr. Charette generously agreed to be interviewed for this chapter. Charette has had very little written about him in the past, but background information came from *This Kind of War: The Classic Korean War History,* by T. R. Fehrenbach (Washington, DC: Brassey's, 1998 [1963]), and Michael Hickey's *The Korean War: The West Confronts Communism* (Woodstock, NY: Overlook Press, 2000).

CHAPTER TEN: DWIGHT JOHNSON

Dwight Christopher Johnson was gracious in passing along his family's memories of his father during an interview. But the most influential work on Johnson will always be Jon Nordheimer's article for the *New York Times.* Similar articles in the *Detroit Free Press* and the *Detroit News* were also extremely helpful.

Also consulted were:

Cole, Tom. *Medal of Honor Rag: A Full Length Play in One Act.* New York: Samuel French, 1977, 1983.

Detroit News. "Medal of Honor Winner to Be Buried in Arlington." 1 May 1971, 3.

Friedman, Saul. "Dave's Big Brother's a Hero." *Detroit Free Press,* 20 November 1968, 1A.

Graham, Michael. "Errant Hero Is Forgiven in Death." *Detroit Free Press,* 6 May 1971, 3A.

Hendrickson, Paul. "Holy Orders Rag: The Power and Glory of Charlie Liteky, Hero-Priest of 'Nam No More." *Washington Post,* 20 February 1983, G1.

Lifton, Robert Jay. *Home from the War: Learning from Vietnam Veterans, with a New Preface and Epilogue on the Gulf War.* Boston: Beacon, 1992.

Lochbiler, Peter R. "A Hero Gets His Wish—His Dad Will Return." *Detroit News,* 21 November 1968, 1B.

———. "Officials to Aid War Hero." *Detroit News,* 20 November 1968, 3B.

Martin, Reginald. "An Interview with Michael Harper." *Black American Literature Forum* 24, no. 3 (1990): 441–51.

Murphy, Edward F. *Vietnam Medal of Honor Heroes.* New York: Ballentine, 1987.

New York Times. "President, Presenting 5 Medals, Warns of 'Bitter Days' Ahead." 20 November 1968, 1.

―――. "Vietnam Medal of Honor Winner Killed in Detroit Store Holdup." 1 May 1971, 21.

―――. "War Hero's Widow Wins Battle for G.I. Benefits." 23 March 1977, 16.

Nordheimer, Jon. "From Dakto to Detroit: Death of a Troubled Hero." *New York Times*, 26 May 1971, 1.

Peterson, John. "Detroiter Gets Highest Award." *Detroit News*, 19 November 1968, 3.

Popa, Robert A. "Why Did Detroit GI Stray Off Hero's Path?" *Detroit News*, 3 May 1971.

Ricke, Tom. "Medal of Honor Winner Dies in Holdup Attempt." *Detroit Free Press*, 1 May 1971, 1A.

Rosett, Henry L., M.D. "Letters to the Editor: The Post-Vietnam Syndrome." *New York Times*, 12 June 1971.

Rowell, Charles H. "'Down Don't Worry Me': An Interview with Michael Harper." *Callaloo* 13, no. 4 (1990): 780–800.

Russell, Robert. "Letters to the Editor: Medal of Honor Pension." *New York Times*, 11 July 1971.

CHAPTER ELEVEN: THOMAS KELLEY

Thomas Kelley himself provided most of the material for this chapter, granting several interviews and patiently answering many questions. Additional background on the Mobile Riverine Force was found in *Brown Water, Black Berets* by Thomas J. Cutler (Annapolis, MD: Naval Institute Press, 1988).

ACKNOWLEDGMENTS

Highest on my list are the Medal of Honor recipients who agreed to be interviewed for this book—Vernon Baker, Hiroshi Miyamura, William Charette, and Thomas Kelley. Paul Bucha, past president of the Congressional Medal of Honor Society, influenced this project by meeting me at a very early stage. Gerard F. White, a former director of the Medal of Honor Society and co-author of *Medal of Honor Recipients 1863–1994*, brought to my attention some of the candidates in this volume. Gerard was a lively and prolific researcher, who sadly passed away as work on this book drew to a close.

The living relatives of several recipients—Joyce Blackman, Cabell Waller Berge, Maynard Smith Jr., Mary O'Brien, and Dwight Johnson Jr.—were kind enough to share their memories in interviews.

The staffs of several libraries and museums must be thanked, even though their constant refrain when thanked in person was "just doing my job." They are: the Connecticut Valley Historical Museum in Springfield, Massachusetts; the San Diego Public Library; the Public Library of Cincinnati and Hamilton County; the Kenton County Public Library, Kentucky; the John F. Kennedy Presidential Library; the Oral History Research Office at Columbia University; the Caro Area District Library, Michigan; and Michigan's Own Military and Space Museum. And finally, the always incredible staff of the Library of Congress in Washington, D.C.

Edward Murphy, author of several books on the Medal of Honor and president of the Medal of Honor Historical Society, helped clear up a mystery about Maynard Smith. Howard Jablon, Social Science Section Chair and Professor of History at Purdue University North Central, shared information he had about David Shoup. These two historians deserve thanks for keeping alive many more memories than this small volume even attempts.

Having worked in book publishing, I know how fortunate I was to have not one excellent editor, but two. Will Schwalbe and Mark Chait were patient in-house sages who hid their headaches and kept this project on track. And David Lott worked around the clock to see the book through production. Paul McCarthy, of McCarthy Creative Services, took a first crack at vetting the first draft. Gary Paul Gates also lent his able hand and acute eye. And it was Bill Adler and Mike Wallace who got this ship launched and set it on its way.

Back here at home, several people stand out as being greatly supportive during the trying times this project created. But most especially, always there with the right advice at the right time, or at least a smile and a nod, were Mike Taylor, Carey Bodenheimer, Jocelyn Byrne, and Beth Antunez. Thanks. Again.

—Allen Mikaelian

I want to thank my former CBS News colleague Gary Paul Gates for his editorial assistance.

—Mike Wallace